EUI — Series A — 9

Cassese/Weiler (Eds.), Change and Stability in International Law-Making

European University Institute
Institut Universitaire Européen
Europäisches Hochschulinstitut
Istituto Universitario Europeo

Series A

Law/Droit/Recht/Diritto

9

Badia Fiesolana — Firenze

Change and Stability in International Law-Making

Edited by

Antonio Cassese and Joseph H. H. Weiler

1988

Walter de Gruyter · Berlin · New York

Library of Congress Cataloging-in-Publication Data

Change and stability in international law-making / edited by
Antonio Cassese and Joseph H. H. Weiler.
X, 214 p. 15.5 × 23 cm. — (Series A — Law = Droit ; 9)
Based on the proceedings of two international colloquia held at
the European University Institute, Florence.
Includes indexes.
ISBN 0-89925-420-9 (U.S.) : $55.00 (est.)
1. International law — Congresses. I. Cassese, Antonio.
II. Weiler, Joseph, 1951— . III. European University Institute.
IV. Series: Series A — Law ; 9.
JX1245.C48 1988
341 — dc 19 88—3680
CIP

CIP-Titelaufnahme der Deutschen Bibliothek

Change and stability in international law making / ed. by
Antonio Cassese and Joseph H. H. Weiler. — Berlin ; New York :
de Gruyter, 1988
(European University Institute : Ser. A, Law ; 9)
ISBN 3-11-011494-1

NE: Cassese, Antonio [Hrsg.]; Istituto Universitario Europeo
<Fiesole>: European University Institute / A

Dust Cover Design: Rudolf Hübler, Berlin.
Typesetting and Printing: Arthur Collignon GmbH., Berlin
Binding: Verlagsbuchbinderei Dieter Mikolai, Berlin.
Printed in Germany

Preface

Although the international community is changing at an increasingly rapid pace (chiefly at the instigation of developing and Socialist countries), some of its basic features remain unaffected or at least are being eroded only marginally, due to strong resistance from the traditional "actors". Thus, there is a deep rift between the "old" and the "new" patterns of the community, the cause of continual tension. The motivations and ramifications of this cleavage must be grasped, if one wishes to understand where the international community is heading at present. This theme was chosen as the focus of two international colloquia held at the European University Institute, Florence.*

We decided to look at this phenomenon from a particular vantage point: that of the mechanisms existing at world level for creating, updating, modifying or eliminating the "rules of the game" of the international community: in short, those mechanisms which are traditionally called "the sources of law". We thought that this area, if looked upon as a dynamic process, could show, as if seen through a prism, the resistance of the "old" and the innovations of the "new". We thought that by examining the microcosm of the law-creating processes, we might perhaps better understand some general trends of the macrocosm of the world community.

In order to take a fresh look at this much-trodden area, we thought that we should adopt a rather novel approach. For this purpose, we decided on a two-pronged strategy. First, we thought that the various issues coming within the purview of our "problématique" should be looked at from the viewpoints of the three major "families of nations", namely Western countries, Socialist States and developing nations. Accordingly we invited a small number of international lawyers from the three major areas to two round-table discussions and recorded their views and comments. We thought, indeed, that the various views would come to the fore better in the course of such a discussion than in a set of essays produced by individual scholars.

Our second "strategy" consisted in dividing our discussion of the subject into two parts. First, we endeavoured to *"revisit" the classical sources of international law*, by scrutinizing the way those sources affect the present international community. In particular, we wanted to focus on the question

* The holding of the colloquia was made possible by the financial support of the Italian "National Council for Research" (research project no. 86.01158.09).

of which sources are resorted to most frequently, and which are becoming to some extent obsolete. In addition, we raised the question of whether resolutions adopted by international organizations have an impact on traditional sources, or whether they constitute a new and distinct law-making process.

In the second part of our discussion (distinct from the first, because it took place at a colloquium held a few months later), we wanted to *rediscuss* all the various issues *in a different order*: our agenda was no longer to work source by source but to tackle certain questions which cut across all or most sources. Accordingly, we focussed on what we felt were three fundamental questions: (i) is there any evidence of a breakdown in the distinction between *lex lata* and *lex ferenda*, and has the introduction of *jus cogens* led to the emergence within *lex lata* of a hierarchy of different norms? (ii) is there sufficient evidence that *voluntarism* as the underpinning of international obligations is being replaced by a *majoritarian* norm-setting process? (iii) what effect, if any, has the current *ideological cleavage* in the structure and process of international law on the creation, content and acceptability of international rules and procedures?

We believe, that, on the whole, the two round table discussions (held in Florence in late 1984 and early 1985) were successful. In spite of the necessary pruning and editing, we have kept the format of oral delivery so as to make the book as lively and interesting as possible. The discussion is rounded off by some general concluding remarks by A. Cassese. They were written when the manuscript of the proceedings had been finalized, and are intended not to sum up the whole discussion, but merely to highlight some of the trends that emerged as well as the main points of convergence or dissent. We should like to thank Attila Tanzi and Liliane Markewiecz who prepared the analytical index and the index of statements respectively.

We end this preface on a sad note. One of the conference participants — among the most promising of the new generation of American international lawyers — Professor Ted Stein, died shortly after his return to the U.S.A. We mourn his death. We have decided to dedicate this book to his memory.

Antonio Cassese
Joseph H. H. Weiler

Table of Contents

List of Participants

G. Abi-Saab, Professor of International Law, Institut Universitaire de Hautes Etudes Internationales; Member of the Institut de Droit International (I and II)

G. Arangio-Ruiz, Professor of International Law, University of Rome I; Member of the U.N. International Law Commission; Member of the Institut de Droit International (II)

I. Brownlie, Q.C., D.C.L., F.B.A., Chichele Professor of International Law, University of Oxford; Fellow of All Souls College, Oxford; Member of the Institut de Droit International (II)

A. Cassese, Professor of International Law, University of Florence and European University Institute (I and II)

L. Condorelli, Professor of International Law, University of Geneva (I and II)

H. de Fiumel, Professor of International Law, Institute of State and Law, Polish Academy of Science, Warsaw

B. de Witte, Assistant Professor of Law, European University Institute (I)

R. R. Falk, Milbank Professor of International Law and Relations, University of Princeton (II)

G. Gaja, Professor of International Law, University of Florence (I and II)

B. Graefrath, Professor of International Law, Academy of Science of the German Democratic Republic, Berlin (I)

E. Jimenez de Arechaga, Former President of the International Court of Justice; President of the Administrative Tribunal of the World Bank; Member of the Institut de Droit International (I)

J. Hazard, Former Professor of Comparative Law, Columbia University; Honorary President, American Society of International Law; Visiting Professor, European University Institute (I and II)

M. Mendelson, Professor of International Law, University of London (II)

T. Meron, Professor of International Law, New York University School of Law (I and II)

W. Riphagen, Professor of Law, University of Rotterdam; Former Member of the U.N. International Law Commission; Member of the Institut de Droit International (I)

Eric Stein, Emeritus Professor of European and International Law, Michigan University Law School (I)

Edward Stein, Late Professor of Law, University of Washington (I)

S. Sur, Professor of International Law, University of Paris X (Nanterre); Deputy Director, U.N. Institute for Disarmament Research (II)

E. Suy, Professor of International Law, University of Louvain; Former Under-Secretary General, United Nations; Member of the Institut de Droit International

M. Virally, Professor of International Law, University of Paris II and Institut Universitaire de Hautes Etudes Internationales, Geneva; Chairman of one of the Chambers of the Iran — U.S. Claims Tribunal; Member of the Institut de Droit International (II)

J. H. H. Weiler, Former Professor and Head of the Law Department, European University Institute; Professor of Law, Michigan University School of Law (I and II)

A. Yankov, Professor of International Law, University of Sophia; Member of the U.N. International Law Commission; Member of the Institut de Droit International (II)

It is indicated in brackets whether participants took part in the first or the second round table discussion, or in both.

Part I

The Classical "Sources" of International Law Revisited

Chapter I

Custom and Treaties

I. Presentations

A. Custom

JIMENEZ DE ARECHAGA

Article 38(1) of the Statute of the International Court of Justice is a rule about rules. It is what Hart calls a "secondary rule", putting a legal stamp on those "primary rules" which result mainly from two different and predetermined procedures: either the treaty procedure with its various stages, or the procedure of customary law which results from the general practice of States accepted as law.

Under the influence of a clear-cut distinction made in separate clauses between these two main sources of international law, and also of a jurisprudential approach developed mainly on the basis of municipal law, a prevailing tendency is to consider these two sources as entirely different: as separate and independent one of the other.

Many writers emphasize their antithetical features. Treaty law is identified as *lex scripta*, the result of a deliberate intellectual effort, as having the qualities of precision, clarity, systematic order; while customary law is *lex non scripta*, described as spontaneous, unintentional, unconscious in its origin, disorderly, uncertain in its form, slow in its establishment. Some writers even qualify it as a "procédé artisanal", not well-adapted to the rapid pace of evolution in the modern world.

Such an antithesis may be correct in the municipal field, where statutes and codes are rightly opposed to customary law, but it is not true in the international sphere. Treaty law and customary law do not exist in sealed compartments in contemporary international law.

It has been recognized for a long time that rules of law formulated in the text of a treaty may at the same time constitute or become rules of customary international law. What is important to emphasize is that this process of interaction between the two sources has acquired a greatly increased significance in the contemporary world.

This phenomenon has been a somewhat unexpected by-product of the efforts made, in the last forty years, under the auspices of the United Nations, towards the codification and progressive development of international law. The procedures and the organs established for this purpose, while designed to obtain as an end-product codification conventions, have resulted in practice in the establishment of customary law on an unprecedented scale.

The preparation of texts by the International Law Commission or by expert bodies with a wide geographical representation allows the auxiliary means of doctrine and jurisprudence to influence the elaboration of drafts. Governmental representatives in the General Assembly and at plenipotentiary conferences bring in the direct experience of diplomats and of legal advisors on the practice of States. There can be no better way of making the evidence of general practice directly available to all. Finally, the submission of proposal and amendments, the vote, abstentions or tacit acceptance of a given provision reveal the *opinio juris* of each government represented. *Travaux préparatoires* may then be utilized not to interpret the text of a treaty but to determine the presence of the two elements of customary law: whether a proposal was submitted *de lege lata* or *de lege ferenda*; whether it was voted unanimously or by a very large marjority. It is an often-forgotten truism that whenever it appears that all nations constituting the international community accept the application in their mutual relations of a specific rule of conduct, that rule becomes part of customary international law.

Customary international law is thus secreted by the procedure for codification and progressive development, on the basis of the equal participation of all States and not by the *fiat* of a few preponderant States. A consensus achieved in these conferences confers on the resulting provisions an authority of their own, even prior to the formal entry into force of the conventions so elaborated. In this way, the codification process, far from pushing customary international law into the background – into an eclipse as Thirlway anticipated; or into regression, as Charpentier feared – has on the contrary reinvigorated it, increased its "tempo" and combined customary and conventional law into a harmonious whole, like two pillars which support each other.

The International Court of Justice has had an important role in this contemporary resurrection of customary international law. It is a fact that the Court, particularly in the last fifteen years, has had to grapple, in practically every case, not with treaty law, as the Permanent Court did, but with what an intelligent observer of the Third U.N. Conference on the Law of the Sea called "the amorphous but formidable jellyfish of customary international law". In 1969, in the *North Sea Continental Shelf* cases, the Court not only had to apply rules of customary international law; it was also called upon to make a number of pronouncements about the nature of customary international law, the elements composing it, the process of its formation and its relation with treaty provisions.

Personally, I believe that the most important contribution made by the Court to the progressive development of international law is to be found, rather than in its judgments or advisory opinions, in the flexibility of the jurisprudential conceptions it adopted on this subject of sources, particularly with respect to customary international law. This contribution, which is for me the crucial test of an international tribunal, is one aspect of the Court's work which has passed somewhat unobserved, despite its being of more lasting significance for the development of the law than the settlement of a particular dispute, or the actual contents of a specific judgment or opinion.

A general comment which may be made at the outset is that in dealing with customary international law the Court has shown an innovative and potentially fruitful approach, without however falling into the extremes of legal heterodoxy.

It has searched for the general consensus of States and not for unanimous or universal practice. It has not required strict proof of the specific acceptance of the defendant State, thus rejecting the voluntarist conception of custom and placing in a broader perspective earlier *dicta* concerning regional and local custom. It has accepted a short period of time — 12 to 15 years — as the basis for a maturing practice, thus recognizing that the development of custom is to be measured by the rhythm of contemporary life. But at the same time, by requiring the existence of the two classic elements — a common and repeated behaviour stretching over some period of time and *opinio juris* — it has rejected the notion of "instant custom". It has recognized that customary law does not necessarily grow up independently of treaties, but may be expressed or secreted in the widely attended codification conferences. And it has expressly accepted that this kind of customary law resulting from the codification process may operate in three different ways. First, the *declaratory effect,* when the conventional text, not yet in force as such, merely restates a pre-existing rule of customary law; second, what the Court has called the "*crystallizing effect*", i. e. when the incorporation of a given provision in a conventional text has the catalytic effect of crystallizing an emergent rule, one that was *in statu nascendi*, and thus the *imprimatur* of the Conference attests to its legal character; third, the *generating or constituting effect*, when a treaty provision *de lege ferenda*, or a proposal at one of these conferences, becomes what has been called a "conduct model", that is to say, it constitutes the focal point of a subsequent practice of States which, in due course, hardens into a rule of customary international law.

B. Treaties

HAZARD

In approaching my subject of treaties as a source of international law, I am mindful of a dicussion we used to amuse ourselves with in the American Society of International Law. The question was: does an education in law or political science fit one better to understand international law? Our seniors here will recall the prominent American scholars who were trained in political science – Quincy Wright and Herbert Briggs. Those trained in law included James Brown Scott and Philip Jessup. Of course, there was no consensus on appropriate training for the discipline, but the point being made is important to our discussion of today. Perhaps the topic should be studied as a feature of international politics rather than as a study in hard legal science.

I shall refer in my brief intervention only to some of the controversial issues relating to treaties, as the fundamental principles are well known. The principal question being mooted these days is: are treaties legislation or contracts? The debate was initiated because of Third World pressure for recognition in law of their aspirations and the fact that in their position as the majority of the members of the United Nations they have the power of numbers. They cannot be ignored.

The debate is by no means new. Fifty years ago Judge Manley O. Hudson entitled a series of multilateral treaties he edited "International Legislation". He was an enthusiast, hoping to make international law binding upon the world. Of course he knew that few would accept the idea that treaties bound any State not a party, but he hoped to insinuate the idea into the minds of scholars that multilateral treaties were the beginning of a legislative process that could bind non-parties.

Years later it was clear that Hudson's effort had failed. When Judge Sir Gerald Fitzmaurice wrote in 1958 on the topic he said "... the treaty and the 'law' it contains only applies to the parties to it." In short, for Fitzmaurice a treaty was no more than a contract.

J. L. Brierly took a middle position in the little volume on which many of us cut our teeth. He wrote: "Such treaties are the substitute in the international system for legislation, and they are conveniently referred to as 'law-making'. ... But even a law-making treaty is subject to a limitation which applies to other treaties, that it does not bind States which are not parties to it."

The matter would appear to have been settled by Art. 34 of the Vienna Convention on the Law of Treaties, which reads: "A treaty does not create either obligations or rights for a third State without its consent." In elaboration of this rule Charles Rousseau in his massive treatise points out that there may be a difference when the matter is one of obligations rather than rights. While he follows the Vienna Convention rule that a benefit accrues to a third State when it communicates its willingness to receive the benefit, there are instances when an obligation binds a non-party who remains silent. He refers to treaties creating an objective situation, such as the demilitarization of the Aaland Islands which was enforced against Finland and Sweden even though they were non-parties.

Those who take the position that modern multilateral treaties have a wider impact on the world community call attention to the United Nations Charter. Art. 2, para. 6 reads: "The Organization shall ensure that States which are not members of the United Nations act in accordance with the principles so far as may be necessary for the maintenance of international peace and security." There are two schools of thought on the Charter. One sees it as no more than another multilateral treaty. The other sees it as the starting point for an entirely new body of law.

The latter school, in which many Third World scholars place themselves hails the Charter as establishing a new rule for treaties generally. Since this school sees the Charter as binding non-parties such as Switzerland, at least as regards threats to peace and security, they, in their enthusiasm for treaties as binding "legislation" argue that multilateral treaties other than the Charter also have an impact upon third parties. That impact is possible in application of the theory that multilateral treaties establish principles which, after a time, become "custom", binding on all. This is where my topic relates to what Judge Jiminez de Arechaga has just said. Some treaties have been found to incorporate not only new law, but to codify customary law as well. As to this codification, the law incorporated in the treaty would have bound the world as general international law even had there been no new treaty.

Judge Richard Baxter in his Hague lectures took this position, when he says: "My thesis is that general practice or international custom may be found in treaties, and that treaties may, therefore, exercise their effects, *qua* evidence of customary international law, upon non-parties."

Professor Derek Bowett has added an argument along these lines when he surveys the status of signatories of a treaty who fail subsequently to ratify it. He says that such a State cannot later deny that the treaty reflects an accurate statement of customary law by which it is willing to be bound. He calls this "estoppel". Sir Frederick Pollock, in 1902, put the third party situation in the imperialist terms being used at the time when he said that if most Great Powers have agreed, non-parties are subject to their principles unless there is prompt and effective dissent by some Power of first rank. In short, treaties could be taken to be evidence of the existence of a customary rule established by the Great Powers of his time.

Pollock's position raises the question of the status of former colonies with regard to treaties executed on their behalf by former metropoles. After liberation, many of their scholars argued that such treaties had no automatic binding effect, although the new State's officers might decide to honour one or another treaty inherited from the past. Traditionalists in the field of international law tended to argue to the contrary, namely that former colonies were bound by the treaties made in their name. Third World scholars countered by pointing to what the Russian revolutionaries had done when reviewing the Tsarist files. They had rejected treaties creating financial obligations but continued to rely on treaties advantageous to them, such as those creating parts of the frontier with China. With this "precedent" the Third World claimed that it could pick and choose the treaties it wished to continue in force. Socialist scholars were content to accept this claim, provided that the choice was made promptly and communicated to the world so that the state of the law might be clear.

The International Law Commission in its report of 1974 expressed its view that a newly independent State may have a clean slate in regard to any obligation to continue to be bound by its predecessor's treaties. As to its claim of rights under such a treaty the Commission found that international practice appears to support the conclusion that a newly independent State has a general right of option to be a party to certain categories of multilateral treaties in virtue of its character as a successor State. It must, however, notify the world of its own consent to be considered a separate party to the treaty.

A major dispute over the relation of non-signatories to a multilateral Convention has arisen since completion of the Convention of the Law of the Sea. Some major States have refused to sign the Convention, while claiming rights which its signatories deny to non-signatories. Ambassador Tommy Koh, who presided over the conference drafting the Convention, has declared that non-parties have no right to claim under the Convention privileges created by the Convention as *new* law. Ambassador Elliott Richardson, who headed the United States delegation prior to the change of personnel by President Ronald Reagan, agrees with him. In short, Koh and some others argue that the Convention must be seen as a "package", in that the new law was "purchased" by those States who were willing to abandon some of their rights under old law, and States unwilling to pay the price have no right to the new law's benefits.

As might be supposed, the non-signatories who want to enjoy those aspects of the new law which have to do with the right to traverse straits in a submerged submarine, or in an aeroplane, or to avoid regulation of passage by surface vessels are arguing that they may claim these new rights. Their argument rests on the ground that the Convention not only codifies customary law, but it also creates evidence of the existence of norms which are already or, at least, are becoming norms of customary law. Thus

Professor Anthony D'Amato of Northwestern University in the United States argues that the Convention through its creation of new treaty law is leading to recognition of new customary law. To a degree the Vienna Convention on the Law of Treaties supports the argument, for its Art. 38 reads: "Nothing in Article 34 to 37 precludes a rule set forth in the treaty from becoming binding upon a third State as a customary rule of international law recognized as such".

Professor Luke Lee, formerly a member of the negotiating group from the United States, also argues that the Convention, through its Art. 38, creates an attitude, namely that constitutive treaties creating new law may initiate the creation of customary law. In support of his argument Lee points to the *North Sea Continental Shelf* cases (1969) before the International Court of Justice. The Court foresaw the possibility of such a transition under four conditions — notably, that there be widespread and representative participation in the Convention and extensive and virtual uniformity of State practice evidencing recognition of the new rule, and also that there be passage of some time, however short. Lee notes, however, that a claimant must meet the burden of proof on State practice.

Time is too short today to raise all treaty law questions being debated. Some of the issues are raised with regard to the invalidity of treaties. No one debates the invalidity of treaties obtained by fraud, and Art. 49 of the Vienna Convention applies to vitiate them. If treaties are obtained because of the application of force, the issue is not so clear. Art. 2(4) of the United Nations Charter, requiring member States to refrain from the threat or use of force, would seem to make a treaty executed under such circumstances unenforcible, but earlier treaties present a problem. The People's Republic of China has claimed that the frontier treaties forced upon it by the Russian Tsar have no validity, but the Soviet Government continues to resist any change in the frontier.

Unconscionable treaties present a question, especially to jurists not trained in Romanist systems, where the doctrine of *lésion* is recognized to invalidate an unconscionable private contract. Charles Rousseau notes that no organ has as yet been qualified to declare a treaty unconscionable, and that only one case has been reported (the *Létitia* case). Regrettably, at least for scholars who seek the law in arbitral decisions, the case was settled by the Rio de Janeiro protocol recognizing validity.

A far more debated issue is the influence of *jus cogens* upon a treaty which establishes a norm violating what is now called modern *jus cogens*. No court or arbitral tribunal has ever declared a treaty void on the grounds of such a violation but there was much debate during the drafting of the Vienna Convention on the Law of Treaties over the vitality of the new version of the concept. Authors and diplomats from the developing and Socialist worlds did their utmost to insert in the Convention such a concept, and succeeded. Art. 64 introduces the principle, but with the limitation set forth in Art. 65. There must be notification by the claimant of nullity of the action it proposes to take. If objection to the claim is raised within three months, a proceeding under Art. 33 of the Charter must be initiated to resolve the dispute peacefully. Only thereafter, and following a waiting period of twelve months, must the issue be submitted to one of three methods of resolution – the International Court of Justice, arbitration (with the parties' consent) or the Secretary General of the United Nations, with request for initiation of a procedure specified in the Annex to the Convention on the Law of Treaties.

A major problem for scholars opposed to introduction of the new *jus cogens* principle into the Convention was determination of what is the new *jus cogens*. Some proponents argued that the new *jus cogens* is comprised of the commonly accepted principles set forth in resolutions adopted by the General Assembly of the United Nations. There is argument over the type of majority required for recognition of such resolutions as *jus cogens*, but most authors now seem to accept those denouncing slavery, racism and environmental pollution, and the resolution supporting the concept of permanent sovereignty over natural resources. As the list is by no means closed, there was fear among the traditionalists that the Third World, supported perhaps by the Socialist World, would use its majority to introduce topics that could not be accepted by the long-established States.

In view of this mistrust of resolutions likely to be adopted by the General Assembly, it becomes important to consider the positions being taken on the status of resolutions of the General Assembly of the United Nations. This topic falls within the next topic on our agenda.

II. Discussion

WEILER

There are two points in the presentation by Judge de Arechaga which caught my attention. I just want to throw them in as possible points for debate. First he said that the modern trend is to reject voluntarism as a necessary element in the creation of custom. But he did not spell out really the meaning of this rejection of voluntarism. Does it for example mean that the rule of the "persistent objector" is eliminated? I would like someone to deal with this theme: has voluntarism been eliminated, and what are the consequences of that?

The second point is one which comes up in any course of international law on sources and custom: to what extent is violation of the law a necessary condition of changing custom? President de Arechaga pointed out without elaborating that the 200 mile zone initiated as a possible violation. But does change in customary law necessarily mean as a *conditio sine qua non*, that someone somewhere has to break the law in order to move ahead towards a change? I am not taking a position on this, but I would like these two points, voluntarism and breaking the law in order to change the law, as two points for discussion.

Abi-Saab

I want to make two points. The first is an apology, because you have circulated an article of mine, which I wrote when I was a very young graduate student ("The Newly Independent States and the Rules of International Law", 8 *Howard Law Journal* (1962), 94–121). But since 1962, much water has run under the bridge. That article was written before the Vienna Convention on the Law of Treaties and long before all the work leading to the two Conventions on State Succession. In fact, if I have to pick an example indicative of how quickly law changes, there is none better than succession to treaties. Take, for instance, Dan O'Connell's thesis on State Succession in its first version of 1954; he represents the law then as prescribing almost total succession. Take the second edition of the same book in the late sixties, and you notice a turn-about of almost 180 degrees. He has to admit that the rule has become that of the clean slate, with exceptions. And that is what was more or less adopted in the Vienna Convention. Of course I know this is an over-generalization, but we are now speaking of general trends.

When I wrote this small article – and this brings me to the point raised by Professor Hazard – the full succession position was very strong. And there was also a kind of double-think: people speaking the language of progress, like Jenks and others, were in fact trying to impose on the Third World, lock, stock and barrel, all the 19th century system of international law. I am not referring to the Grotian system of the 17th century – which was ideological, but idealistic – but to that of the 19th century, which was the Great Powers' law, the Congress of Vienna, a hierarchical type of law, willed by the centre and imposed on the periphery through colonialism. But once colonialism began to recede, this law was supposed to be maintained and generalized through such arguments as the idea of a world law and the necessity of maintaining objective treaties, etc. As a result new States came to existence, like children, in an already-existing legal system which was binding on them even before they were born.

This was the general context in which that article was written; one had to react very strongly to it by saying that those who were speaking the language of progress were really defending a retrogressive case and trying to deny any choice to the newcomers. Of course, one State cannot contest the law which is already there, but if whole segments of the international community consider this law as no longer adequate, it is a different matter. I just wanted to clarify this point, because I am all for general international law, but for a general international law different from that of the 19th century.

This brings me to my second point, which is a comment on the very innovatory presentation of custom we have just heard from Judge de Arechaga. In fact as he was speaking, I was thinking "are we really still speaking of custom?" And I think the custom he described to us, which represents much of the actual situation, has only episodic resemblance to the custom we know from books. My impression is that through these new processes, what the international community is groping for is a technique for creating general international law. We have material interdependence – I insist on the adjective material – with the great division of labour resulting from technological advances and so on. For instance, we can all suffer from airway or railway strikes and things of that sort; and think what will happen to all of us tomorrow when data bank strikes deprive us of our sources and we no longer have books to fall back on. We have very strong and growing material interdependence.

But at the same time, there is politically a very heterogeneous international community which is universal, and very large. We are in dire need of rules of general international law to cope with all these new and rapidly changing phenomena; we are groping for these rules by extrapolation from existing rules and techniques, whether by trying to push treaties beyond the conventional community – and this is the custom-creating potential of codification treaties (and in a similar but different way, of General Assembly resolutions) – or through interpretation by the International Court (which sometimes goes beyond the limits of what is foreseeable from existing rules, but can only justify this by calling on custom again).

We are calling different things custom, we are keeping the name but *expanding the phenomenon*. After all, custom, if considered from a technical point of view, is not so much the rule; it is the procedure of creating the rule. These procedures are changing under our very eyes but we are still calling them custom because of the general recognition of custom as a source capable of creating general international law, while other procedures (or sources) are not or not yet generally recognized or accepted as having this potential. In fact we have new wine, but we are trying to put it in the old bottle of custom. At some point this qualitative change will have to be taken into consideration, and we will have to recognize that we are no longer speaking of the same source, but that we are in the presence of a very new type of law-making. The problem with this recognition, however, is that it may provide an argument for breaking the system altogether. This is why it may be safer, at least for the time being, to keep the old label, while using the new techniques. All the same, we have to be conscious of the qualitative change that is taking place in our instruments.

CASSESE

Although Georges Abi-Saab is trying to play down his paper of 1962, I think we should still try to stick to it. One point in particular which he made in 1962 is very important, and that has to do with reciprocity: customary international law and *reciprocity*. I will focus mainly on the attitude of different groupings of States towards international custom. The point Abi-Saab made in 1962 was that on the whole the attitude of developing countries towards customary international law was rather negative. At least at that stage, they tended to reject, not the whole body of general international law, but most customary rules, except for those based on reciprocity. I think at that stage, it was right to say that they favoured the rules (such as those on diplomatic immunities, State sovereignty and so on) which are based on reciprocity.

I wonder if this is still true today. Can we not see a gradual shift on the part of developing countries away from this notion of reciprocity toward a broader notion of solidarity or something which anyway goes beyond reciprocity? I am thinking of course of some cardinal concepts of international law which owe their origin to the Socialist countries and probably also to developing States. Take the concept of obligations *erga omnes*, for example. This is a kind of negation of the notion of reciprocity and as far as I know, developing countries are strongly behind it. Or the notion of *jus cogens*; again this is at variance with the principle of reciprocity, as is also the notion of a common heritage of mankind. As far as I know, even the Socialist countries at the outset were somewhat lukewarm vis-à-vis the concept of a common heritage of mankind, but there again reciprocity seems to have been jettisoned. If what I am saying is correct, this would constitute a very important development in the attitude of one major segment of the international community toward international law-making.

I should like to take up another vital point which was raised by Jo Weiler; namely what I would call the "objective" versus the "consensualist" or "voluntarist" approach to customary international law. Does the notion of what Ian Brownlie calls the "persistent objector" still play a role in the international community? Or to put it differently, can a State that opposes a nascent customary rule consistently from the outset nevertheless be considered bound by that rule? Now we all of course know the splendid paper written by Prof. Prosper Weil, and particularly the English version in the *American Journal of International Law*, in which, in a very subtle and clever way, he complains, among other things of course, about these new developments. Commenting on the *North Sea Continental Shelf* cases, he says "the International Court of Justice gave a negative answer to the question of the role of customary international law for countries which have objected to the rule when it was *in statu nascendi*". However, according to Professor Weil, "the implication was that the equidistance rule could otherwise have been imposed upon the Federal Republic of Germany even though it had expressly opposed that rule. And even though it was that very position which had lain behind its refusal to ratify the Convention". He goes on to say, "The opposability of custom was admittedly hitherto a presumption, but one which could be overturned by a State in its own particular case. Henceforth custom is opposable to all, with no possibility of escape. Explicit acceptance of a customary rule has never been required. From now on, even explicit rejection is effective." Of course he holds this to be a very bad thing, because it would mean a move from an anarchical society with traditional law, based on sovereign equality and as a consequence on a consensualist or voluntarist approach to international law, to a state of affairs based on majority rule where the majority is able to impose the new rule of international law on the minority, even with binding force. This would be equivalent to international legislation.

Now my view is that Professor Weil's misgivings are not justified because what he claims is not in actual fact true. The "persistent objector" still plays a role: a State cannot be bound by a rule which it has consistently opposed from the outset. There is evidence for this both in some very important cases heard by the International Court of Justice — the famous *Asylum* case and also the *Fisheries* case in which it was stated in fairly clear terms that the role of persistent objector cannot be discarded — and, probably even more important, in the position taken by the *Socialist countries*. You cannot disregard the political and legal stand taken by an important segment of the international community. To the best of my knowledge — but Bernhard Graefrath can correct me if I am wrong — all the Socialist countries are very keen to stress the importance of their participation in the adoption of either treaty rules or customary international rules. They very strongly believe that they cannot be bound by any rule "enacted", by any international body or gathering, whatever the majority, if they are not agreeable. In the light of the attitude of the Socialist countries and also of the cases decided by the Court I think that customary international law is still based on a kind of tacit agreement.

TED STEIN

I find myself somewhat in the situation of a child in a candy store, all the goodies being supplied here by the very distinguished speakers. I am honoured to be here and I wish to take advantage of the presence of so many luminaries whose writings I have studied and read before. I have heard a number of themes sounded that I want to try to put together, and suggest some directions I think the international legal order may be moving in, and some dangers that are posed by moving in those directions.

I think first we have to start with what I think is an evident truth but not often stated: the distinction between custom and treaties began as an empirical observation that there were obligations that States cited to one another and rights that they claimed with respect to one another which were not based on treaties concluded and binding on a bilateral basis. This observation was systematized through the work of publicists and others and then codified in Article 38 of the Statute of the Permanent Court of

International Justice. But the real point here is that we must begin our discussion of the international process of generating obligations and rights with empirical observation of the international system.

In his presentation Judge de Arechaga suggested a number of differences that can be observed between the classic process for generating universal rules of international law, and the contemporary process. I should like to put those contrasts in sharp form, as *a set of paired opposites*. In classical terms, general international law was unwritten; today it is written. It was unconscious; today it is conscious. Here is one of my own devising: before, customary law was accreted, it was generated over time through the accumulation of discrete instances; today it is instant and captured in some legislative formulation. It was bilateral (think back to classic chestnuts of customary international law learning like the *Caroline* incident); customary international law was always generated through bilateral interchanges; today they are multilateral interchanges. It was generated through processes that were not influenced by the procedures of any established forum; today general international law is generated in settings where formal procedural rules of the forum have a tremendous influence. One has only to think of the difference between the classical law of the sea generated through the practices of maritime powers in the 19th century and the contemporary law of the sea in the last portion of the 20th century.

I should like to make two predictions, based on the differences just referred to. First, the style of reasoning and argument about general international law is going to change from empirical or inductive to principally *interpretative*. We are going to look at texts and what was said about texts, we are going to be analyzing the rules of general international law in much the same way as we analyzed rules that are binding as a matter of treaty law. Second — and here I want to connect up with Professor Cassese's comment about the "persistent objector" — I believe the rule of the "persistent objector" is going to be of increasing importance in this new general era of international law. This is so because, first, the consent idea has, and always will have, an enormously powerful moral as well as social strength; second, we have moved into an era where the most powerful States are no longer capable of controlling the customary international law process as they once were. These two factors will result in States that have not characterized themselves in the past as "persistent objectors" in any particular field, characterizing themselves as "persistent objectors" in relation to rules generated by these new processes. I believe, for example, that the United States will one day claim the status of "persistent objector" with respect to certain rules of the law of the sea (e. g. the rule relating to deep-seabed mining which would reserve the deep-seabed to exploitation by the international deep-seabed authority).

There are however some dangers in these new processes. First of all it seems to me that some kinds of obligations do not seem very readily generalizable. Somehow the processes that the international system has generated do not seem capable of producing general obligations to submit to *binding third-party settlement*. And here I want to go back to one of the examples utilized by Judge de Arechaga: the near-consensus in the 1960 Conference on the Law of the Sea, with respect to preferential rights, and the 6+6 formula. This 6+6 formula was not tied to the dispute settlement, but the idea of preferential rights was tied to a binding arbitral mechanism for determining the existence of the objective conditions in which preferential rights would be justified. In the Court's opinion, where it treats that resolution as provoking a general right for a coastal State in a situation of dependence, what we have instead of an obligation to submit to binding third-party determination is a very mealy-mouthed reference to Art. 33 of the U.N. Charter.

The same is true of the area of *jus cogens* to which both Professor Hazard and Professor Cassese made reference. In the Vienna Convention on the Law of Treaties, the idea of *jus cogens* is linked absolutely to an obligation to submit to binding third-party dispute settlement. Loose references to *jus cogens* (there are so many such references in the international community and in the international scholarly community as well) are divorced from this condition. Somehow this problem has to be faced up to.

I would like to make one final point about the *danger* of some of these new processes. The status of the Exclusive Economic Zone (EEZ) is probably, as Judge de Arechaga states, the outstanding example of what he has termed the generative or constitutive effect of provisions contained initially in multilateral treaties, which then become the focal point of future practice, which in turn gives the rules the status of law. If in fact we look at the practice of States which have adopted EEZs, the practice is actually quite divergent from the text of the Law of the Sea Convention. We must at some point make a choice. Either the *practice* is what counts, or the *general acceptance* of the treaty text in the conference is what counts. On important points, such as the right to restrict navigation, many of the States that have adopted EEZs go much further than the conference text would permit. And, here too, we find a failure to generate anything like the dispute settlement obligations contained in the treaty in the general international law process.

De Witte

I have some questions on customary international law. First of all, I wonder whether it is more appropriate to speak of general rather than customary international law, or whether the two terms are synonymous. Secondly, it seems that more and more State practice is decided through the declarations of States in international *fora*. I wonder, then, whether there is still a difference between practice and *opinio juris* in the element of custom. Does the *material practice* of the State still count? For instance, does it count at internal level, if it is in opposition with declarations of the State in international *fora*? Furthermore, what theoretical objection is there to recognizing ***instant custom***? I understand that in most cases it is unacceptable, but there could be instances of all States agreeing in a very short time on a new rule. Is there any theoretical objection to this?

De Fiumel

I should like to throw out a few ideas regarding treaties and practice based on the relations among Socialist countries, which I think may be of interest. They are raised by some new phenomena (I do not know to what extent they can be generalized) in the ***conventional practice among Socialist countries***, particularly the Council for Mutual Economic Assistance (CMEA), known in the West as Comecon, We see an increasing number of agreements, called interministerial agreements, made between ministers in various sectors, and this large number of interministerial agreements raises a number of interesting legal questions. First, of course, the problem arises of the hierarchical relationship between intergovernmental agreements and these interministerial agreements: to what extent are interministerial agreements inferior to those of governments as such? In principle, of course, we see these arguments concluded by ministers as also being intergovernmental agreements, since the ministers are acting as State organs. In legal literature, however, the question is raised whether these interministerial agreements may sometimes be of a civil law character. That is, it is sometimes stressed that the ministries themselves are rather complex in nature; not only are the ministers State organs, but the economic ministries are also engaged in economic activity. From this new point, one may conceive the possibility that economic ministers in the various sectors might sometimes reach agreements among themselves that need not be of intergovernmental character, but perhaps may have the nature of civil law. This is still a very controversial point, but there are many authors in Socialist doctrine, for instance some Soviet authors, who are beginning to ask this question.

Another point is that sometimes the appropriate ministers reach agreements and sign them, not so much as ministers for a particular area of governmental economic activity, but rather as the heads of particular State enterprises. An instance might be a multilateral agreement signed by the communications ministers regulating railway problems among the Socialist states. In the literature, the question is then raised whether this multilateral agreement is to be treated as an intergovernmental agreement ***stricto sensu***, since the communications ministers who are the parties to the agreement are acting as heads of State railway enterprises, and these State enterprises are entities distinct from the State. From this viewpoint, we can of course treat such an agreement either as an intergovernmental agreement or perhaps as an agreement in civil law, if we accept that the real parties to the agreement are not the ministers as such, but the heads of the State railway enterprises.

Another phenomenon that arises in this area is that very often these agreements, particularly interministerial ones, concern problems which, properly speaking, are not aimed at regulating intergovernmental relations, but relations of civil law between physical persons or State enterprises. This is very frequent in the economic area. In these cases, the problem also arises of the internal authority of such an agreement. You perhaps know that in principle Socialist doctrine, and in particular Soviet doctrine, does not accept the possibility that international agreements may have direct effect in the internal sphere of States. They necessarily require *conversion*, an internal act of the State allowing an international norm to produce legal effects in the internal sphere of the State. This point too is far from clear. Even some Soviet authors accept the possibility of direct authority of international norms in the internal sphere and when one comes to Polish doctrine in this area, it is practically unanimous in accepting the internal authority of conventional norms without need for conversion. We then say that the international agreements may act *proprio vigore* in the internal sphere. It may logically be accepted that such a norm can act directly in the internal sphere because the will of the States has already been expressed by their signing the agreement, clearly with a view to relating relations that are in principle part of civil law, and that these norms have been formulated in such a way as to be directly applied. No additional procedure is required for them to be directly applied to relations of civil law of an international character. This problem too is much discussed in Socialist literature.

GAJA

A revival of "voluntarism" has recently taken place with regard to sources of international law. Thus, rules of general international law are considered to be applicable to a State only when that State has accepted them. If *acceptance* is not a mere fiction, this attitude causes considerable difficulties when one attempts to define the content of most rules and identify their legal addressees. The practice of very few States is usually known and even for those States the existence of acceptance of the rule may be hard to establish. In some cases, a rule appears to be operative with regard to a certain State, although the State concerned may not have accepted the rule or may even have objected to it. Acceptance of a rule contributes to its effectiveness; however, it cannot be held that no effective rule exists until it has been accepted. A compelling reason for excluding a rule which is effective in international society from the rules of international law has yet to be given. On the other hand, there are cases when a rule has been accepted by certain States but their conduct shows that there is no rule which can be said to be operative in respect of the same States. It is questionable whether acceptance should in these cases be taken as the decisive factor for asserting the existence of a rule of international law.

MERON

First a small comment about Prosper Weil's article in the *American Journal*. I think it would not be realistic to ignore the fact that that article has had a tremendous impact in the United States. For the time being in analyzing these questions, we must be aware of the fact that this article is probably the first very comprehensive paper covering these theoretical issues, and that it has been well and seriously received.

Now, with regard to the interministerial agreements mentioned by Professor de Fiumel, I think that it would be fair to suggest that the problem is not peculiar to relations between Socialist countries. You may be acquainted with a very famous Department of State circular on treaty making produced by an editor of the *American Journal*. This circular deals in great detail with the distinction between agreements made within the domain of public law, or international law, and agreements made between agencies of different States but which deal with what Professor de Fiumel called civil law. We could probably generalize somewhat, because it need not necessarily be civil law, but basically internal law. Put in terms of the Vienna Convention, we would be talking about agreements which are governed, or not governed, by international law. In any event there is a fair body of writing on this question, including the famous article by Oscar Schachter in the *American Journal of International Law* on agreements in the twilight zone: one of the problems he discusses is the status of those agreements which are not classical agreements under public international law.

Now I would like to move briefly on to more general subjects. In his presentation Professor de Arechaga spoke of the role of multilateral conventions, and their impact on reform, revision, change, and maybe even, though he did not put it this way, termination of customs. He referred to certain areas, for instance the law of the sea, in which the conclusion of agreements, (and one could almost have said the negotiation over a long period of years of certain agreements) and a developing consensus on certain issues, did affect the existing custom. This leads me to a point which was suggested by Professor Weiler which I believe we have not really answered, but which to me is basic: what is the effect of breach of custom on the future existence of certain customary rules? This can be related to the problem of treaty making or treaty negotiation, but can also be discussed *in abstracto*, not in the context of new treaties: how does breach of something that has been accepted in the past as representing a customary norm, affect the present and future status of that norm? Bruno De Witte referred to the relevance in this context of *internal practice of States*. Let me illustrate these problems with more specific examples to make them somewhat clearer. We know that in the whole domain of the law of the sea, the developments since 1958 which preceded the final conclusion of the U.N. Law of the Sea treaty did have a tremendous impact in the direction at least of destabilizing the custom.

Moving from this to different areas, let us suppose that we have a norm that is stated in international agreements very widely, but is also generally recognized as reflecting a customary rule. An obvious example of this would be the statements, which appear in so many international instruments, against *torture.* The recent report of Amnesty International suggests, to the shame of all of us, that the majority of the international community practises governmental torture. How does the element of practice relate to an area where every government will be willing to condemn the practice and to say that it violates international law? How does this relate to the basic components that we have to bear in mind with regard to any question of custom? To take a different area in which there has also been recognition (including the recent Restatement of the Foreign Relations Law of the United States) that the norm which emerged subsequent to the U.N. Charter has by now been accepted into the corpus of customary law, let us refer to *racial discrimination.* The last report of the United Nations commenting on the subject and referring to a number of basic questions, states openly that the majority of the international community does not comply with the requirements of the U.N. Convention on Racial Discrimination. These requirements are not only important *per se*, they are important because the prohibition of racial discrimination reflects a customary rule.

Should we try to aim at a distinction between the example of the modification of the law of the sea norms, and these other examples, by working out some kind of formula in which the psychological element would have the highest importance? Maybe States do violate rules regarding torture, and other subjects, such as race, but we do not hold this practice to negate or even weaken the existence of a customary international law because it is accompanied by continuing recognition. We should be aware that in this area the law compels us in fact to act differently, while with regard to the law of the sea the impact of the international negotiations, the impact of the development of new rules, has led in a different direction, namely to the weakening *per se* of certain norms, and growing doubt as to whether these norms as such still represent binding rules that ought to be taken into account.

There is no doubt in my mind, and this is my concluding point, that because of this growing interplay of emerging treaty rules and the many doubts being thrown on the past practices of forming customary rules, the role and the function of the "persistent objector" not only continues to exist, but will be a very vital one. There is no question that at least in what John Hazard referred to as the First World, the sort of standard practice to be envisaged in the future in the foreign offices will be that the

Senior Legal Advisor will tell the Junior Legal Advisor: "When in doubt, object. Do not get us into a situation in which we may be faced with being boxed in".

GRAEFRATH

I would like to confine myself to a short remark. It seems to me that nowadays there is a general tendency to stress the common aspects of customary and treaty law. I want to underline this trend, because it reflects a change in international relations. Of course, there was a time when Socialist lawyers had to stress the antithetical aspect between customary and treaty law to make clear that a Socialist State as a new State could not be bound by custom from colonial times or by rules established without its consent. This was true for most of the former colonial countries as well as for Socialist countries. But even at that time, this did not mean that every general rule of customary international law was rejected by Socialist States. The reason for this suspicion of customary law was clearly the fear of being bound without consent by rules which would be contrary to the interests of Socialist States; and this consideration continues to be important. But because there has been a fundamental change in the international situation and Socialist and newly independent States participate equally in the international law-making process, other aspects have come to the fore.

Professor de Arechaga has stressed the interaction between treaty law and customary law and I basically agree with this approach. Indeed, I would stress that it is even more than interaction: it is the common ground that is so important and makes the interaction possible, this common ground being agreement between States of one form or the other. It is important for custom to become law and for treaties to become real binding law; and it is because of this common ground that it is possible to codify customary law in treaties, to change customary law by treaties and treaty law by customary law.

Another important point is that State practice itself has changed. Today State practice in international relations, to a much greater extent than fifty years ago, is, or at least results, in treaty-making. I think we should not forget that when we speak about customary law, we are generally thinking, even without realizing it, of the past, when customary law was made by a restricted number of States. When lawyers speak about customary law quite often they simply refer as a source to one or two old decisions of small arbitration courts or individual umpires. Relying on an old decision concerning a special case under specific circumstances, they then try to elaborate a customary rule or attempt to prove that this decision was already the result of an existing customary rule. Referring to State practice now, what we have in mind is much more practice as reflected in treaties and acts of foreign policy at international conferences and in international organizations, than decisions of isolated arbitration courts. Nowadays, when we speak about emerging rules the main thing to look for is the treaty-making process for evidence of one kind of State practice. Today most peoples have an independent State and are in a position to take part in this process. They can articulate their wishes and intentions and therefore treaty making and implementation are essential pointers to the practice of States which is decisive for the creation of customary law. Of course, customary law may be bilateral, regional or general, and it would be wrong to identify a customary rule always with a general rule under international law.

Georges Abi-Saab has pointed to the "procedure" that is the norm-creating process as a new element; but hasn't it always been a "procedure" that was under review when we looked for State practice? I rather believe that what has really changed is the nature of the "procedure". Formally it tended to be State practice between certain, mainly European or European influenced, States, and not that of Socialist States or African and Asian countries. It was not so much the drafting and implementation of multilateral treaties as a restricted bilateral practice. Now we have a different kind of practice: there are many more States, States with extremely different backgrounds and interests; also, international communication and cooperation have developed enormously and produce widespread interdependence. It is hard to imagine any practice between two States that could not affect other States and even a bilateral treaty may affect some other or even all States. It is as a result of all these changes that it looks as though we are more concerned with procedure than before. I simply think the norm-creating process has changed and has become a more important function, an organizational function in international law-making.

There is another element which is very much related to the trend towards greater cooperation and interdependence between States. We are now in a situation where we really need some general rules to ensure that sovereign equality is in fact enjoyed by all States. It is not enough to rely on general principles; in the main areas of international cooperation generally agreed rules are necessary to guarantee that small States as well as big States, coastal States as well as landlocked States, developing States as well as industrial States, may exercise their sovereign rights. It is no longer sufficient simply to proclaim equal rights for every people; in practice this may mean to privilege some against others, because only some are in a position to use their rights effectively. It is for this reason that Socialist States have always favoured the process of codifying international law and efforts to ensure the equal enjoyment of rights by all States.

For instance, it is common knowledge that Socialist States have very much stressed that there is a type of general multilateral treaty, the object and purpose of which are of interest to the international community as a whole, and that therefore all States have an equal right to participate in them. While it was not possible to refer to these treaties directly in the Vienna Convention on the Law of Treaties, Socialist lawyers continue to emphasize the existence and the importance of these general rules of international law.

The approach to the conventions on *succession of States* is on the same lines. Here again Socialist States not only hold the opinion that new States have a right to determine their position towards preexisting treaty obligations, but they have always stressed that there are general multilateral treaties which are so basic for the international community as a whole and for ensuring the exercise of sovereign rights by all States, that the validity of these treaties should not be questioned. I think that this is a very well known position which reflects a development we witness every day.

I do not think, therefore, that we can really speak in general terms of a revival of voluntarism. There are two basic trends: one is the continuing importance of the principle that States cannot be bound against their will, that a practice which is said to have a law-creating feature must also be the practice of the State concerned. The other trend is that we are establishing more and more general rules of international law based on *jus cogens* and aimed at universal application. We use the codification process of treaty-making to restate a common and useful practice and try at the same time progressively to develop such rules to make sure that they correspond to the needs for peaceful cooperation in a world that is composed of States with different socio-economic systems. And in that sense the treaty-making process itself becomes an important element of State practice.

Abi-Saab

I have two small remarks to make. The first is in response to what Professor Cassese said about *reciprocity* underlying custom. I apologize in advance for having to defend myself again with regard to something I wrote a very long time ago, under different circumstances. What I meant there was that many of the customary rules are models of behaviour in which certain types of States usually found themselves in the role of beneficiary, while others rarely found themselves in that role, if at all: take, for example, all that used to be said about the protection of foreign economic interests, the theory of vested interests, and so on – you could immediately imagine who would be on one side, and who would always be on the other. I used the term "reciprocity" in this context, not in its technical sense, in order to say something like what Professor Graefrath was just saying: namely that the rules of customary law which really reflect sovereign equality – in the sense that all States can really benefit from them, in contrast to those exclusively used by and for the benefit of a particular segment of the international community – had stronger possibilities of not being contested in the long run, and could thus harden much more than others. And this is exactly what happened.

Take, for example, what happened in the field of State responsibility between Garcia Amador's draft articles in the fifties, which so strongly emphasized the protection of foreign economic interests, and Ago's followed by Riphagen's, from the late seventies up to now. These are a very different kettle of fish, with the emphasis on "secondary rules", in relation to which any type of State can find itself on either side, and not on "primary rules" (such as those dealing with foreign economic interests, or any other subject of international law, for that matter). It was in this sense, and not at all in the technical legal sense that I used the term "reciprocity", or, more exactly, "effective reciprocity", in that article. I just wanted to clarify this point, and of course I agree that much of the newly emerging international law is community-oriented, and puts the emphasis not so much on the exchange of benefits, as on the theory of the "common good". This orientation underlies international environmental law, *jus cogens*, article 19, etc., regardless of all the problems they may give rise to.

This is the first point I wanted to make. But I should like to add a footnote to it, in response to Ted Stein's idea that much of the new law is fuzzy because there is no clear agreement on the details, and also because of the lack of compulsory jurisdiction or guarantee of application. I agree that these are inconveniences, but we have to come back to the general "problématique", which I see as follows: we have an international community groping for a law which is general, which does not merely consist of bilateral agreements. If there is no neat procedure for producing general international law, there being no legislature which can render pre-existing law obsolete and replace it by new law, complete in all its details — it can only come about through a cumulative process; a process which by definition cannot produce an instant product. We may start off with a text which underlines the general idea, but does not provide all the details, as in the case of the restrictions on the Exclusive Economic Zone, and then gradually, by slow approximations, we will hopefully move on to such qualifications, as well as to the question of guarantees. The same or a parallel process is put into motion as far as participation in the rules is concerned. The whole idea behind Weil's article is that you cannot impose on everybody willy nilly what the majority wants. Agreed. We then get the syndrome of the "persistent objector", and the paradox of the pace setters of yesterday becoming the "persistent objectors" of today. But consolidation through widening acceptance, through the progressive "erosion of oppositions", may come gradually as a cumulative process. In other words, what we cannot have immediately in final shape should not be rejected completely, i. e. dismissed for being incomplete, as it may still be perfected, given time.

WEILER

In a way we have also been looking at a historical process which I will dichotomize artificially, because of course it is more gradual than a dichotomy. As a result of the emergence of new international law (U.N. Charter law) the new States are rejecting rigid rules of treaty succession etc., on the grounds that they did not participate in making that law (and claim that they would have been "persistent objectors" to it had they been around when it was made). It is the old family of nations, the First World, which at that time was trying to impose universal principles, that is now insisting on the "persistent objector" and is "anti-universalist". Of course this is a pure reflection of politics. You insist on the "persistent objector" when you are in a minority, and you accept the universal principle when you feel that you control it. In the fifties in the United Nations the Occidental World dominated the scene and was in a position to insist on universalism. Now the tables have been turned.

CASSESE

I would like to make three disparate points. First of all, I think I should reply to the query made by Bruno De Witte about whether we should talk of *general* or *customary* international law. Traditionally, for instance by distinguished positivists such as Heinrich Triepel and Dionisio Anzilotti, the terms customary international law and general, international law were used as equivalents. I think, though, that we should probably make a distinction between them; we should in my view talk of customary international law being either general or universal.

By general I mean rules which do not necessarily bind all the members of the international community. By contrast some fundamental principles of international law, say the seven basic principles laid down in the Declaration on Friendly Relations adopted by the U.N. General Assembly — and here I am taking up an idea advanced by Professor Graefrath — plus the principle on respect for human rights, are universal; that is, they are binding on all member States of the international community. I think that even South Africa is bound by the general principle of respect for human rights or the principle of self-determination, and could not claim the role of "persistent objector". In other words some customary rules of international law have evolved to such an extent as to be binding on everybody.

I may recall in passing that the use of the two different terms general and universal can already be found in some State constitutions. Thus, you may remember that Article 4 of the Weimar Constitution of 1919 actually spoke of "generally accepted" rules of international law, meaning by that expression customary law, whereas Article 55 of the Spanish Constitution of 1931 — one of the most forward-looking constitutions and very much geared to international law, though "killed", of course, by the Franco Revolution — stated that "universal" rules of international law were binding in the Spanish legal order.

Now let me move on to another important topic: what do we mean by *State practice*? This is a point raised by Bruno De Witte and it is a question which gives rise to a lot of argument among international lawyers. By this expression do we mean, say, the pronouncements made by delegates of the various countries within the General Assembly? If you go through the summary records of the Sixth Committee you come across a lot of important statements on rules of international law. Should we conclude that they reflect the State practice of the various countries concerned, or ought we to go further and look into the actual conduct of States, their domestic courts, how officials within the domestic setting of each country actually behave, and so an?

This becomes even more crucial when one turns to the problems relating to the laws of warfare. I remember having a discussion once about the rules of the First Geneva Protocol of 1977 protecting civilians. I had argued that to a very large extent these rules are not merely treaty rules, but have become customary international law. Why? Because of the various pronouncements made by so many delegates in the diplomatic conference on humanitarian law held in 1974—77. But a clever and articulate member of the Judge Advocate's Office of the United States objected to this in a way that made it clear that he thought I was crazy. He said: "That is not State practice. State practice on humanitarian law and the laws or warfare is the practice of the battlefield; it is the members of the army who make practice. You do not want to pay too much attention to the official statements made in the nice relaxed atmosphere of New York or Geneva. It is we who are engaged in the battle who by our behaviour can show whether our respective States consider that a particular rule of international law is, or is not, binding, has, or has not, emerged".

My third point is in effect an illustration. This is mainly for those who might be interested in one particular example of how difficult it is to decide, even from a scholarly point of view, whether a rule of customary international law has really evolved. Here I take up one of the points made by Professor Jimenez de Arechaga about the crystallizing or catalytic effect of international conferences where treaty rules are hammered out. Let me just show you how the various arguments can be put forward for and against a certain view. I shall be referring to Article 1(4) of the First Geneva Protocol of 1977, which states that wars of national liberation should be regarded not as internal or civil conflicts, but as international armed conflicts. A large number of political and also legal consequences ensue from this. The rule was adopted in Geneva, by a very strong majority and I have put forward the view that the adoption of this rule had a crystallizing effect. By this I mean that the rule is a treaty rule but also embodies a rule of customary international law, a rule that is binding even on States which did not vote for it in Geneva.

I put forward three arguments in defence of this view. First, before the adoption of the rule, very important resolutions to the same effect had been adopted by the General Assembly. Of course, Western countries had often voted against these resolutions, but then my second argument is that in Geneva the U.S. delegation made a proposal that the rule should be adopted by consensus, without a vote being taken. Israel objected, a vote was taken and the only country that voted against was Israel, whereas the majority of the members of the diplomatic conference were in favour of the rule (there were a few abstentions). What had been lacking before in the General Assembly was no longer so in Geneva, because most Western countries which until 1977 had been opposed to a rule of this kind, came out in favour of it (except of course for Israel, which in this case acted as a "persistent objector"). Even those Western countries which to some extent expressed reservations or misgivings did not actually challenge the new rule; they merely criticized it on the grounds that it was "bad law".

My third argument is that Egypt, Greece and Australia, (two Western countries and one Third World nation) stated formally that by the adoption of this treaty rule the international community had meant to demonstrate the opinion that a customary rule of international law had evolved. They very clearly stated that this was a rule of customary law and none of the other delegations objected to this contention.

These are the three arguments in favour of this process of general international law, but of course there are also arguments against. First of all, my first argument may be countered on the grounds that one should not attach too much importance to General Assembly resolutions, because they do not amount to actual practice. This is exactly what the member of the Judge Advocate's office said on that other occasion. Pronouncements by the General Assembly are not tantamount to practice, and therefore one element of the formation of customary international law is missing, namely actual practice of States.

A second argument can be based on the attitude of some Western countries, and in particular the United States of America. True enough, the head of the American delegation, George Aldrich proposed the adoption of the rule by consensus. But the argument to which I am referring points to the real motivations behind the attitude of the American delegation and claims that the American delegation was in favour of this new rule on wars of national liberation only because they thought that it was pointless. They thought this because it related only to South Africa, to Israel and to colonial countries: now, South Africa of course would never be bound by the rule because there was no South African delegation in Geneva in 1977, Israel voted against, and the Portuguese colonies at that stage were no longer under the colonial yoke. The rule would therefore have no importance or impact whatsoever. So why not support it?

The problem is, then, whether we also need to look at the motivations behind the attitude of States. Should we consider, for instance, that the attitude of the American delegation is part of this process of custom formation, and if so must we also take into account the political or ideological motivations behind these rules?

The third and last objection was that of course nobody objected to what Egypt, Greece and Australia said with regard to the rule having general value going beyond the contractual effect of the treaty, simply because they considered that they were involved in a process of treaty-making at a diplomatic conference which had the purpose of working out treaty rules. This being the case, they did not feel the need to reply to Egypt, Greece and Australia because they felt that what these countries were saying did not make sense.

So you can see, then, what different arguments can be put forward when dealing with this problem, which I think is one of the most crucial we have to discuss.

Meron

I think that Nino Cassese has just made a great contribution to our discussion by really putting these things in a sort of comprehensive scope. Two or three questions come to mind. How does a government commit itself to the formation of a custom? Is it conceptually a once off operation, expressed for instance by a vote, by a statement? Or is it something like a continuing gradual process? If it is the latter that we have in mind, do we not have to look at the "ensemble" of the positions taken by the same government on the same issue, say in the General Assembly, and positions subsequently taken by the same government in a different *forum*, say a domestic *forum*, in reports to Congress and so on? What is the significance for the formation of customary international law of just one particular position which is not in accordance with either previous or subsequent positions?

The second problem I wanted to refer to is this: how do we relate the entire question that we are now discussing, i. e. governmental acts which contribute to the creation of a binding international commitment for a particular government, to *constitutional* law?

Let me now turn to the First Geneva Protocol of 1977. I myself will agree that quite a few provisions of the Protocol are declaratory of customary international law. We may differ about this or that provision, but quite a few do reflect customary international law. Surely the delegations that participated in the negotiating process in Geneva were fully aware that, constitutionally, whatever was being said and voted upon was not *per se, ipso facto*, binding on governments, because of basic constitutional provisions regarding ratification. In other words, if we press too hard on statements, if we attribute too much importance to this or that vote taken in isolation, how do we then relate this to the whole underlying constitutional obligations of governments?

And finally — it is probably more a question of political science or psychology than a question of law — what liberty do we have, what discretion, in reading or interpreting governmental statements? You say quite rightly that the governments that challenged certain propositions in Geneva did not necessarily challenge the basic concept of law. But isn't it true as a basic political science proposition that if a government wants to express reservations about something, or water something down, or help erode it in the future, it will choose for its statement, not something that will get it into trouble, but something that will cause it minimum political difficulties. I am not suggesting that this process of interpretation is not legitimate: it is legitimate, but requires in every case a fairly serious historical *ad hominem* in the sense of a detailed analysis of what brought about this particular position.

WEILER

There is a footnote to that. The more you press for greater value to be given to this type of "intraconvention" statements and practice, the more reluctant will delegations be to reach an accord, thus diminishing what Georges Abi-Saab said: let us have some sort of document, and then by accretion have customary law. There can be a dialectical process: the more value you give to it, the more reluctant they will be to come out with any kind of consensus because of the fear that they are binding themselves more than traditional canons of treaty law would suggest.

JIMENEZ DE ARECHAGA

I would like first to try to answer the two main questions that were raised, which were really so provocative that they became the focus of the discussion. The first question is that of the "persistent objector". I agree with Professor Cassese that the principle remains, but perhaps, at least with respect to certain very essential norms of international law, there is a contemporary tendency not to allow individual "persistent objectors", but only groups of States to veto the establishment of a customary rule. Take for instance, the position of South Africa with respect to *apartheid*. Its individual opposition is not something that would lead us to consider that the rule against *apartheid* is not a general customary rule binding all States. I think that in this respect the provision on *jus cogens* which refers to the international community as a whole, a formula which has also been adopted in connection with international crimes, indicates that what is required is a consensus of the three worlds: the Western developed countries, the Socialist States and the Third World. This means that one cannot consider that a general customary rule has been accepted if there is persistent objection on the part of one of the three worlds, by groups of States rather than individual objectors. In this respect there is clearly a political background to these problems.

Now, to admit the possibility of "persistent objectors" against a certain rule, when such opposition emanates from one of these groups of States, is not equivalent to holding a voluntarist view of customary law. To me these are different things. The idea of tacit agreement as the basis of customary law was rejected by the International Court of Justice in the 1969 *North Sea Continental Shelf* cases. Basing itself on the words of Article 38, the Court looked for general rather than unanimous practices and in particular did not take into consideration whether the Federal Republic of Germany had or had not agreed to the rule relating to equidistance. It considered the broad spectrum of the practice of States and this is quite a different thing from the question of the "persistent objector".

The second question that was put, very provocatively, is whether we can allow a breach of the law to be the source of a customary rule. It all depends on what you take to be a breach of law. Before 1974 many States held the Latin American policy on the 200 miles limit to be a breach of law, but we did not. The question hinged, of course, on what one considered to be the established law: was it or was it not that of the three mile limit affirmed by the big maritime powers? For the Latin American States, the fact that at three conferences, held in 1930, 1958 and 1960, there had been no agreement on the extent of territorial waters, meant that there was no such 3 mile rule. They were therefore not violating any law. Besides, all law, international or municipal, has to be considered in a time perspective. Since all systems of law tend to perpetuate themselves, to become established and permanent, they must be elastic enough to admit evolution and a persistent penetration and incorporation of considerations of justice. It is clear now to everybody that fisheries in coastal waters were completely unfair and gave an inadmissible advantage to the big maritime powers, which fished in the waters of a State, and when the resources were exhausted moved their fleets to the waters of another coastal State.

In the *Icelandic Fisheries* case, decided while the Caracas conference was being held, the Court recognized the preferential rights of the coastal State to the fishing in its adjacent waters. In support of this view the Court admitted that certain customary rules had become established in the practice of States around the nucleus of a proposal which had failed to pass by a single vote at the Second U.N. Conference on the Law of the Sea. In other words it accepted the generating effect of a mere proposal *de lege ferenda* which had not been approved. The emphasis was thus shifted from the formal instrument to the conference process itself, as being capable of revealing a consensus, or what the Court called the "near-agreement" of a large majority of the participating States. The implications of this judicial pronouncement with respect to the work of the Third Conference on the Law of the Sea proved to be far-reaching.

At the Caracas Conference the States, acting as legislators, went beyond the Court and overruled its conclusions, as they are entitled to do. The big maritime powers yielded one after the other and accepted the Exclusive Economic Zone concept, proposed by the Third World countries. On the basis of this consensus almost all coastal States have today proclaimed

Exclusive Economic Zones, or Fishery Zones. In the *Tunisia-Libya* case the special agreement authorized the Court to take into account "the new accepted trends in the Third Conference on the Law of the Sea". As Professor Abi-Saab said in his successful pleading, this was a tribute paid to the innovative work of the Conference and a recognition of its great impact on the evolution of the law. The Court answered this invitation by saying that "it could not ignore any provision of the draft convention if it came to the conclusion that the content of such provision ... embodies or crystallizes a pre-existing or emergent rule of customary law".

This *dictum* signifies two things: first, that there are in the unratified convention provisions which already constitute rules of customary international law, and second, that not all the provisions of the Convention have attained such status. This should answer the question put by one of the participants in this conference. The problem is, though, how one is to select and recognize, among the 320 articles, those which may be considered as part of customary law. And here the tripartite distinction advanced before between *declaratory*, *crystallizing* and *generating* effects, may be of assistance.

One finds some provisions in the Convention which merely restate or codify existing principles and rules of international customary law, such as the articles defining the legal status of the territorial sea; its baselines; rights with respect to the continental shelf; the regime of the High Seas, etc. Most of these provisions reiterate those already established in the 1958 Conventions.

Other provisions have had the effect of crystallizing new or emergent rules of customary law which were *in-statu nascendi*. One of these is that most elusive and intractable issue, the breadth of the territorial sea, about which three conferences, in 1930, 1958 and 1960, had failed to reach agreement. It may be considered that this long-standing issue, which constituted a serious gap in the Law of the Sea, has now been settled at 12 miles by the consensus of the conference, embodied in Article 3 of the Convention. Other examples may be the new definition of the continental shelf, rejecting the exploitability test; the rights and limitations of scientific research; the powers and obligations of States concerning pollution of the marine environment, etc.

Finally, the obvious example of an already accomplished generating effect is the Exclusive Economic Zone. The Conference demonstrated the emergence of a consensus between those Latin-American, Asian and African States which advocated the zone and the maritime powers, which, one after the other, at Caracas, became resigned to it. But this acceptance and the incorporation of the Zone in the Conference texts was not sufficient to create a new rule of customary law. What was decivise for the building of this new institution was what took place after the Conference: on the basis of the consensus revealed at Caracas, practically all coastal States have now proclaimed an Exclusive Economic Zone or a Fisheries Zone. The rules of the Convention thus served as the model or guide for a consistent and uniform practice of States, which has now become an irreversible part of today's law of the sea. This development constitutes a radical and fundamental change in the law of the sea. The 200 miles claim originated in Latin-America and was for a long time considered a violation of classic international law and of the Grotian dogma of the freedom of the sea. Today, with a time perspective, we realize that the alleged violation really constituted the initial stage in the process of improvement of existing, but outmoded and inequitable rules.

States, confronted with the fact that it takes many years for the entry into force of a treaty, have become impatient and prefer, as an alternative solution, the customary source, which, contrary to doctrinal expectations, has shown itself to be much quicker than the conventional one. And the customary source has not led, as some feared, to the stagnation of the *status quo*. On the contrary, it has functioned as an efficient mechanism, not just for law-making, but for law-reforming and the adaptation of fundamental rules to the new circumstances and requirements of the international community of today.

Professor Stein has said that in some EEZ proclamations certain countries have gone beyond the terms of the 1982 Convention on the Law of the Sea, by equating their Exclusive Economic Zone to territorial sea. If that is so, then we have another advantage of the Convention as a source of customary law. The terms of the Convention, which contain clear limitations to the rights recognized to the coastal State over its Exclusive Economic Zone, would govern any dispute.

While the Exclusive Economic Zone has become an established institution, as recently recognized by the Chamber of the Court in the *Gulf of Maine* case, the same cannot be said of the common heritage of mankind with respect to sea-bed resources. This is a consequence of the persistent objection of the Western group of economically developed States. Conversely, it would be difficult to accept the thesis advanced at the Conference by Ambassador Richardson of the United States, to the effect that in accordance with the customary law principle of the freedom of the seas, any State or group of States may validly exploit those resources unilaterally. This cannot be a customary rule of international law since it is strongly objected to by the other two groups of States: the Third World and the Socialist countries. Until the question is settled no one can claim that they may exploit sea-bed resources in accordance with international law.

As for the role of *practice* and *opinion*, I think the answer was given by Professor Meron: both are required, because the practice which is relevant is that which coincides with *opinio juris*. But of course, the two elements are very much interrelated: for instance, if a State makes a claim against another, the advancing of such a claim is, at the same time, an implicit admission that the rule cited would also apply against itself. This is an obvious consequence of a basic rule of equity. As to the *question of time* for the establishment of custom, of course there is no theoretical objection to all States at the same time agreeing in a codification conference on a certain rule; that rule then immediately becomes part of international law, as was said long ago by a judge of the Permanent Court, Judge Weil. Now, the need for a time element arises because only time reveals the emergence of a consensus; consider the Law of the Sea Convention: it took ten years to produce some customary rules. Finally, we may ask where the Court will place these developments, bound as it is by Article 38 of the Statute. Since they are neither treaty law nor general principles, there is no place to deposit all these new elements emerging in general international law, except by reference to the paragraph on custom and general practice accepted as law.

HAZARD

If I were presiding in the Sixth Committee I would have a difficult time determining what the consensus on this really is. It seems to me we have agreed really only on one very important point, that customary law and treaty law are so intertwined that they cannot be separated. I am glad that Judge de Arechaga in his final comment mentioned the famous Article 38 of the Statute of the Court which, I suppose, at that time was drafted because the two – customary law and treaty law – were seen as rather separate sources. If it were to be redrafted in the light of what we have been hearing this morning I am not sure that there would be such a distinction. In fact I am not certain that the treaties or conventions would have been placed first. I have always been taught that the order in which the sources of law appear in Article 38 is not necessarily a hierarchy, but it is true that conventions are placed first because, at the time it was drafted, conventions were believed to be the best source of law, it being possible to see and detail what was in them. And, for customary law, as Professor Brierly used to say, you have to search through the files of the Great Powers (he did not think it was necessary to look at those of the Small Powers!). If we go into a system of codification of all customary law, we will lose some of the practice that I consider very important as a source of law, but most of the world then believed that treaties were the answer and conventions the hope of the future. Everything would be written down, and customary law would finally take the form of a sort of American Restatement of Law. This has not happened.

I think we are in total agreement that there is an interrelationship between treaties and customary law and from what I have been hearing here this morning it seems that customary law is taking the ascendency at the moment. Treaties are now looked upon as a first step towards the creation of customary law, instead of the reverse. It used to be customary law that was put into treaties through the codification process, and now, to many people's minds, customary law is apparently created by the negotiation of a treaty; and even if not everybody signs the treaty, they are all bound it, because it is custom. There is certainly no consensus on this, but, as I started out by saying, one has to consider the politics of the situation. I think that most of the arguments that are heard in the world are by way of being lawyer's briefs and like you, because I am a common lawyer too, I like to think that maybe somewhere in the background there is a court which is going to determine which of the two briefs, or which combination of the two briefs to accept as the existing law. So I do not take the conflict terribly seriously, because I see it in terms of arguments put by good lawyers before the court of public opinion, (regrettably the whole world is not yet prepared to go before the International Court of Justice for final determinations). Public opinion is the last resort. The difficulty is that we academics have a hard time determining what public opinion really is. I suppose because we are academics we rather tend to look at what all the scholars of the world are saying and see what that adds up to, but I know that other people are not entirely prepared to accept this. I find that there certainly is in this room an "inquiètude", as the French would call it, about these progressive steps, about the development of a customary law from a treaty, whether you consider it instant custom, or whether the treaty is only a step towards the custom.

Chapter II

The Role of General Principles of Law and General Assembly Resolutions

I. Presentations

A. General Principles of Law

RIPHAGEN

I have been struck today, not for the first time, by the abstract character of discussion about the sources of international law. Perhaps this is because nobody wishes to accept any source without qualification. This holds for domestic legal systems to a certain extent and much more so for States which want some sort of ideal procedural or substantive guarantee that the product of the source does not upset what they regard as the right balance between *liberté*, which corresponds to sovereignty in international law, *egalité*, equality, and *fraternité* or solidarity, which now has a more important place in international relations than previously.

What kind of guarantee do States want? There are procedural guarantees involving some sort of consent, implicit or otherwise, and there is the guarantee that what is put forward as a rule of international law is somehow a logical implication of another accepted rule of international law. This brings us to a question that has already been referred to during our dicussions: whether we can really distinguish between source proper on the one hand and what comes out of it, that is, primary, secondary or tertiary rules, in what is called the system of international law. What strikes me also about today's discussions is that no reference has been made to what is called soft law. There exist various degrees of hardness or softness of law, and this may be important for the determination of the sources of that law.

The point I wish to stress with regard to the so-called general principles of law is the fact that every abstract rule of law is surrounded and even counterbalanced by other rules of international law. This too is a point we touched upon this morning, when we were discussing a possible hierarchy in the various sources. I suggest that there is not so much a hierarchy in the sources, as a hierarchy in the product of those sources.

Anyway, as I said, every single abstract rule is somehow counterbalanced (or surrounded, if you prefer a more neutral expression) by other rules, and in this respect it is perhaps significant to refer to what are called the rules of interpretation of treaties. When you look at the Vienna Convention you see this relationship between various sources reflected in the rules of interpretation. You have the natural meaning, you have the context, you have the object and purpose which should somehow be derived from the treaty as a whole, and you also have the other rules of international law applicable between the parties to the treaty; these are actually mentioned in the Vienna Convention. Here again, then, each particular rule is surrounded by other rules of international law. It is interesting to note that for the first time in the 1970 General Assembly Declaration on Principles concerning Friendly Relations, there is a final clause which states that every principle enumerated has to be interpreted in the context of other principles. This of course poses the question of the relationship between the various principles and particularly of conflict between them. Now that clause which appeared first in the Declaration on Friendly Relations — and I have some sympathy for it, having suggested it myself! — is once again the final clause both in the General Assembly Definition of Aggression, and in the Helsinki Final Act. It seems to be a sort of guarantee for the States involved that they are not bound by the strict formulation of the various rules but can interpret them in the context of other rules. I think this is important, now that I come to the specific subject of the so-called principles of international law as a source of international law.

I notice in our discussion that we agree on customary law and treaty law intertwining and perhaps we can agree even to admit the existence of general principles of law, but when it comes to concrete instances we are bound to disagree. It was quite clear during this morning's discussion that while everyone accepts customary law and treaties, there is no consensus on the interrelationship between the two, or when concrete examples are considered. This makes determination of the sources of international law as such a very hazardous job indeed. But I suggest that this is partly a consequence of insufficient attention being paid to the fact that any rule of law from any source is somehow either counterbalanced or extended by rules from other sources of international law. This is certainly even more the case as regards general principles of law, because principles, however you define the word, are always even more abstract than rules.

Another point I would like to highlight is the mention of the general principles of law in Article 38 of the Statute of the International Court of Justice, which in a certain sense counterbalances the fact that, by the particular wording of the article, the Court is limited in its actions since it has to apply rules of international law. I suggest that under these circumstances it is absolutely necessary that aside from customary law and treaties, the Court should have a certain latitude, and this latitude is given by reference to general principles of law. Now the proof of the pudding is in the eating. For instance, when accepting the concept of *jus cogens* a lot of delegates at the conference of Vienna tried to give examples; but if you start giving examples, you get disagreement. Even those who accepted the idea of *jus cogens* as a possibility were wary about certain examples of *jus cogens* made by other States. And the same would probably apply to the general principles of law as referred to in Article 38.

As I said, the proof of the pudding lies in the eating. What are supposed to be general principles of law? In the *travaux préparatoires* relating to the Statute of the Permanent Court of International Justice certain examples are given of general principles of international law and it is very interesting to look at them. There is for instance a reference to the principle of *res judicata*, a principle which does apply, but not to all types of settlement of disputes. In the case of the dispute settlement which was provided for but did not succeed in the 1958 Geneva Convention on fishing, etc., there is no *res judicata* at all: the decision of the dispute settlement body could be changed in the face of changing conditions. Then there is the principle of good faith; nobody could quarrel with that of course, but the result is something that needs to be discussed. There are certain principles relating to procedure, and again nobody would deny that anybody charged with the settlement of a dispute needs to invent some rules of procedure. He would not be able to do his job otherwise; he may have to fill in *lacunae* in the *compromis* or even choose between conflicting provisions in it. As regards the latter I can cite the example of the *Air Services* award: there the *compromis* contained clearly conflicting ideas and the arbitral tribunal had to decide which to apply. In short, when you have third-party procedures, the third-party is necessarily required to fill in some gaps left by the *compromis*.

Going back to the *travaux préparatoires* we find another, to my mind, amusing principle, to the effect – and I quote – "that what is not forbidden is allowed". Now this principle in present day international law is very much disputed, otherwise we would not have a topic like liability for injurious consequences of acts not prohibited by international law. You do not find it very much referred to in any doctrine or judiciary pronouncement. The *travaux préparatoires* also talk of a principle proscribing the abuse of rights. This is all very well, but it begs the question, as when the idea of *abus du droit* first came up in France, there were writers who, in a sense correctly, said "le droit cesse où l'abus commence". By proscribing abuse of rights you put a question rather than give an answer. There is also reference in the *travaux préparatoires* to the principle by which under special circumstances the stronger takes a rightful precedence over the weaker. That is something that nobody is going to accept nowadays, except possibly by underlining these special circumstances, of course.

Now, so as not to make my introduction too long, I would just like to comment briefly on what Bin Cheng, one of the best known writers on the subject of general principles of law, included in 1953 as general principles of law. The first principle he talks about is that of self-preservation, and he goes on to discuss its internal application. When one looks at this nowadays one asks oneself what he needed this principle for. He needed it as a counterbalance to what you could call the extraterritoriality of aliens and their property, a rule which is not really considered as a principle nowadays, although it necessarily reflects on the usefulness of the international application of the principle of self-preservation. As to the external application of this principle, when looking at what Bin Cheng gives us as an example, we are reminded of the fact that this type of situation has now been dealt with in the Draft Articles on State Responsibility, for instance in the case of the so-called state of necessity. Here again when we look at the draft prepared by the International Law Commission on this question, we see that it was very careful not to give too great a scope to the principle of self-preservation. Of course the principle itself of self-preservation is clearly linked with another thing that we do not consider as a principle nowadays, and that is sovereignty itself.

Then we have the principle of good faith, which according to Bin Cheng implies the principle of the non-abuse of rights. Again one cannot avoid the feeling that the whole principle is introduced as a counterbalance to the somewhat outdated concept of complete sovereignty of States. And to the extent that complete sovereignty of States is limited by rules of customary or treaty law, the scope of the principle of good faith becomes less far reaching than it was before. But that of course is partly to be explained by developments in international relations and procedures since Bin Cheng wrote his famous book on this topic. I think the same holds, up to a point, with regard to another principle, the juridical concept of responsibility, which covers things like imputability, fault, integral reparation and approximate causality. One may well ask whether these are really derived from a concept of responsibility or whether they do not rather constitute a particular customary law explication of that concept. Talking of customary law, we can refer again to the work of the International Law Commission on State responsibility where most of these things have been dealt with in terms of written law, or possibly future written law. Looking at the concept of State responsibility, one cannot really say that the rules of imputability, fault, etc. are implicitly in or derived from a concept of responsibility, in particular – and here we have to take into account later developments – since we nowadays recognize that international law is not necessarily limited to such rights and obligations as entail legal consequences provided for by real breaches of international obligations, but also has a part which deals, as I say, with liability for injurious consequences of acts not prohibited by international law. So there may be no logical derivation involved in the concept of State responsibility at all.

Further general principles put forward by Bin Cheng on the basis of decisions of arbitral tribunals and so on are the principles on judicial proceedings. Obviously when there is a basis for judicial proceedings by an independent third party, then you have to invent some criteria to enable it to fulfil its task. But there is nothing very logical here either, because it all depends on the type of dispute settlement agreed upon. I have had occasion already to refer to the non-applicability of the *res judicata* principle to the sort of dispute settlement which comes close to a form of international management; similarly *res judicata* does not apply in matters of administrative decisions. It is doubtful therefore whether these principles on judicial proceedings mentioned by Bin Cheng are really universal.

Now I might perhaps sum up what the meaning or function of general principles of law as a source of international law is. But before I do this, I should also mention a more recent claim for a general principle of law, put forward by some writers on environmental law. G. Handl, for instance, who has written extensively on environmental law, considers as a general principle of law the rule that where "States or private persons controlled by them engage in activities that carry a recognizable significant risk of transnational harm, they will be held strictly liable without having violated international obligation if harm typical of the risk created materializes". This is claimed to be a general principle of law deriving directly from the principle of the sovereign equality of States. Now it is superfluous to point out that in the present-day world there is no general agreement on this principle at all. But perhaps this is also a consequence of the fact that by talking about source, one abstracts from the product of the source and particularly one abstracts from the relationship of the product of that source and the product of other sources. As I see it, the *function of general principles of law is twofold*: first of all to take some rules deriving from other sources to their logical consequences, and secondly to counterbalance rules deriving from other sources. In both cases, the claiming of a general principle of law only fulfils one step of the function. It poses something next to other rules of international law, but it does not provide a solution to the conflict between this rule and the other rules derived from other sources. And it is this second function, this second problem, which should in my mind get more attention from international lawyers.

B. The Role of General Assembly Resolutions

Condorelli

It was only three or four days ago that the organizers of this workshop asked me to introduce the discussion on the effects of resolutions of international organizations. Out of friendship I accepted without the slightest hesitation; an indubitable demonstration of rashness. But the fact that I was given so little time to prepare this statement ultimately puts me in an easier position: no one will be able to complain of the banalities and absurdities I utter in the course of it. I shall therefore take advantage of an enviable position of total freedom: being absolved in advance of responsibility, I may cheerfully say whatever passes through my head. Thus I shall, on some of the subjects I shall mention, seek first of all to say the banalities and then the absurdities. At bottom this is perhaps the best method to ensure the success of a colloquium of this kind; in other words, one may hope that the ensuing debate will be all the richer and more stimulating because the participants feel the need to react to "provocation".

Before coming to the heart of the matter, I must still interpret it. I have been asked to introduce the theme "the effect of resolutions" but am not supposed to talk about all possible effects of all possible resolutions: I am not to forget that what we are discussing here is the "sources of international law". By that I understand the ways, mechanisms and procedures whereby new rules of law are created or old rules are amended or abrogated. So from the outset I will exclude from my subject anything to do with the effects of resolutions other than those relating specifically to the elaboration, amendment or cancellation of international law (that is those with "normative effects"). The majority of resolutions, in all international organizations, have to do broadly with the application of the existing law, and not the creation of new rules. We need not therefore concern ourselves with these resolutions to the extent that they are confined to organizing the work of the organization concerned, running its institutional activity, pursuing, through the means provided for, the common interests of the Member States, on the basis of pre-established rules of applicable law. The binding effect or otherwise of such rules changes nothing from this viewpoint. For instance, the fact that a resolution of the U.N. Security Council adopted under Article 41 of the Charter is, where appropriate, binding on States, does not make this resolution produce a new legal rule, since all that happens here is the application to a specific case — with binding effect — of a pre-existing provision. The case is conceptually equivalent, to give another example, to a resolution whereby the General Assembly asks one of its subsidiary agencies, or the Secretary General, or ECOSOC, to do something or refrain from doing something.

The distinction just drawn should not of course be understood too rigidly, since the boundary between the area of the formation of rules of law and that of their application cannot be represented by a clear line, whether in domestic or (*a fortiori*) in international law. Thus the resolutions of an international organization constitute an essential element in its practice, that must carefully be taken account of in evaluating both the content of the rules applied and their evolution. Subject to this reservation the distinction should nevertheless be retained, so as to determine better what questions are to be discussed.

This preliminary (and fundamental) delimitation of our subject does not bring us directly to focus on the problems that are at the heart of our concern, which the organizers of this colloquium were no doubt thinking of when they decided to bring us together. The fact is that resolutions of international organizations may play a part in the process of elaborating rules of international law in very different ways and through many different channels. The resolutions may themselves constitute the *direct source* of rules, or else represent a more or less important *contribution to their formation*, but as one element in a more complex process.

Here I shall concentrate attention on questions relating to resolutions as "a direct source", and therefore avoid going over all the efforts and contributions that the various international organizations make, for instance to the formation of international agreements between States (encouragement, preparation, adoption, publication, etc.). Moreover, I shall only in passing mention the fact that organizations can also, as is well known, be parties to international agreements or else called upon to take part in procedures aimed at amending treaties, as is the case with Article 108 of the U.N. Charter regarding its amendment. Nor will the resolutions whereby many international organizations engage in various activities hold our attention: it will suffice to mention them, without forgetting to note that close participation by international organizations in normative processes is a typical feature of the contemporary international community.

I now come to those cases in which the resolution of the international organization appears as (or aspires to constitute) the *direct source of rules of law*. Here too an operation of reconnaissance and ground clearing seems necessary, so as to pick out and leave aside those situations which, although falling within the area under observation, are of less interest from our viewpoint.

The international organizations, as instruments created by States for cooperation in specific sectors, consist of a more or less sophisticated organic apparatus made up of a set of agencies and bureaucratic structures. The functioning of this apparatus obviously requires appropriate rules of law. But experience has shown that, since the founding treaties inevitably contain gaps as regards the system of relationships between agencies (and between officials and the organization), it is advisable to give the organization concerned the power to regulate these areas in detail itself through unilaterally enacted measures. Moreover, these provisions must be constantly amendable to meet new needs.

Thoughts about the regulatory power of international organizations have led to the development of a number of notions such as that of the internal legal order of international organizations. I do not wish here to discuss issues relating to this, interesting though they are in more than one respect.

I shall merely point out that the relevant resolutions of the international organizations concerned must indubitably be counted among the sources of each of the internal legal orders that have just been mentioned. The legal force of these resolutions is here based entirely on explicit or implicit provisions of the international treaty whereby each international organization was set up and given regulatory powers.

The same approach may be used to understand other particularly significant, though doubtless rarer phenomena. I am alluding here to what the legal literature – particularly in the English language – frequently calls international legislation.

It is well known that a few rare international organizations are given by the treaty setting them up a genuine external, normative power, in no way to be confused with the regulatory power mentioned above. The rules in question now do not relate to the organization's internal operation, but are addressed to the member States, giving them obligations or rights that complement and extend the norms contained in the founding treaty. Some legal scholars talk in this connection of "derived law", so as to highlight the fact that the power to issue new norms is given to the international organization concerned by the founding treaty. In other words, an international agreement between States may very well establish and organize a new source of international law which will be different from the agreement itself but subordinate to it. The resolutions whereby the international organization in question (for instance the International Civil Aviation Organization, the World Health Organization or the European Communities) exercises this normative power may, then, properly be counted among the sources of international law, though in the limited sense (as "secondary sources") that has just been described.

The importance of this type of mechanism should not – it must be said in passing – be overestimated, as it is by certain authors. First, as we have just seen, it falls entirely within the scope of the even-handed logic that is characteristic of the present international community, since it finds its legal foundation in and draws its normative power from an international agreement between States: in this sense there is not really any analogy between international legislation and domestic legislation. Secondly, it is only with difficulty, and in very technical areas, that States agree in principle to be subjected to international legislation, the quantitative importance of which consequently remains very slight. Thirdly, even when it is accepted, the mechanism in question is often accompanied by all sorts of arrangements which allow States to considerably reduce or even eliminate the "legislative" effect. These arrangements are indicated in current language by the expression "contracting out". In some of the U.N. specialized agencies a body made up of Member States adopts by majority "regulations" that are binding only on those Member States that have not, within prescribed time limits in various forms, notified the organization concerned of any objections. Other systems of contracting out are applied by the Fisheries Commissions set up by various international conventions.

The provisions adopted through contracting out do not, as can be seen, constitute only secondary or derived norms whose binding force derives from primary norms of conventional character. In essence, these provisions have themselves a genuinely conventional nature, since they represent the outcome of genuine international agreements with the special characteristic of being arrived at without need for explicit consent by all States involved. It is however clear that this consent is required: it is deduced implicitly from the absence of objections.

The European Communities is the only international organization in which, under the founding treaties, a body of intergovernmental character (the Council of the European Communities) is supposed to be able – in many cases – to adopt by majority secondary norms, binding also on the minority. The relevant procedure is, to be sure, rather complex, since it brings in two other bodies: the Commission, made up of independent figures, which has an initiative role, and the European Parliament, elected by direct universal suffrage, which must be consulted, but whose opinions have no binding force in the matter. In short, it is the Council that holds effective decision making power. Leaving aside other important peculiarities of the Community system, it is clear that what we have to do with here is a case in which the expression "international legislation" might seem particularly appropriate.

It should nevertheless be observed that practice does not bear much resemblance to what is laid down in the texts. Since 1966, in fact, the Member States have agreed at the highest level (at a summit of heads of State and government) that the majority principle would not be applied to matters regarded as "important" by any one of them. In reality, therefore, all normative acts are in practice adopted by unanimity: it is, in short, diplomatic, consensual logic of the traditional type that has ultimately prevailed over the innovative logic (called "supranational") that largely inspired the founding treaties. Because of this, Community normative acts in essence strongly resemble international agreements: it is merely that these agreements are not arrived at through the ordinary methods established by international practice and regulated by national constitutions, but through special, simplified, anomalous procedures. In conclusion, international legislation not only has agreement for its basis, but also shows a clear tendency to take agreement as its model, in a more or less disguised form.

Let it be said in passing (and by way of conclusion on this point) that if it is true that in all these cases some formal disguise hides real international agreements, then all the appropriate consequences ought to be drawn. This is an observation I have put forward on other occasions, which should be insisted on especially as regards Community acts of general scope (regulations and directives). If these are in reality intergovernmental agreements, it is hard to see why they should not be subjected to the relevant legal system. I would point out that I am not referring to the international system of treaty law alone; I am also thinking of domestic legal systems, more specifically the constitutional rules relating to treaty making power. Since the needs are exactly the same, what I shall here call Community law-making power should in my view be governed by the same principles. I have the impression that the opinion I am setting forth is very heretical; but I did say at the start that absurdities were to be expected.

So far I have reviewed the normative effects of resolutions provided for and regulated by the founding treaty of the international organization concerned. Let us now come to the central issue, namely when and to what extent these resolutions may appear among the sources of international law independently of any explicit or implicit provision of the founding treaty. In asking this question, especially as regards U.N. General Assembly resolutions, one should never forget to point out that the Charter nowhere gives normative effect to these resolutions, nor even binding effect (with some exceptions), terming them as it does mere "recommendations". This problem must therefore be approached, and an answer to it sought, by looking at international law in general (apart from the basic treaty).

There is no question of summarizing here the whole set of doctrinal positions that have been put forward, defended and attacked in this connection. That would be an impossible task, given the number of authors that have discussed the subject and the seas of ink used writing about it, in more or less stimulating articles. As for myself, I intend to start by putting forward some simple preliminary remarks aimed at singling out and fixing — as far as possible — a number of sure points, from which it will then be possible for me to expand into critical remarks likely to arouse discussion.

There is no doubt that Third Worldist enthusiasm resulting from the gradual conquest of a majority on the General Assembly by the Third World, supported by the East, led to theories of the General Assembly as a sort of international legislator capable of imposing a new international law, of a strongly progressive nature, by majority. It is, however, easy to see that in their extreme versions these views are no longer fashionable: they have been replaced by more moderate, less absolute ideas, the extreme diversity of which does not prevent the picking out of a number of common features. The general conviction is that there are resolutions and resolutions: only some have a truly normative character (not even all those called "declarations of principle"), those which meet a number of conditions. These are then evaluated and described very differently by the various schools of thought: there may be references to the tenor of the resolution itself, to the fact that it was adopted by consensus or by a large majority, to the voting declarations of States and to the reservations made, to subsequent practice and to the presence of machinery for ensuring observance, to reiteration, etc.

In brief, according to this view, the resolution as such has no normative effect, even though the circumstances surrounding its adoption may be favourable and promising. Nor is reiteration sufficient: as one author says, in indubitably excessive language, if one resolution is worth zero, multiplying it by 10, 100 or 1000 still gives you nothing but zero. The same thing must, moreover, be said of each of the factors, conditions or elements indicated, taken in isolation. On the other hand, an all-round synthetic evaluation of them may lead to the conclusion that a given resolution is the expression of general international law in a particular sector. For such a conclusion to be justified, international practice must also appear to have genuinely undergone the effect of the resolution and been significantly changed by it; in other words the resolution must have penetrated from the world of words into the world of reality, of the actual behavior of social actors; it must have appreciably influenced international relations.

The position that sought to make the U.N. General Assembly into a genuine international legislator is, then, untenable and is in fact no longer maintained, since it is in radical contradiction with the institutionalized structure that continues to characterize the contemporary international community, despite the profound changes it has undergone during this century. As for current views, the common features that have been pointed out imply fundamental acceptance of an underlying logic and approach that deserve to be strongly emphasized. It is now generally recognized, I feel, that the resolutions of international organizations represent a remarkable enrichment and acceleration of the law-making process in the present-day international community. This enrichment and acceleration is not however, brought about through any new source: they occur within the system of traditional sources, through far-reaching changes in the processes of formation, amendment and annulment of conventional customary norms. Regarding international custom in particular, resolutions have neither supplanted it nor truly changed its essence. They have rather brought important novelties in respect of the times, forms, procedures and mechanisms whereby the two constitutive elements of custom are made manifest and can be evaluated: the practice of States and the *opinio juris*.

As to the specific identification of these novelties and the exact size of the gap between today and yesterday, as to the weighing-up of the respective importance that the two elements have taken on nowadays and of the changes in the relationship between them, opinions diverge considerably between realists and idealists, progressives and conservatives, between northerners and southerners, etc. But whether or not the *opinio juris* has tended to anticipate and influence the *repetitio facti*, whether the latter has lost or kept its traditional "supremacy", does not change things fundamentally: the question is still one of custom, even if it is increasingly less "wise" and more "wild".

The question of the normative effect of resolutions has thus been considerably transformed under our eyes: it can now be seen as one of the aspects of a much broader question, relating to the new manifestations of international custom (or if one prefers, of general international law). But customary law, because of the well-known upsets that the international community has undergone during our century, is well known to be in a state of crisis. What remains to us, then, is to make a quick study of how resolutions act in this crisis situation: do they manage to remedy it one way or another, or are they caught up in it?

It seems to me that the second hypothesis is much more plausible and of more frequent occurrence. To illustrate my point, I wish to look at examples of the two most typical situations that may arise: first that of a resolution adopted by majority, and second that of one adopted by consensus.

The fact that, following preliminary negotiations that may sometimes have taken years and years, a resolution has been adopted by a majority, quite obviously indicates that some States have not been convinced of the validity of its content (or of part of it). If the gap between the viewpoint of these States and that of the majority is considerable, and if the weight of the States in question is significant, adoption of the resolution has very little chance of leading to uniform practice on the part of the generality of States. In these circumstances, a new norm of general international law could not normally arise, given that a significant number of States refuse to recognize it and demonstrate the intention of not aligning their own conduct to it. One might even go so far as to assert that proclamation of a principle of international law by majority declaration is proof that the principle proclaimed is not genuinely part of general international law.

The example I wish very briefly to present (with great simplification) is *G.A. Resolution 37/92 of 1982* on the principles governing use by States of artificial earth satellites for direct international television. Despite some twenty years of negotiations, it was not possible for the resolution to be adopted by consensus. This represents an absolute novelty in the area handled by the General Assembly's subsidiary agency for space matters. The reason is that a whole group of States (a minority, to be sure, but an important one, the West) resisted stubbornly to the end the adoption of a number of principles firmly held to by the majority States, in this case, the Third World and the East. The clear split in the voting (107 Ayes, 15 Nos and 15 abstentions), shows that an important, homogeneous group of States refuses to accept the innovatory principles incorporated in the resolution. This is the case in particular with regard to the one whereby each State should on the one hand guarantee that television programmes sent out by private individuals subject to its jurisdiction via direct broadcasting satellites should conform in content to the rules laid down in the resolution, and on the other should bear direct international responsibility in the event of breach attributable to one of these private individuals. It is clear that this refusal by a whole block of States, though a minority (including, among others, all the countries equipped with the appropriate technology) deprives the principle in question of any chance of being incorporated into general international law.

I will not here give any more details concerning the specific question of direct broadcasting by satellite, which I have in any case gone into on other occasions. Here I shall merely repeat, in the light of this example, the conclusion already put forward: the majority proclamation of certain principles by resolution is normally a serious indication of the fact that these principles do not form part of general international law, however numerous the States that would like it to be so.

It is no accident that the practice of *consensus* has become general in all international venues. This is particularly true for the adoption of resolutions for which a properly normative role is hoped, particularly the "declarations of principle" of the General Assembly: no effort is spared, at the price of interminable negotiations, in the endeavour to arrive at a consensus text. If it is not arrived at and the resolution is adopted by majority, this is considered to be a failure. It is, in brief, realized that adoption by a majority severely compromises the chances of the principles asserted becoming general international law; on the contrary only adoption by unanimity or by consensus (or even by overwhelming majority, as long as the minority carries little weight) can preserve or increase this chance. In other words, the fact that all States display a conviction that it is highly desirable or indeed necessary to reach consensus proves that they are aware of the impossibility of creating general international law through majorities.

Unfortunately, the serious tensions running through the international community, the dividing factors (cultural, ideological, economic, political) that make it a split society, make consensus, and *a fortiori* unanimity, extremely difficult, not to say impossible. Deep disagreement as to the consistency and the continued force of old general international law inevitably engenders equally deep disagreement about the content that the new law should be given. While the range of social interests is expanding, while law is becoming the object of a fundamental split between those who would like to keep it unchanged in substance, and those who would like to reform it thoroughly (and thereby reform international society), how can it be possible to reach major planet-wide social compromises, capable of renewing general international law?

Sometimes consensus is reached: but only at a heavy price. This is one of the chief observations I wished to bring to your attention. To secure consensus (or a majority close to unanimity, that is, without significant dissociations), the text to be adopted must be a consensus text, that is, acceptable (or not unacceptable) to all. In view of the frequently radically opposed starting positions of the various groups of States, the search for a consensus text tends to end with ambiguous, anodyne, vague and inadequate formulas, so that all and sundry can then maintain that their point of view has not been rejected. In brief, the real issues will not have been resolved, but merely hidden under suitable verbal camouflage. In other words, resolutions proclaiming principles by consensus (or by a very large majority) may — it is true — be better at producing normative effects in general international law; but it is almost inevitable that the tenor of the principles so proclaimed will be sufficiently vague to deprive them of all true practical utility, of all meaningful legal force.

Here is the last of the absurdities I have the intention of throwing at you, and it is a big one. As planned, I shall illustrate it with one example only, drawn from recent U.N. practice: the *Manila Declaration on the Peaceful Settlement of International Disputes among States*, adopted by consensus by the General Assembly in 1982 (resolution 32/10), after years of negotiations.

This Declaration starts with a general statement, repeated several times, that international disputes ought to be settled peacefully, that the use or threat of force is forbidden, that the principle of free choice of methods ought to be respected, and other scintillating novelties of the same kind.

The second part of the Declaration "reinforces" the role of the United Nations in the area, and goes on to review the relevant functions of the various bodies. As is well known the Third World gives a clear preference to the General Assembly, whose role it would like to see strengthened, and readily accepts the Secretary-General, but detests the Security Council for being under the thumb of the big powers, and mistrusts the International Court of Justice. The East, in contrast (secretly), mistrusts the General Assembly, does not like the Secretary-General at all, detests the Court and likes the Security Council. The West, in turn, declares its sympathy for the Court, defends the Security Council and the Secretary-General, and feels a general antipathy towards the General Assembly, since the majority is no longer what it used to be. How, then, can one, by consensus, strengthen the role of these bodies in settling differences, faced with this situation of "criss-cross vetoes"?

The final result could only be what emerges from a close reading of the text under consideration: a text which says it wants to strengthen the role of those bodies, but in actual fact proclaims, in a rich panoply of entirely useless verbiage, that each body must do everything that the Charter tells is to do, that States are invited to use these bodies within the limits of their respective competences as laid down in the Charter, that States "ought ... to take due account, as appropriate ..." of the relevant resolutions of (for instance) the Security Council or the General Assembly, but also that they "ought not to lose sight ... of the desirability ... of contemplating the possibility ..." of making more use of the Court, and other platitudes of similar scope.

My final observations on the central question to be discussed (that of the normative effect of resolutions of international organizations at the level of general international law) are simple, and I shall simplify them still further. In principle, these resolutions, if adopted by a majority in the face of a significant, decided minority, cannot create new general international law; if they are adopted by consensus or unanimity (or else by a majority close to it), then their content will almost inevitably be so imprecise and incomplete that no significant normative effect can attach to it.

II. Discussion

WEILER

I would like to make a point concerning general principles of international law. I think that in the "old law" general principles tended to be procedural, and more general – in terms of their content – than norms. In more recent years (late sixties, early seventies) there has increasingly been a demand to have recognized as general principles of law norms with a much stronger substantive content, norms of the environmental type: often the source of these new substantive norms is attributed to repeated resolutions of the United Nations, especially the General Assembly.

HAZARD

May I ask a question of Professor Riphagen? Our colleagues in the East have been very critical of general principles of law if they are held to mean something that is related to municipal law. They say that they accept general principles only if they are part of international law and not part of municipal law. Now I am not quite certain, from what you said, which falls into which category: which are the principles of international law that are general, and when do they fall into the field of domestic law?

RIPHAGEN

That was one of the things I should have said in the first instance, but for the sake of brevity I did not refer to it. One commentator, Schwarzenberger, said that general principles are introduced for the good reason that rules that have been accepted in the more mature and integrated field of municipal law can also be accepted in the international field. I suggest that this is not the case; on the contrary. We all know that international society is in no way comparable to a national society, so that what has been tested in the more mature and integrated field of domestic law is almost by definition not applicable to international relations.

On the other hand, if you look at the general principles of law as a sort of logical development then you can of course take a particular domestic rule and say in view of the fact that every domestic legal system considers it as a logical link between one rule and another, then it should be accepted in international law. But I am afraid that this does not often happen. As a result think that this reference to *forum domesticum* is not really applicable to the international field, with the exception, as I say, of those cases where conclusions are drawn as a matter of logic in national legal systems. These will also apply in the international field because in a certain sense you can say logic is by definition universal.

Jimenez de Arechaga

If the aim of this workshop was to provoke discussion, I think the two statements we had this morning were very provocative and, as far as I am concerned provoked disagreement. I think the position which was put forward by Professor Condorelli concerning General Assembly resolutions does not take into account a factor which we discussed this morning: the fact that if States, properly represented, agree by consensus on certain rules, those rules become rules of international law. Now if codification conferences have been appropriate vehicles for reaching that consensus, why should this not be the case with the General Assembly, where all States are represented? Why should this organ not be an appropriate vehicle for reaching consensus and determining the agreement of States on certain rules to govern their own conduct? There is nothing preventing it. Of course, the Charter says that resolutions of the General Assembly are merely recommendations, but this is immaterial since it concerns other sources of international law. The proof of the existence of this possibility is simply that certain resolutions of the General Assembly have been judicially recognized as sources of law. I am thinking particularly of certain resolutions by which the General Assembly intends to declare or establish principles of conduct for State Members, not internal resolutions, but those which are in general called declarations.

This type of resolution may have the effects we saw this morning. They may have a declaratory effect, merely restating already established rules of international law; one such is the Declaration of Principles on Friendly Relations between States. Other General Assembly resolutions adopted unanimously or by consensus crystallize emerging rules of international law. I refer, for instance, to the resolution establishing the freedom of outer space which preceded the treaty, and which would survive the treaty if it were denounced. Finally, resolutions of the General Assembly prescribing principles of conduct may, in their application by Member States and also by General Assembly organs, constitute a model of conduct which, followed by the practice of States and of the Organization, becomes a rule of international law. I am thinking, for instance, of resolution 1514 which abolished the legitimacy of colonial rule. This resolution was considered by the International Court of Justice as part of existing customary law on the basis of the practice of States in accordance with it. What more evidence do we need of the seal of a rule of law than a declaration by the Court that it is part of customary law, as occurred both in the case of Namibia and of the Western Sahara? I remember that in the *Western Sahara* case not even the colonial State attempted to justify its domination, but only required, before leaving the country, a plebiscite in accordance with resolution 1514.

These are rules of law which have emerged from General Assembly declarations; you cannot just dismiss them on the grounds that first World countries do not attach any importance to this type of resolution. Of course there are some resolutions which are not adopted by unanimity or by consensus, but only by a majority vote, such as the one just mentioned concerning direct television, and these do not attain the status of customary law. (May I mention in passing a point made by a diplomat: how could one accept that a bull fight in Spain be broadcast, live, on Indian television?). This has to do with the question examined this morning of persistent objection by groups of States which represent an important part of the world.

However, even some of these resolutions not adopted by broad consensus nevertheless contain elements which constitute part of international law. I refer for instance to the Charter of Economic Rights and Duties of States, which was objected to on certain grounds. Yet some parts of it are undisputedly rules of international law: take the principle of permanent sovereignty over natural resources, which has been the basis for recent developments in the world concerning, for instance, nationalizations. Of course there are still controversies over the amount of compensation, but the right of a State to nationalize its natural resources cannot be disputed today. Thus, the Charter contains some provisions which declare existing international law, like the one concerning permanent sovereignty; others which crystallize certain rules, like the rule requiring appropriate compensation; and others again which may in the future have a generating effect, like the rules which concern the terms of trade. They are not positive international law at the present date, but these principles have been accepted by all States, and constitute a goal which nobody would question today. No one doubts the necessity of establishing greater equity in international economic relations; what is in question is not the objective, which has been universally accepted, but the methods used to reach this objective. I think it is going too far, therefore, to entirely dismiss the law-making and the reforming effect of General Assembly resolutions of this nature.

Professor Riphagen also presented a very sceptical picture of general principles of law. I agree that from the point of view of a lawyer, pleading general principles may not be so satisfactory as invoking a treaty or a customary law rule. From the point of view of the judge, however, these principles are essential because of the possibility they afford of filling in gaps to reach a certain conclusion. I am thinking for instance of the equitable principle concerning the delimitation of the continental shelf in the *North Sea Continental Shelf* cases (in which he presided as a judge).

In this judgment the Court rejected the submissions of Denmark and the Netherlands advocating the principle of equidistance as a mandatory rule of customary international law. But the Court did not accept that there was a *lacuna* in the law of nations on the subject: it stated that, on the contrary, "there are still rules and principles of law to be applied". The Court found that the most fundamental of these rules is that delimitation should be agreed on or decided in accordance with equitable principles. It added that "in this field it is precisely a rule of law that calls for the application of equitable principles. There is consequently no question in this case of any decision *ex aequo et bono*."

So general principles of law, though rarely mentioned in the Court's judgments, should not be underestimated as to their influence on the minds and the intellectual processes of judges. As Judge Cardozo said, "it is these generalities and abstractions that give direction to legal thinking, that sway the minds of judges, that determine, when the balance wavers, the outcome of the doubtful lawsuit".

Abi-Saab

I think that Luigi Condorelli's presentation was stimulating and he managed to provoke many of us. In fact, much of what I wanted to say has been said, and much better, by Judge de Arechaga. I think the total effect of the presentation was very restrictive and negative, and perhaps the example chosen is a special case which does not reflect the full possibilities of resolutions. First of all, Condorelli neglected a significant role of resolutions which is related to sources, though in a negative way. A resolution may have a *destructive effect* on an existing rule, even if it is not adopted by consensus, if it reflects very strongly the *opinio juris* of large segments of the international community that a rule is no longer a rule, or never was. Although this is a negative effect, normatively speaking, it is still very important. And if we take the example that has just been given about nationalization, I think it also provides a good example of resolutions which may not create a new rule, but which at least reveal that the old one does not exist any more.

If we look more positively at what resolutions can do, *grosso modo* I agree with what Luigi Condorelli said. Still I think resolutions can have an important role in law-creation, even if they start by being only majority resolutions. This is of course if we do not think in terms of immediate creation of law, which is the attribute of legislation. After all, what is law if not social ideas which take hold and become so generally and widely shared that at some point they are formally sanctioned as law. Now in the first place these ideas have to be formulated; and sometimes resolutions, by registering positions, put certain ideas on the negotiating table which later on develop into law. I shall give you another example from the economic field: the idea of general trade preferences for developing countries. Preferences were mentioned for the first time in UNCTAD I, in 1964, in Principle 8, I think, which was adopted by majority vote, and against which the Western powers took a very strong line on the grounds that it revealed fuzzy thinking, that it was unworkable, etc. But the formulation of the resolution for the first time in UNCTAD I led after 4 years to UNCTAD II, to the general acceptance of preferences as a matter of principle, and to agreement on a general scheme for preferences (GSP), in UNCTAD III, in 1972.

Thus, although the first resolution started by reflecting a confrontational attitude on the part of a majority, it was a registration of position which, with time, and with the erosion of opposition, eventually led somewhere. The first resolution was very important; it was the *seed*, and although we can say it did not create law, it definitely was ***a building block in the process towards creating law***. I would not therefore discount it completely as zero, that if you multiply by zero or add to other zeros, can still only amount to nought. I think it is a building block, but not sufficient by itself. This is an important role of resolutions to add to the three roles mentioned by Judge de Arechaga.

I also want to make a point about resolutions and soft law. Some people prefer softness to hardness; Professor Seidl-Hohenveldern once spoke of "le charme discret du soft law". He said that some States, especially those in the rear-guard (in the sense of States resisting legal change), preferred to abide by a non-binding instrument than to accept a hard and fast obligation. However, this contributes to law-creation through what was described by Judge de Arechaga as the generating effect.

There are many ways, then, in which one can say that resolutions can help, and not only help but constitute buildings blocks in the process of law-creation. I do not think that they should be considered as an all or nothing proposition: that you either have consensus, which means you have law (but not, anyway, as a result of the resolution); or you do not have consensus, which means you have nothing at all. I think that this is to see things too much in black and white, whereas in reality grey predominates, especially if we follow the situation on a time map, that is as an evolutive rather than an instantaneous phenomenon or process, and gauge its effects cumulatively as a trend or a curve rather than a mere point in time.

Finally, I have a small comment on general principles. Again I am defending myself in relation to that article which was distributed in the morning, in which I was very optimistic about the role of general principles. I considered them as one vehicle through which the newly-independent States might contribute to the development of a new international law; i. e. by taking into consideration their own legal systems together with others in order to identify new principles. In the last 20 years this source has not after all proved to be very fertile, perhaps in part because of the increasing tendency to emphasize voluntarism. After all, general principles are not supposed to be a voluntary source, but a device to overcome the lack of a rule, and the lack of clear agreement. This perhaps explains why they have not proved as fruitful a source as they could have been. I just wanted to preempt any attacks on this point in the article. I had the great honour of being attacked on it by Professor Tunkin in his general course at the Hague Academy, but on different grounds; his position being that there are no general principles, generally shared in a substantive way by all components of the international community.

GAJA

While I agree with Luigi Condorelli's view that General Assembly resolutions can hardly be taken as evidence of rules of general international law when there is a significant opposition within the Assembly, I would hesitate to accept that the situation is different with regard to most resolutions adopted by consensus, even when no State makes a reservation to them. First, it is not uncommon for State practice not to conform with resolutions which were adopted with an affirmative vote of the States concerned. For the sake of ascertaining whether a rule of general international law exists, the conduct of those State organs whose activity would be governed by the hypothetical rule is without a doubt more important than an intent expressed by the same or other organs. Moreover, State delegates at the United Nations generally have insufficient standing to bind their respective States. Only rarely can it be assumed that specific instructions were issued for the delegates' vote and, in any case, instructions are usually given only by Foreign Ministry officials. In these circumstances, it is questionable whether one may consider this an adequate acceptance on the part of States of the existence of a rule of international law.

I shall now turn to the "general principles of law recognized by civilized nations". The International Court of Justice appears to have used the concept of "principles" mainly to characterize rules of international law that do not derive from custom or treaties. The Court has sometimes asserted that a certain principle finds a parallel in municipal systems; however, this is never taken as a fundamental element for holding that the relevant principle exists in international law. In spite of the opportunities apparently granted by Articles 38 (1)(*c*) of its Statute, the Court has refrained from using principles prevailing in municipal law to draw new rules of international law from. The Court has understandably been reluctant to depart from rules of existing law when deciding disputes. Moreover, as arbitration awards show, a decision can hardly ever be taken on the basis of principles that may be termed as "common" to municipal systems. Applying "general principles of law" has often involved the search for the "best rule" from amongst the conflicting principles which prevail in the different systems. The use of discretionary powers is inherent in this method. Had the Court applied it, States would no doubt have shown even greater reluctance in submitting to the Court's jurisdiction.

CASSESE

I would like to address myself to the question of general principles of international law, and here I tend to share the pessimistic view put forward by Professor Riphagen. I think, however, that we should try to place a constructive interpretation on the famous provision of Article 38 and what I now mean to do is put the whole question into historical and political perspective.

I have gone through the very interesting debates which took place in 1921 within the Advisory Committee of Jurists, the body which actually drafted Article 38. It may be interesting to remember that there were ten people on the Committee, eight Westerners, a Brazilian and a Japanese; which was equivalent, at that time, to saying that there were ten people from the West or whose attitudes in a way reflected the Western outlook. If you look at these discussions, however, you become aware that there was a split, with a majority led by the Chairman, the Belgian Baron Descamps, suggesting that "principles of objective justice" should be applied by the Permanent Court of International Justice. Let me just quote one sentence which I think is very important. He said the following: "We should apply the fundamental law of justice and injustice, deeply engraved on the heart of every human being and which is given its highest and most authoritative expression in the legal conscience of civilized nations". Now in my view this was a rather revolutionary attempt to introduce a new source of international law over and above the will of States, a third source which did not attach any importance to the will of States.

This, as I said, was the majority position. The minority, which was made up of the American Root, the Englishman Lord Phillimore and the Italian Ricci Busatti, took an extremely positivist approach. Their view was that the majority position was unacceptable because international law is what States decide that it should be, as the American Root emphatically stated in one meeting: "Nations will submit to positive law but will not submit to principles that have not been developed into positive rules supported by an accord between all States". The contrast is quite clear and the interesting point is that it was a rift within a group of Western countries, or people representing Western countries, not between two areas of the world.

The final solution was a compromise in so far as the idea of objective justice, a kind of new natural law, was rejected. The acceptance of the majority view would have meant that the Permanent Court of International Justice would have created new law, and this was against the basic principles of the world community at that time. The compromise solution was that the Court was called upon to apply general principles, not objective justice, only those general principles which were to be found in domestic legislation. Thus there was a "reference point" and this was rooted in the domestic legislation of Western States. It was quite clear at that time that they were referring to Western countries — "civilized nations" meant the West.

I think that as a result of this compromise and the general acceptance of Article 38 by Member States of the League of Nations, a customary rule evolved on this new source of international law. However, if we look at the case law both of the Permanent Court and of the present International Court of Justice, we can see that the record on this topic is very poor. Actually international courts have never applied general principles in the sense advocated at that time. Later Article 38 was attacked very harshly, and I think rightly, by Tunkin and other leading jurists from the Socialist countries, on the very real grounds that it was contrary to the will of States. International law can only consist of rules made by States and freely accepted by States, that is to say autonomous, and not heteronomous law. The result of these new developments was that the customary rule on the third source of international law gradually began to wither away, to such an extent that I think it has now fallen into disuse.

If this is the case, one could immediately object, what then is the value of the provision in Article 38? As a matter of fact this article is now part and parcel of the Statute of the Court and the Court is therefore bound to apply it. I think, though, that one might perhaps give a different interpretation of the provision in question. That is to say, one could hold that general principles of international law recognized by civilized nations now mean those universal principles of international law accepted by all member States of the international community. They would include the seven famous principles laid down in the Friendly Relations Declaration of 1970 as well as the Principle on respect for human rights. It follows that when applying the provision the Court should apply these fundamental principles because of their basic importance for the international community.

If this view is accepted, its logical consequence is that the Court would have to reverse the sequence established in Article 38. We all know that under Article 38 the Court is supposed first of all to look at international treaties, and then, if there is no treaty governing the specific issue brought before it, at international custom, and finally, as a third step, at the general principles of law recognized by civilized nations. Now, if we take the general principles as meaning fundamental principles of universal importance, then the Court should of necessity start by seeing if the issue under consideration is covered by a general principle. Why? Because those principles constitute *jus cogens*. If the Court were then to find that the issue was regulated by a treaty and that this treaty was contrary to one of the eight general principles, the treaty would be null and void, and the Court would have to discard it.

De Fiumel

I wish to make a few observations on the subject of general principles of law which has already given rise to a good deal of discussion. I would find it very hard to accept that general principles of law should be regarded as a distinct source of international law. Why? First, this idea is very controversial; there are many diverging opinions as to what these general principles of law truly represent, and no legal text provides us with a list of them. We have, to be sure, Article 38(c) of the Statute of the Court, but in my opinion that article was conceived not so much as a catalogue of sources of international law, but as a catalogue of sources of decisions of the Court. That is quite a different thing. The sources of international law are one thing, and the sources of the Court's jurisdiction, of its case law, are another.

We know, as Professor Cassese has already said, how prudent and reticent the Court itself is in applying these general principles in its decisions. Reference is made to general principles of law in certain contracts arrived at between States and legal persons. These may, for instance, concern investments in a foreign State or concessions, but in these cases it is not intergovernmental relations that are involved but relations of quite a different nature. This shows, in my opinion, that it is very hard to treat them as a source of international law. If we accept international law to be norms created by States, or at least accepted by States, it is hard to conceive how it can come about other than through custom, through international treaties or through resolutions of international organizations, accepted by the States to which they are addressed. In my opinion, then, we can only speak of these three sources of international law: custom, treaty and resolutions of international organizations.

Coming now to resolutions of international organizations, I think they have perhaps a more effective chance of being applied in the context of organizations of a regional type, that is those that bring together a limited group of States, than in organizations of world type, since in the latter case the problem arises of who is to be the judge. This is certainly true of organizations of an integrationist type such as the European Community, as we well know. It is also, true, however in the context of, for instance, the C.M.E.A. (Comecon) that many resolutions are adopted that are of considerable importance in the context of the organization which in principle have the character of recommendations. These recommendations are in general endorsed by the Member States, and entail obligations among these States and also between them and the organization. The resolutions are often such as to constitute a normative text that regulates relations of civil law, if one may say so, that is, mutual relations between enterprises in the various Member States. Sometimes they are also of the type which we may call "programmatic". That is to say, they establish a multilateral programme of cooperation in one area or another. As to their contents, they provide for duties and obligations on the Member States to arrive at certain international agreements in order to achieve goals set in these programmes. This then is a rather interesting field, which perhaps shows us a fairly close link between resolutions of international organizations and treaties, since the resolutions themselves provide for an obligation on the Member States to which they are addressed to arrive at agreements in one area or another in order to implement these programmes.

STEIN (ERIC)

Professor Hazard raised the question of the use of the comparative method in international law. As I understand from Professor Riphagen, he is quite sceptical about the possibility of getting at a general principle through a comparative method investigation of national legal systems. My question is whether what appears on the surface as a rather promising method these days should be simply discarded altogether because of the vast ideological differences in the world. I have in mind, for instance, a case between Venezuela and Italy, the *Gentini* case, in which the Italian Government asked the Court to consider a reparation claim of some thirty years before, a thirty year stale claim. The Court proceeded, looking at the major systems and looking at the major policy considerations of the rule of prescription, what we call statutes of limitation, and rather ingenuously concluded that a plaintiff before a national court and a government plaintiff before an international court, and of course the defendants, are essentially in a comparable position when you have a stale claim of thirty or forty more years. The witnesses are dead, the documents are lost. Anybody who has had anything to do with an archive in a Foreign Office knows what an incredible mess it is (Ted Stein knows the U.S. State Department situation and I have some dealing with it too), so that policy considerations, plus the national legal systems, clearly indicate that there is a general principle of prescription or statute of limitation.

My question to Professor Riphagen would be whether he feels that this is really an isolated and completely unique case, or whether it could be applied to somewhat similar situations. I am entirely in agreement that this is a method that has to be used very carefully and by very sophisticated people. And I assume that the people on the Court know enough about their national legal systems to speak authoritatively on the question of whether a particular principle is an idiosyncratic development in one or two or thirty Western or Eastern systems or whether there is anything to the proposition that instead it is really a general principle recognized in national legal systems?

TED STEIN

I would like to pick up almost exactly where Eric left off, and talk about the use of the comparative method in relation to general principles of law. It seems to me that there is a perfectly useful place for the comparative method in relation to Article 38/1/c. And the purpose of the comparative method is to show that a particular principle is so central to the idea of the legal order as such that we find it in a very wide variety of legal systems. It is a test of the proposition that in a legal order that exists as such, and that can be conceived of as such, the principle must be found. That is the enquiry into which I believe Art 38/1/c directs the Court. Understanding it in this way, I see no cause to be distressed if it turns out that only a relatively narrow range of principles fit the bill.

Now I would like to turn to the question of General Assembly resolutions. And first I would like to stress one point: the need to be definitively empirical about what one chooses to regard as a source of international law. One cannot simply derive a list of the sources of international law deductively, or determine as a matter of derivationist logic what is or is not a source. One could otherwise proceed to take the view that since law is a social institution designed to serve social ends, and social ends are understood best by men and women of deep learning and profound insight, and they all happen to be in this room, we could between us come up with a list of rules and call them international law. That would be an interesting exercise, but it would certainly not tell us about the international legal order in reality. It would not be a very useful approach to law and its sources. You have to begin (and H. L. A. Hart makes this point very clearly) with what is accepted within the particular legal order as a source. And I take that approach in relation to General Assembly resolutions as well. The question must be: do States, and under what circumstances, accept General Assembly resolutions as sources of obligation? This question I think is one that you cannot answer on any general grounds. I think one has to look rather carefully at particular resolutions and how they are used. I would suggest two tests. The first test is whether the State that claims the rule in the resolution is indeed a rule of law, is prepared to have that rule applied against itself. And secondly whether that State is prepared to treat the rule as non-voluntary, that is not one that it can subsequently opt out of. If these criteria are met, and we find evidence that they are met in fact, then I am prepared to say that that State regards the General Assembly resolution as a source of law.

WEILER

I shall just make one little comment on the last intervention. In a sense I think it begs the question. Because what you have ended up by saying is that you are not accepting a General Assembly resolution, but something else we should call custom or a general principle of law.

RIPHAGEN

I would like first to set right what to my mind is a misunderstanding of what I said before. I am not sceptical about general principles of law; I merely say that they are only a starting point. You can say that something is against the rules of customary law or treaties, but then you still have to find a solution to the conflict between the two. What I said is that if you wish to arrive at the right solution, you have to take into account the general principles of law; so my position is not really negative. And of course this links up with the observation I made about comparative law, that is about the application of principles deriving from a comparative study of domestic laws to international law. In some cases this may be quite right, particularly when we talk about extinctive prescription. Extinctive prescription is after all an application of the principle that you have to put an end to disputes and it is therefore applied by international courts and tribunals; I think quite rightly.

But this is an entirely different context from that of substantive rules of law. Now this field is related to dispute settlement, and of course, as I said, the dispute settlement body is practically forced to find new elements which are not yet in any particular rule which proclaims its competence. The same goes for general principles; the Court has to decide on its own competence up to a point, even without being able to give binding decisions on the substance. As you know, we now have the "soft" dispute settlement procedure of compulsory conciliation. Well, here, according to the Annex to the Law of the Sea Convention, the conciliatory body is competent to make decisions. That does not mean, and of course cannot mean, that its decision or recommendation will be binding on the parties. But the decision that it is competent to deal with the question is binding on the parties, because this is a preliminary matter which is the obvious logical corollary of the fact that the procedure as such is compulsory. It would not be compulsory if the conciliatory body did not have to decide on its own competence to conciliate.

So I think we should avoid any kind of oversimplification in this matter. We should look at exactly what is claimed to be a general principle of law and even if we find that it is a general principle of law we still have to balance it against other rules of international law, like the principle of good faith. Good faith is actually meant to counterbalance too strict an interpretation of treaty rules. And here again, it is quite difficult in practice to see where the treaty rules apply, and where the principle of good faith modifies them. In sum, if you take general principles as a source of international law you are only at the beginning; you do not have an applicable rule of international law. I submit that this is not a negative view at all, all I am saying is that to admit general principles of law does not take one the whole way to determining what rule is applicable in a particular situation. And that is again what my objection would be to the qualification of principles of international law as principles essential for a legal order as such. Here again, what is the legal order as such? It is very difficult to know, because we refer mostly to domestic orders, and if one thing is clear it is that the international legal order is not comparable with the domestic legal order at all.

Professor Cassese said that my view was a bit too negative with regard to the general principles of law relating to friendly relations, and so on. Having worked for six years on these general principles, I certainly do not mean to throw them out of the field of international law at all! Still, it is quite clear from the final clause (I refer to the clause whereby principles have to be taken together, and one principle has to qualify another principle etc.) that by defining those principles you have only taken the first step. The second essential step is to see how they interrelate. And that is the point which is not given sufficient attention in the treatment of this topic, because the topic itself is perhaps too abstract.

In that connection I would also like to refer to Professor Jimenez de Arechaga's remarks about a general principle of law relating to equitable solution; I think he referred to the continental shelf limitation. Once again, this all well and good, but it is only one step. The next step is: what is the equitable solution? If you do not accept a severe formula such as equidistance, then you still have to decide what the equitable solution is; particularly in view of the fact that there is absolutely nothing equitable in disputes between nations! It was stated in the *Continental Shelf* cases that equitable principles were not meant to correct the consequences of history and geography. These are points which have to be discussed, and it is not sufficient simply to proclaim a general principle of law to get a rule of law.

CONDORELLI

I find that my manner of introducing the debate has helped to make it particularly interesting, rich and lively, and I am very satisfied. I wish to take advantage of the chance to speak that I have now been given, not to comment on or criticize the positions taken by other participants, which would be of no particular use, but simply to supply a few clarifications so as to remove any ambiguities there may have been in some of my possibly too blunt and unqualified opening statements.

The point is the central question of the normative effect of resolutions at the level of general international law: my remarks were understood by some as amounting to a refusal to grant these resolutions any effect whatsoever. That was not my intention. Though denying that resolutions constitute a direct source of general international law, I certainly admitted that they can play an important part in the law-making process; not as a new and original source, but as a new element capable of enriching the traditional sources, particularly the customary process.

I would add that I have no difficulty in applying to resolutions, *mutatis mutandis*, the same set of arguments as the International Court of Justice has put forward to indicate the ways in which codification conventions may, where appropriate, become part of customary international law. I am thinking of the three possibilities mentioned by the Court, notably in the celebrated ruling on the *North Sea Continental Shelf*: the codification convention may represent either the "consecration" of a preexisting customary norm, or the "crystallization" of a norm in the process of formation, or again the starting point for (or one of the components of) the subsequent formation of a new customary rule.

It is beyond all doubt that resolutions that merely confirm, underline, or reiterate (or in the language of the Court "consecrate") a principle already indisputably in force are particularly numerous. For instance, it seems to me that the Manila Declaration – which I mentioned in my statement – essentially does only that, even if in the particular case this consecration seems to be of no practical use, dealing as it does with principles already consecrated innumerable times. In my opinion a large number of the resolutions cited during the debate should be counted in this first category.

The idea of crystallization is probably well adapted to a number of different situations, as Judge Arechaga clearly brought out. These are cases where the resolution constitutes the final stage in the process of formation of the customary rule; a process that was already in hand but which the resolution completes, so that the outcome of the process takes on its definitive form. The image of crystallization is particularly apt here, since it makes one think of something still fluid which – thanks to a further contribution represented here by the resolution – finally assumes the solid state and thus the fixed form of a crystal (a norm in our case) which it will keep until a new process of liquefaction (or erosion, or shattering, or whatever) intervenes. As for the "starting-point" or ("component"), I readily accept the observations made by Georges Abi-Saab; in fact, in the legal construction that a customary norm represents, the resolution may very well have the function of a foundation, or a brick or a column or whatever: in brief, a part of a more complex whole. Once all that has been admitted, two observations still remain to be added.

The first is that if this type of analytical grid is used in connection with resolutions, the idea I set out in my introduction is being implicitly accepted: namely that the resolutions of international organizations, in particular the U.N. General Assembly, are in no case to be counted among the sources of international law. On the contrary, they represent important material to be taken into account in evaluating and weighing the practice of States and their *opinio juris*, that is, in assessing the formation of customary rules. In this sense the situation is somewhat paradoxical; resolutions are often stressed because custom is accused of not responding to current needs; yet these resolutions can reach the goal aimed at only by way of the customary process! In other words, there can be no success as regards the normative effect of resolutions (at the level of general international law) until one has fallen right back into the source of law one was seeking to get away from!

The second observation is that, as I tried to show in the introduction, it is one thing to note that certain possibilities exist, and quite another to claim that these possibilities are actually (and frequently) realized. In my view, of the three hypotheses considered, only the first is frequent (the consecration in a resolution of a preexisting customary rule); the two other hypotheses are rarely realized in the international community. But it is my opinion that the characteristic of that community represents a serious obstacle to resolutions playing any important part in the process of formation of customary rules. If a resolution is adopted by majority, it normally testifies to the existence of a division among the international actors, which is hardly favourable to the generation of a new rule of general international law. If a resolution is adopted by consensus (or by a very large majority), then it normally has to be worded in such an anodyne and ambiguous manner that it can contribute very little to the development of general international law.

To these observations, I must now add a self-criticism. Hitherto, I have spoken of normative effects of resolutions essentially in the sense of the formation of new rules. However, that is not complete. A remark made by Georges Abi-Saab induces me to clarify one important point. I feel that in fact resolutions are often incapable, for the reasons described, of contributing in any really significant way to the formation of new rules; however, they can easily produce a destructive effect. From this viewpoint, a majority resolution may very well constitute proof that the *opinio juris* of a significant number of States is no longer in its favour, which might be enough to assert that a former customary rule is truly dead, without necessarily being replaced by a new one.

In closing, I wish to touch on one last point. I am led to make a rapid analysis of it by an extremely interesting remark made by Giorgio Gaja.

He expressed doubts as to whether the people participating on behalf of each State in the various bodies of international organizations, where the resolutions are adopted, are truly representative. I am among those who share those doubts, but I wish here to use a similar argument as a basic element in a criticism of a thesis regarding the normative effect of resolutions which Professor De Fiumel rightly referred to during the discussion.

Some scholars have in fact put forward the view that resolutions, particularly those of the General Assembly, might be binding at least on States which, by vote and/or by other means, have expressed the wish to observe them. The basis of the obligations (allegedly) deriving from these resolutions would, according to this thesis, be of a conventional nature: resulting from a sort of agreement in simplified form among the States concerned, including an undertaking to observe the resolution in question.

Many arguments have been put forward to refute such a theory, but never this one, which seems to me personally to be decisive: namely that those representing States in the General Assembly normally do not have (at any rate, not all of them) the necessary treaty-making power, pursuant to their domestic legal systems. In fact the "full powers" given these people by their various States quite obviously refer only to the statutory activity of the organization concerned and its Assembly. Where appropriate, pursuant to Article 7(2)(c) of the Vienna Convention on treaty law, full powers may include adoption of the text of conventions negotiated (and thereafter adopted) in the Assembly; but they could not cover the power to express States' consent to be bound by these conventions or by any other international agreement.

This argument may be technical, but it is far from being formalist. Many democratic constitutions regulate the process of formation of the State's will in respect of assent to international undertakings in a complex way, so as to prevent the Executive having the sole say in the matter. When the undertaking is politically significant, the national parliament must in most cases give its authorization to the Executive in order for the latter to be able to bind the State. These national constitutional principles — the importance of which needs no stressing, touching as they do on the delicate balance between powers in the modern State — would be violated in an arbitrary and unaccepted manner if the Executive's emissaries, seated in the General Assembly, sent to take part in adopting a statutorily non-binding resolution, could through their vote (and/or declaration) bind their State to observe the resolution, so that subsequent contrary conduct would entail the State's international responsibility as culprit of a wrongful act.

Part II

Are we Heading for a New Normativity in the International Community?

Introduction

J. H. H. Weiler

In order to give some direction to the discussion I would like to identify some focal points for debate. I think we should concentrate on three basic issues:

Is there evidence for a breakdown in the distinction between *lex lata* and *lex ferenda* and the emergence within *lex lata* of a hierarchy of different norms? If so what is the significance of this development? Are there sufficient indications that voluntarism as the underpinning of international obligations is being replaced by the emergence of majoritarian norm setting processes. If so what impact would this have on the international system? What effect, if any, has the current ideological cleavage in the structure and process of international law on the creation, content and acceptability of international rules and procedures?

In some respects these issues can be characterized as crisis symptoms of the system. For some observers they represent a breakdown of the existing fragile structure and as such a retrograde development. For others they represent, instead, the inevitable and thus positive adaptation of the international legal system to the demands of a larger, more complex and politically differentiated world system.

The most clamorous phenomenon in this context is the emergence of so-called soft law, such as General Assembly resolutions like the Charter of Economic Rights and Duties of States, and "non-binding agreements" (Helsinki), and so forth. The first question concerns of course the status of soft law. Is it a theoretical aberration which is contrary to meaningful legal discourse, or is it part of the norm setting process as an intermediate category between *lex lata* and *lex ferenda*. Is soft law really a modern phenomenon? Did international law really enjoy a higher level of certainty in the past? Of even greater interest would be the function and effect of soft law. Does it have the effect of blurring international normativity and increasing the uncertainty of rules in an already fragile system or is it an important mechanism for the progressive development of a new and more representative international law?

Within *lex lata* we would just mention the problem of *jus cogens*. There is the problem of whether the notion of *jus cogens* has really become part of customary international law. We should spend some, but not too much, time on this question. More interesting for our purposes would be to analyze the effect, positive or negative, which a double tier of norms, would or could have on the operation of the international legal system. Could such a double tier system work? On what basis and with what criteria could one (even the International Court of Justice itself) decide which norms were imperative and which, instead were ordinary? If we limit the content of *jus cogens* to those few areas (e. g. genocide) in relation to which there would be consensus among the major components of the international system, does *jus cogens* retain its importance?

The second theme merges in some respects into the first. Here as well, we have the question of the value of General Assembly resolutions, though this time in a cumulative, quantitative sense. Posed in more general terms the critical question may be phrased as follows: are there any circumstances in international life in which a State may be held to be bound by a norm to the creation of which it objected. This is principally a problem in the context of customary law. Has the traditionally affirmed right of the "persistent objector" to opt out a customary rule been eroded? There are more subtle variations on this theme. What is the meaning of silence in the evolution of custom? What effect can one give to world-wide diplomatic conferences and conventions which claim to state or crystallize customary law which would therefore bind non-participants and non-signatories as well.

Another issue relates to the respective value to be given to statements and actual practice. How does one determine the position of a State and its acceptance of an international norm: through statements in international fora or through its actual conduct?

Naturally we would wish to discuss in relation to all of these items their positive or negative significance for the current international system.

It is a commonplace that no law can be neutral. A legal system is rooted in a set of political values. The same is true for international law. In the past, however, there was to a large extent a consonance between the ideology of international law and the principal actors. The values of international law were those of the Old European World. It is only in today's much more pluralistic world order that the issue of ideology within the international legal system becomes a problem. It is almost inevitable that on many issues new norms, by nature value laden, will displease at least one of the principal components of the world order. The non-neutrality of law emerges thus in bold relief. This in turn creates a series of interesting problems.

Can there exist a basis for consensus in a dichotomized or even trichotimized world order? And if we continue to stipulate consensus as a basis for norm creation, could new norms evolve in all but a few non-controversial areas? Should the majority of States, in say, the United Nations, be allowed to impose their values on the minority? Should by contrast a minority of States be able to thwart the evolution of international law? Is international law beginning to face the age old problem of domestic law: the intractable problem of balancing respect for majoritarian wishes and values with protection of minority interests? The divided world pushes towards a reliance on accepted texts, especially the U.N. Charter. But is not the price paid in widely divergent and often wild interpretation of such texts which reduce their efficacy?

Chapter I

To what Extent are the Traditional Categories of *Lex Lata* and *Lex Ferenda* still viable?

I. Presentation

BROWNLIE

I am going to raise a few issues, and put some pigeons into the air for the members to shoot down. I certainly do think this subject, the sources of international law, and the problems it raises, is an important one. Too often central subjects get rather ignored, people are always looking for conspicuously new subjects, and I have always had the view that some of the more classical subjects remain important, and are not worked out, as is sometimes assumed. A good example of this is Crawford's book "The Creation of States in International Law" – a subject which was assumed to have been worked out long ago, but which remains important. Sources of international law is in the same class, an evergreen; in fact in the International Law Association a new committee has been established devoted to this subject (our colleague Maurice Mendelson is one of the members of that new committee).

The proposition is that recent developments have blurred the distinction between *lex lata* and *lex ferenda* and on the basis of this it is inferred that there are serious threats to the structure of international law, there is a sort of degradation in the normative values of the subject. Prosper Weil, in a highly fluent and almost apocalyptic article in the *American Journal of International Law*, listed his anxieties arising from the problem of distinguishing *lex lata* and *lex ferenda*, and also from the growth of a certain hierarchy of norms, with particular reference to *jus cogens* and obligations *erga omnes*. Now the problem of distinguishing *lex lata* and *lex ferenda* in the recent past has always been related to a reference to the appearance of soft law. And the phrase soft law, because it is a moderately useful shorthand, is one which is constantly repeated. In my view it is very much not a term of art: I only have a very vague idea of what soft law is; it is a trendy phrase. The examples which writers give of soft law are extremely varied; they include United Nations General Assembly resolutions on a great variety of subjects, for instance the Charter of the Economic Rights and Duties of States, relating to the new international economic order; also the Helsinki Final Act, which is a carefully drafted and very extensive instrument; and other instruments, such as the sets of guidelines drawn up in various quarters for the conduct of multinational entities.

The thesis is that the increased difficulty of distinguishing between *lex lata* and *lex ferenda* threatens to cause a sort of breakdown in the structure of international law. Well, I share some of Prosper Weil's concern, and whatever he says is always worth careful consideration, but I think that the nature of the problem has to be appreciated, and I am not quite as gloomy as Prosper appears to be.

I would like to look at some possible causes of what is seen as the problem of distinguishing between *lex lata* and *lex ferenda*. In the first place, I think it is a fact that diplomacy on occasion deliberately chooses soft law techniques. It is not a question of some esoteric problem which clever commentators have spotted; it happens to be a fact of life. Nor is it a question of *lex ferenda* or *lex lata*; it is simply that there is a certain technique of diplomacy which deliberately uses what may be called soft law. The Helsinki Final Act is a current and quite dramatic example of just that. So far as there are ambiguities about the legal status of the Helsinki Final Act, they are deliberately there. It seems to me to be part of the diplomatic exercise that there should be confusion; and some would say it was a highly sucessful diplomatic operation.

A second point is that there is a tendency which is found again in the political sphere, amongst diplomats and politicians, to invoke legal elements, to try and draw legal elements into almost every context. And there is a sort of supreme paradox here because the same gentlemen in other committee rooms, and smoking other cigars, are likely to point in a very knowing way to the weakness of international law. I am not myself particularly happy with this tendency to invoke legal elements on all fronts: on the one hand it stresses the importance of law, but it has a countervailing effect which is to put too much stress, too much strain on the law. People expect the law to do everything: to bring about disarmament, to maintain peace. Apparently such subjects are not the responsibility of diplomats any more, but the responsibility of international law, as a disembodied element. None of these things are done by the law, they are done by persons, by governments, and I think that it causes damage to the law when international law is expected to be able to cope with literally everything. In my view a part of the tendency to bring legal elements into almost every discussion is related to something which is certainly true in the Western World (the only world I really know well): which is that it is very unfashionable to discuss morality. Morality is old hat, and to remain smart, to remain acceptable to your pals, you must discuss morality under some acceptable cloak, and law appears to be an acceptable cloak.

Another aspect of this problem of the distinction between *lex lata* and *lex ferenda* is what I would call the problem of professional formation. I think in law schools in Great Britain and the United States, and perhaps elsewhere, there is a great tendency towards specialization. Students want more and more options, they want more choice, and they are allowed to do the Law of the Sea, or Human Rights, or Protection of the Environment, perhaps before they have done a course in general international law. In some law schools it is perfectly possible to plunge into a specialist subject like the Law of the Sea without having any original knowledge of the sources of international law, or the law of treaties. This leads to a certain lack of professionalism in dealing with fundamentals; that is, it leads to a lack of technique. In the political sphere, too, by which I mean the United Nations, governments, national assemblies, and so forth, precisely because of this invocation of legal elements, legal questions tend to be constantly discussed by persons who are not trained as lawyers. As a result a certain looseness, a certain glibness, a certain amateurism tends to appear in the treatment of questions of law. And so, to a degree, some of the difficulties of distinguishing between *lex lata* and *lex ferenda* are not the fault of the law: they exist, but are caused by factors outside the law.

Now let us have a look at the problem from a slightly different point of view. I think the main problem at the moment is the old one that law-finding is always difficult. Even when you have a treaty, it is necessary to find out what a particular text means; you may have a treaty which has been in existence for 20 years, but if it has not been much interpreted by courts the law-finding remains to be done. There is a curious tendency for people to think that if we can only find the right formula, the right rule, then the business of law-finding is suddenly going to be made more easy for us. I think that is rather unrealistic.

I do not think the problem of law-finding is peculiar to international law. Most of my career I taught a variety of legal subjects — not just international law — and certainly both in common law jurisdictions, and in civil law systems the same problems appear. The problem of stating the law of contract, or the law of tort, or the principles of civil responsibility is just as severe as that of discovering the content of rules of customary international law. This is evident from the very extensive works on the law of civil responsibility in France, for example, with its massive case law, or, in the public law sphere in Great Britain, the evolution of administrative law. The law often has to be guessed at, on the basis of *dicta* in lower court decisions, and for practitioners who have to try and offer a court what evidence there is as to the given rule (the rule they want to use), the evidence is often no more than a sort of forecasting. It cannot be anything else. So I think that the first problem is that law-finding is in practice, and will remain, difficult, however many seminars are held on the problems of distinguishing *lex lata* and *lex ferenda*.

Another point is that many of the examples said to be of soft law are neither of law nor of non-law, neither of *lex lata* nor of *lex ferenda*; they are simply evidence of what the law is or may be on a given subject. Many examples of soft law are not genuine examples of *lex ferenda*. Genuine examples of *lex ferenda* are when research institutes quite consciously offer some new model on the basis of which the law may be developed by those with the authority to develop it. And the examples of soft law (U.N. General Assembly resolutions, for example), which we see in recent periodical literature, are in appropriate cases evidence of the state of the law. In the sixties, for instance, when the General Assembly drew up a declaration of legal principles concerning the exploration and exploitation of outer space and celestial bodies, it was on the basis of four years' work by a particular committee which included a legal subcommittee. Although the resulting declaration was appended to a General Assembly resolution, it was the result of a process of drafting, and constituted law-making every bit as careful and in some ways as formal as that of the making of a treaty. Rather ironically, when the United States and the Soviet Union wanted an easy subject on which to agree, they drew up a treaty which replaced the declaration. The treaty, some of us think, is far less well drafted than the declaration that was adopted by the General Assembly. And so, *some* General Assembly resolutions, not General Asembly resolutions in general, but *some* General Assembly resolutions, are important evidence of the state of general international law. The text of the resolution and the debates leading up to the resolution, the explanation of the votes by delegations, are all evidence, but no more than that, of the state of international law. When I say evidence, I do not necessarily mean to say evidence that is favourable, or positive. Thus the evidence may reveal such differences of opinion on various aspects of the resolution that, viewed in terms of the criteria of customary international law, it suggests that we are still some distance away from customary international law-forming on a given subject.

The Helsinki Final Act, on the other hand, was, as I say, formulated in such a way that it should not be binding, it was not a treaty; on the other hand, in political reality, its effect was meant to be as binding as if it were a treaty. This was a deliberate diplomatic and political strategy. And whether you think it is a good thing or not to use this kind of confusing technique, in politics all sorts of instruments, all sorts of techniques, may be thought to be necessary. I do not think the Helsinki Final Act is *lex ferenda*; it is what it is, a particular technique for making rules. But whether you classify it as *lex ferenda* or not seems to me not to help very much. Of course, even when you have something which is obligatory in principle (a treaty, a bilateral treaty, or even a rule of customary law), some aspects of that may still need to be clarified. Even when you take the clearest type of obligation: for example, bilateral treaties or the kind of treaty which you find listed in the U.N. treaty series, you may find that some such treaties do not have any normative content at all. Some treaties are treaties in form but are really simply pieces of State conduct involving expressions of good will, with the element of actual performance very minor indeed. I am not degrading treaties generally but simply pointing to the variety of types of transaction which fall under the formal category of "treaties", registered as such with the United Nations. In other words even when something is flying the flag of obligation or *lex lata* in particular respects, when you look at it closely, you may find that the normative content is very small and perhaps almost completely absent.

I think that a more interesting way of looking at so-called cases of soft law is to look at their real importance; the fact that certain informal prescriptions, things that are not law as such, obviously have significance in terms of political behaviour between States, and are generally recognized by decision-makers to have an important *catalytic effect*. By informal prescriptions I am referring to anything which can provoke authoritative decision-makers into adopting the normative elements as legal rules. The Truman Proclamation on the Continental Shelf is a classic example. On the day in 1945 when the Proclamation was made its normative value was nil. It was a unilateral act by a particular State, with no obvious standing in its national law at the time, but it was picked up and gradually adopted as State practice in a general way. The same may be said of certain U.N. General Assembly resolutions. The 1962 Resolution on Permanent Sovereignty over Natural Resources has been cited as evidence of international law by a variety of States, including the United Kingdom. It is not just certain States individually or a particular group of States that use U.N. General Assembly resolutions. The Permanent Sovereignty Resolution was adopted after some very careful drafting and a lot of in-fighting. Paragraph 8 on concessions is considered by some to be highly protective of concessions, of investors' rights, and the United Kingdom not very surprisingly invoked it in a dispute with Iraq. The working papers of the Third Law of the Sea Conference are another example of documents which were in essence informal prescriptions; they were literally working papers. While the Conference was moving towards the adoption of a treaty, but before it did so a sucession of working papers appeared. Some aspects of these working papers, particularly in relation to the Exclusive Economic Zone, generated State practice. State practice on the EEZ had thus proliferated before the appearance of the treaty itself in 1982. I think an interesting question to ask is why it is that certain types of informal prescriptions succeed in having a catalytic effect, and others do not?

The last point of this sort I want to make is that even when you have new *lex lata*, even when the International Court and individual governments make the claim that the EEZ has become a concept of customary international law, as it clearly now has, then still the precise modalities have to be worked out. We cannot assume that in all respects the treaty model of

1982 is the customary law model; it probably is, but I am not certain. Whilst it is obviously a leading element in the customary law, quite a lot of State practice relating to the EEZ does not directly reflect the provisions of the 1982 treaty. So you can have a concept which has clearly arrived just as you can have a piece of legislation which is clearly on the statute book, but which needs a further evolution, a refinement. Thus you get a different kind of blurring between *lex lata* and *lex ferenda*.

The subject I have not really had time to elaborate on is the hierarchy problem. It consists of the classification of norms, with the new special classes which are *jus cogens* and obligations *erga omnes*. The category of *jus cogens*, whether you like it or not and whether it creates difficulties or not, has certainly arrived. This is a dogmatic statement, but it is true. The Vienna Convention on the Law of Treaties provides in articles 53 and 64 a very firm basis for the existence of *jus cogens*. Occasionally in practice I have to try and discourage colleagues who are too ready to allege that rules are *jus cogens*. I have to remind then that you should not try to classify something as *jus cogens*, unless you have a real need to do so, because you are taking on a very heavy burden of proof. The criteria for the formation of a rule of *jus cogens* laid down in article 53 are very rigorous indeed, and I think some writers are spreading the concept of *jus cogens* with too much enthusiasm.

Another interesting problem is how you handle the question of exceptions to a principle of *jus cogens*. In the case of the principle of the non-use of force by States as an instrument of national policy, which is certainly a principle of *jus cogens* without any possibility of doubt: how does that proposition affect the way in which you weigh exceptions to the prohibition? How does the concept of *jus cogens* affect the way in which we approach the problems of self-defence?

And apart from *jus cogens*, there is the other special class of obligations *erga omnes* which are very mysterious indeed. They are referred to in the classic passage on page 32 of the 1970. I.C.J. reports on the *Barcelona Traction* case, where the Court makes a general excursion into legal principles, and refers to principles of human rights especially as examples of obligations affecting States generally.

Lastly, although perhaps it is not always thought of as a part of the subject of hierarchy of norms, there is the old problem of special relations: which concerns the so-called "persistent objector", and the "subsequent objector", the State which is trying to change customary international law. I suspect that sometimes it is thought that these problems of special relations are the inventions of academics. But this is not so. They reflect the actual behaviour of States and the example that I offer as my favourite is the behaviour of Japan in respect of the Law of the Sea between 1945 and 1976. Japan, for very good reasons of its own, always withheld recognition of new forms of maritime jurisdiction, including continental shelf claims. This was because of course Japan was the classic distant-water fishing State and only in 1976 did it revise its view and come into the general run of States with respect to the various extensions of jurisdiction over adjacent waters. For a very long time States like New Zealand or Australia had to conduct disputes with Japan, and the new concepts could not be invoked against Japan because it had very assiduously adopted the role of "persistent objector".

II. Discussion

A. Lex lata *and* lex ferenda

VIRALLY

I have only just finished the written version of the course I gave at The Hague two years ago; this has brought before me three series of problems we shall be discussing today, on which I have done a great deal of thinking. For my part I would hesitate to bring under the same heading, though there is obviously a connection between them, the questions of *lex lata* and *lex ferenda* on the one hand, and that of the hierarchy of norms on the other. Clearly, they do go together if one believes in the existence of a whole spectrum of legal rules, but it seems to me that they raise quite different problems, since the problem of the hierarchy arises only within *lex lata*. Consequently, the issues it raises are entirely different. Thus, I shall for the moment leave aside the question of hierarchy, and keep to the first point.

Just now, Professor Brownlie spoke of the use by diplomats of what he called "soft law techniques". It is true that that is an increasingly marked trend in diplomacy, but what exactly does the expression "soft law techniques" mean? More specifically, what is this *soft law*? What is meant by the term? I tend to think that two rather different matters are in fact being confused in it.

The first relates to the *content* of rules. We find that very often diplomats give the impression that the States they represent are making concessions and accepting commitments. But they manage, through artifices of language, through escape clauses, and all sorts of other means, to bring it about that these commitments in fact commit them to nothing. This does not mean that to the small extent that they do nevertheless commit themselves, we are not within the framework of the most classical law, conventional law. But it is a fact that the real constraints resulting from many of these instruments are extremely limited. One well known example is Part IV of GATT, that is the chapter added to the General Agreement on Tariffs and Trade to take account of the situation of developing countries. It largely confines itself to simple declarations of intent, in no way binding on the signatories. To the extent, however, that it does involve specific commitments, such as, for instance, non-reciprocity in tariff negotiations, it does have legal effects.

So much for the first level. There is, however, a second level, quite different — it seems to me — which concerns the *instruments* that are concluded. On this point the example that springs to mind is the Final Act of the Helsinki conference. Here we have an entirely different situation; the Helsinki Final Act contains a number of provisions that are rather ambiguous and equivocal, with consequences not immediately perceivable. But there are also many provisions which, on the contrary, are entirely clear, which proclaim principles that are quite well known and entirely traditional, such as the principle of the inviolability of frontiers and that of respect for sovereignty, and a number of provisions relating to human rights. We are not, then, facing a problem relating to the content of law, but one concerning the significance of the act itself, of the instrument. We can note — and this is what has manifestly struck all lawyers — that the authors of the Act took a number of precautions to make it clearly understood that it did not commit them at legal level, that it did not have legal effect, that it did not need registering as a treaty by the U.N. Secretariat or publication in the collection of treaties.

If our analysis is really to get anywhere, it is important to draw a distinction between these two situations. The first raises no theoretical difficulty, but merely practical ones to do with knowing exactly what the signatories to an instrument have committed themselves to. The other, by contrast, raises problems which are much harder to solve. For the Helsinki Act it is relatively simple, because the authors of the Helsinki Act were clear about what they wanted and what they did not want. When however one comes to consider resolutions of international organizations, especially the General Assembly, differences as to the legal meaning of these resolutions immediately appear. I would be tempted to think that to deal with this problem, the jurist ought to agree to spread the net a little wider, to take in not only law and obligations, but its methods; and in two ways. First, I would say that lawyers ought to be more interested in the process of law formation, which entails many stages; nowadays, probably, still more than in the past, or at least stages that are better marked. This is where we find the distinction between *lex lata* and *lex ferenda*. This distinction can be conceived in entirely static fashion, by contrasting two different situations; *lex lata* and *lex ferenda*. But it can also be considered from a dynamic point of view, since *lex ferenda* is a law which is not yet established, which has not yet become *lex lata*, is in the process of becoming so. This leads us to wonder at what point the threshold is crossed, from one to the other. I do not at this point wish to go into this in any greater detail. Ian Brownlie alluded just now to this question, drawing the distinction between "law" and "evidence of law".

Another extension of the lawyer's field of vision to cope with this problem would be for him to recall that he is not alone in the world. I mean by this that social life — and international life is an aspect of social life — is governed by very many rules, and that not all of these rules are legal ones. In this connection Ian Brownlie also mentioned moral rules, which it is not very fashionable to speak of. There are also the rules of the political game. In many cases, States can agree on certain moral rules; more often, they will come to agreement on certain rules of the political game; but they will not agree to put their agreement on a legal plane.

YANKOV

I agree generally with what Professor Brownlie said, though I am not inclined to overdramatize the distinction between *lex lata* and *lex ferenda*. Sometimes the law-making process may experience an intermediate stage of elaborating draft rules or model rules which need further action by States in order to acquire the effect of legally binding norms of conduct. In some instances the States themselves prefer to establish rules which may entail certain political commitments but do not provide for legal obligations. This may be so not only as a result of "les règles du jeu politique" or diplomatic considerations, but for pragmatic reasons.

In this connection it may be pointed out that on several occasions the International Law Commission has faced the choice as to whether it should elaborate model, or general, rules, without there necessarily being a convention, or draft treaty articles to be embodied in an international instrument in the technical sense. This was the case with the consideration of the draft articles on the Most Favoured Nations clause and later on treaties between States and international organizations, or between international organizations *inter se*. Recently again reference to model rules was made in connection with the draft on the régime of the international non-navigation of water-courses. As rivers have such distinct and specific geographical, hydrological, economic, social, historical, and other features, it may be a tremendous waste of time to try and elaborate a convention which is applicable to all international waterways, a comprehensive convention which will cover all non-navigational uses of water-courses. Perhaps the more pragmatic and realistic course, in similar situations, would be to establish some general rules or framework arrangements to be used as a basis for bilateral, regional or local agreements. A more flexible method of law-making may well serve the requirements of broad international cooperation. The elaboration of general framework arrangements could be very appropriate in the case of international legislation relating to modern issues such as the protection of the environment on a larger global scale. It might be more fitting to work out general guidelines or recommendations which, *stricto sensu* are not binding, but would be at the disposal of governments for use when appropriate.

This idea came to the fore again when the International Law Commission discussed the topic of liability for damage caused by acts not prohibited by international law. The emphasis here has been more on international solidarity and international cooperation rather than on State responsibility for illicit acts in the strict sense. Since this is a twilight zone of legal obligation, perhaps it might be more appropriate to work out rules which are neither *lex lata*, nor *lex ferenda* in the traditional sense. It might be a preliminary stage of law-making, which we can call *lex ferenda*, though it might also be called soft law, consisting of non binding rules. The new methods of law-making may lead to readjustment of some concepts, which reflect a different approach to the true international situation.

I would like also to make a comment on the provisions in the *Helsinki Final Act*. I agree with Professor Virally that the Helsinki Final Act is a mosaic of many things. There are statements of well established and agreed legal principles; there are some specific rules of a technical character; there are reformulations of certain general principles from the U.N. Charter. Thus the Final Act is not a homogeneous document as such; perhaps we need to scrutinize its true content and specific aspects, rather than qualify it as a whole with a general classification.

Another point relates to the functions of *U.N.* resolutions. In this connection I would like to emphasize one aspect – perhaps it ties in with what Professor Brownlie said when he was talking about the catalytic function of General Assembly resolutions. In the international law doctrine of Eastern Europe, there are different views with regard to the nature and effect of General Assembly resolutions. I am not intending to describe in detail the different facets of the conceptual diversity on this matter. However, it should be pointed out that according to one view, if a resolution was generally adopted, or adopted unanimously, such a resolution is more than a recommendation: it might serve as a source of international law. Such an approach entails a differentiation between various resolutions, depending upon their significance or degree of support. In my submission General Assembly resolutions, with the exception of those which relate to the internal law of the United Nations and which have an administrative or budgetary nature are just recommendations. It would be opportunistic, therefore, to say that those resolutions which received general agreement are a source of international law, and those resolutions which were challenged and did not enjoy general consensus are not a source of international law. The way in which a resolution was adopted does not change the legal nature of that resolution.

In many instances U.N. General Assembly resolutions serve as an initial stage coming before the law-making stage *stricto sensu*, when legally binding rules are established. Several resolutions of the U.N. General Assembly, in the field of, say, humanitarian law and human rights, peaceful uses of outer space, the law of the sea, etc., have later become international conventions.

This was also the case with the Declaration on the exploration and exploitation of the sea-bed beyond the limits of national jurisdiction, which had a remarkable impact on the U.N. Convention on the Law of the Sea. General Assembly resolutions on disarmament and arms control matters have served as a starting point and provided the guidelines for disarmament treaties.

The multiple functions of U.N. General Assembly resolutions need further examination in the light of recent developments, as instruments enunciating general principles and rules which have a declaratory nature, or when they serve as an instrument indicating the content of positive law by way of *opinio juris* based on State practice as evidence of customary law. The multiplicity of these functions is substantiated in various ways of stimulating the law-making process, as an important step in the codification and progressive development of international law.

Abi-Saab

I just want to say a few things about the concept of soft law. In the first place, nobody now refers to its real origin. In fact it was Lord McNair who coined the term some forty or fifty years ago, using it to refer to international law formulated in terms of principles rather than through hard cases. It was the abstract structure of the propositions of international law, not buttressed by specific applications as in the common law model of legal elaboration. In recent years the term has gained in currency, but it is used to denote a very different meaning from McNair's. Indeed, there is a great confusion about whether the referent here (that which is qualified as soft) is the *rule* or the *instrument* which vehicles the rule. If we mean by soft law a rule which is not very well shaped, then treaties and very hard instruments can vehicle very soft standards. This is why I agree with Ian Brownlie when he said the important thing is the question of identifying the law; it is not so much the vehicle, but to what extent this vehicle reflects consensus, not in the formal sense of a procedure of adopting texts, but in the political and substantive sense of consensus as the element, or rather the threshold, of emergence of a rule of law.

The question of the threshold of law is of course very important. It was the spearhead of Prosper Weil's attack on many of us; he said that the threshold has disappeared, that everybody slips into the mistake of mixing up law and non-law, or *lex lata* and *lex ferenda*. But law-creation is not only a question of threshold. In my opinion law is not only what would be labelled as such by a court of law sitting and applying article 38 of the Statute of the International Court, so that if a proposition fails that test, it is no law; and if it is no law, then it is nothing at all from the legal point of view. The conservatives who argue these lines subscribe consciously or unconsciously to a restrictive and narrow view of the process for the creation of law: there is a legal "vacuum"; then suddenly there is a big bang bringing something into "being", and this is the law. This idea of law being created by a big bang, ignoring all the rest, *i. e.* all the preceding steps, the cumulative process that led to it, is a reductionist simplification. Besides, the imposition of thresholds and boundaries to legal concepts and phenomena always comprises a dose of artificiality and arbitrariness.

Reducing the whole issue of the legal character of a normative proposition to a mere question of threshold is indeed a simplification; and the real question is not only whether it is legally binding or not, for it can be legally relevant without being legally binding. I think we can all agree as lawyers that certain propositions will be upheld before the Court with great certainty, and others perhaps will not; but that does not mean that they are legally irrelevant. The question is then how to determine this relevance? Is the mission of lawyers, particularly academic lawyers or jurists, simply to interpret and apply the law once it is there? Or is it to try to comprehend the phenomenon of law in its entirety? If the answer is the latter, we have to envisage the creation of law as a cumulative process. Then the steps, the stages which precede the threshold are legally relevant, to the extent that they determine what will happen once the threshold is past. If we consider law as not only the final edifice but also the building blocks that make it, then we have to take them into consideration too, whatever we call them; soft law, hard law, *lex lata*, *lex ferenda*. In the final analysis, this is an epistemological question, a question of sociology of knowledge. If we consider law exclusively as that which can pass through a court, then we have to stop at the problem of threshold. If on the other hand, we consider law as all the components which make the whole, then we have to go back far beyond the threshold, and retrace all the steps, *i.e.*, the cumulative process, that led to it.

GAJA

As Professor Brownlie said in his introduction, non-binding instruments may well produce a catalytic effect with regard to the formation of new rules of general international law.

The authoritativeness of the body stating the law clearly represents an important factor. For instance, statements contained in judgments or advisory opinions of the International Court of Justice may find their origin in the views expressed by authors or in the practice of some States; however, the fact that statements are made by the Court commands far greater attention in international society. The same could be said of resolutions adopted by the General Assembly, if their authoritativeness had not been undermined by their number and by the deliberate ambiguities that they often contain. No doubt, clarity and careful preparation are factors which contribute to the catalytic effect. However, what often appears to be the decisive factor is the content of the stated rule.

When an instrument of a non-binding character or the text of an international convention which is not yet in force sets out some technical rules of a non-controversial nature, State practice may well conform to them whether they are innovative or not. With regard to these matters, legal security often represents the States' primary concern. Thus, many provisions contained in codification conventions come to be accepted by States which are not parties to them, as substantially corresponding to rules of general international law.

In matters in which more significant State interests are at stake, the success of a non-binding instrument mainly depends on the way in which the stated rule relates to the prevailing needs of international society. When a text appears to be satisfactory in the light of those needs, States will often refer to it and eventually a rule of general international law may emerge. As an illustration one may quote the impact of the negotiating texts in the Law of the Sea Conference with regard to the régime of the exclusive economic zone, as compared with the lack of influence exerted by the almost contemporary *dicta* on the coastal States' rights in the *Fisheries* cases.

CONDORELLI

I should like to take as my starting point the very pertinent observation put forward by Professor Virally. In fact in any discussion on the boundaries between *lex lata* and *lex ferenda* in international law, when one comes to consider the type of phenomenon currently denoted by the term soft law, the first difficulty one meets with is a terminological one; Georges Abi-Saab has rightly pointed this out. No doubt we use very vague and ambiguous terms because, deliberately or not, we use them to cover a whole series of fundamentally different situations. In this sense, Professor Virally's remark is very welcome, since it provides useful illumination. In fact, what may be termed soft in certain cases is the *content* of a rule of law, and in other cases is the *instrument* whereby a given rule is promulgated.

That should be accepted; but in my opinion things are much more complicated. To be sure a hard instrument (for instance an international treaty in due form) may have a content which is not hard, but more or less soft. We all know treaties that lay upon those they are addressed to one of those vague "obligations to cooperate" to which Abi-Saab has just alluded. It is often not easy to understand exactly what these obligations bind the States to. In consequence it is still harder to establish when such obligations may have been breached by a State, which would then be guilty of an internationally wrongful act involving its responsibility towards one or several other States (and again, which, in the case of multilateral treaties?). But apart from "obligations to cooperate", we are also acquainted with innumerable conventional norms that contain formulas of the type: "the High Contracting Parties will endeavour, as far as possible, to progressively attain this or that result". International economic law, international human rights law or the law of armed conflict, for instance, are full of provisions of this type.

Hard instruments may exist with a more or less soft content, then. Let us now look at soft instruments, such as the non-binding declarations of international organizations, or the "Final Acts" of international conferences, which, like the Helsinki one, are documents about which it has been decided beforehand that they will not constitute treaties and will consequently not be subject to ratification or registration. Experience teaches us that these documents too may have all sorts of contents, going from the strictest of orders to the gentlest of exhortations. No doubt the Manila Declaration on the Peaceful Settlement of International Disputes (General Assembly resolution 37/10 of 14 November 1982) is one of the broadest and most impressive collections of this spread of possibilities. There are provisions in it whereby States "are bound to" or "must", for instance, avoid disputes among themselves or refrain from aggravating the situation. There are others whereby States "ought to" or "may" do this or that. Then there are principles according to which States "ought ... to take due account as far as appropriate ..." of certain factors. Finally, we find that in other cases States "ought not to lose sight of the fact that ... it is desirable that ... they consider the possibility ..."; not forgetting yet more curious formulae such as that whereby U.N. organs and specialized agencies "ought to study the appropriateness of making use of the possibility ..."!

In sum, all combinations and permutations are possible between hardness and softness in instruments laying down rules of law and their content. The distinction indicated by Professor Virally should be retained, but without forgetting that between the two extreme poles of the hardest on the one hand and the softest on the other, there is a continuum that does not lend itself to any operation of precise delimitation. We are, in short, in an area where the boundary between law and non-law can certainly not be drawn with any degree of accuracy, since it is represented by a zone of uncertain width rather than by a sharp dividing line. In fact, if one claims to trace the boundary on the basis of an instrument, one will find that on both sides of the line can be found, to a variable extent, the same phenomenon of "softening" of the law; ought one then to allow greater normative value to a duly ratified treaty binding the parties to "endeavour as far as possible to cooperate in such and such an area" or a non-binding document signed by some States (or a unanimously adopted declaration) whereby the States in question "recognize" that they "must" comport themselves in such and such a manner? Conversely, were the boundary to be traced essentially according to the duration or flexibility of the content of the rules, ought one not then to treat as soft many customary or conventional rules, and as hard many non-binding documents, especially as some of these are very widely observed? I am leaving aside here the additional difficulties concerning, on the one hand, the question of the formation of rules of general or conventional international law on the basis of resolutions or declarations not binding in themselves, and, on the other, the problem of the consequences for the effectiveness of treaties of a widespread attitude of non-respect for their rules.

In conclusion, between the world of hard law on the one hand (made up of binding rules specifically requiring or forbidding a particular conduct, or authorizing it, thereby obliging the other addressees of the same rule to tolerate such authorized behaviour), and the world of non-law on the other, there is a transition zone in which the elements characterizing these two worlds are mixed in very variable proportions, similar to the situation at the crossover between temperate climates and desert climates. But we have to admit that at present this transitional zone is becoming steadily wider than it was in the past. The term soft law has become fashionable for precisely that reason; the phenomenon has no doubt always existed, but it has today taken on such gigantic dimensions that it could no longer go unnoticed by even the most distracted observer.

Faced with this situation, one may of course adopt the attitude we have taken hitherto in this debate, which was also taken by Professor Weil in his article on "Relative Normativity". By this, I mean that one may seek all the same to specify and distinguish (with greater or lesser rigour according to the academic and/or ideological approach adopted), by weighing the factors capable of making the balance swing to one side more than to the other. My concern here is different. I wish to seek to present a few observations in answer to the following question: why are we seeing this extraordinary growth in the extent of the "transition zone"? What is the real cause of this striking phenomenon affecting the international community, which is manifested in the softening or progressive weakening of international law as a whole?

The answer to this question, which in my view is fundamental, is on the whole rather simple. The international community today is well known to be riven by deep tensions that are tending to tear it apart; the social homogeneity that characterized it in other epochs has exploded. Vast areas of "traditional" international law are, as we know, the object of contestation by some, and are on the other hand bitterly defended by others, who, in return, oppose many aspects of the "new" international law that the former are fighting for. But this situation of crisis is ultimately damaging to all, since noone any longer knows what the "rules of the game" are. In other words, the splitting up of international society brings about the splitting up of international law. This implies legal uncertainty and insecurity, a tendency to regionalization, increased danger of tensions and conflicts, etc. What inevitably arises is a need to recreate, on new bases, a minimum of unity; that is, the need to reconstitute a set of universal rules that could be accepted by all.

How can one seek to secure such a result in a profoundly fragmented society? There is, in fact, only one way: that of major compromises, such as are sought after in all the venues of multilateral negotiation on a world-wide scale. But the price to be paid for this kind of compromise is usually a heavy one, and it is represented precisely by the very often non-binding or weakly-binding, vague, flexible, ambiguous or contradictory character of the "rules" that are worked out. It is because of this that the rules in question seem acceptable (or not unacceptable) to very many States; this is the fundamental reason why such a broad area of current international law (which Professor Weil calls "the pathological international normative system") is affected by "softness". This can, as we have seen, be brought about, depending on the need, by giving a more or less soft content to rules established by hard instruments, or else by using soft instruments to work out provisions with a more or less hard content. In conclusion, today more than ever the international community has need of a *jus commune* if it is to recover a minimum of unity, and to this end it regards it as preferable to have "a" law that is widely accepted even if soft, rather than not have any law at all.

This point seems to me essential. There is little point in comparing (as Professor Weil does) the merits of hard and soft law and concluding that the former is the only good kind, while the second is worthless. The real crux is not there. The question is not whether it is more worthwhile to make hard law or soft law; the point is that in present-day international society, most of the time, either one makes soft law or one makes nothing at all. In other words, rejecting soft law amounts in essence to accepting the irremediable disruption of contemporary international law.

Arangio-Ruiz

I am not at all happy about the manner in which soft law is being envisaged around this table. Since I first heard about the concept I have regretted that McNair's original definition, which Georges Abi-Saab reminded us of, was so quickly forgotten. It was forgotten, I suspect, because States, all States — old, middle-aged and new — are taking advantage of the concept of soft law. They are using soft law as opium, in the same way as religion was once said to be the opium of the people. They use it for their own public opinion and "international" public opinion and for other States too, in order to make peoples and States feel that certain problems are being taken care of at international level while they are in fact not being taken care of at all.

Of course, I would not deny that in given cases, as Professor Yankov reminded us, there may be a necessity, especially for a technical body not empowered to enact binding rules or decisions, to produce recommendations or suggestions for governments to consider the necessity of adopting binding (written or unwritten) rules. I understand, in other words, that there are cases where the adoption of soft law may represent a first step towards the possible adoption — through further adequate steps — of hard law, or just *law* without any adjective. This does not, however, justify recourse to soft law devices on the part of States in order to cover up unwillingness to achieve more substantial law-making results, presenting peoples or other States with a poor substitute for what is needed. Nor does it justify attitudes of complacency on the part of those scholars who seem at times too anxious to applaud as achievements soft law solutions which are only illusory.

For scholars to avoid such attitudes, one should go back more often to the fundamental notions we learnt at law school. Among these is the distinction between rule-making instruments and the content of the rules they "make". Obviously, as Professor Condorelli pointed out, there are instruments normally used to set forth binding rules, which may contain — alongside binding rules — some non-binding or soft law rules. A treaty can include, either mere recommendations (clearly soft) or what are known as "programmatory" rules, namely rules which need some kind of further elaboration or completion. There is nothing strange in the fact that a binding law-making instrument should create non-binding or less than perfect rules.

On the other hand, there are plenty of non-binding instruments — a typical case being General Assembly recommendations — containing formulations or elaborations of Charter rules or principles or of other written or unwritten rules already in existence. Of course, the question may arise here whether the formulation contained in a non-binding instrument represents a (non-binding) interpretation of Charter or other rules. There is no doubt, however, that there are cases in which non-binding statements by the General Assembly formulate or reiterate Charter rules, namely binding rules.

This does not mean however, that the recommendation itself (the instrument) thus becomes a binding instrument. The recommendation remains what it is, namely a non-binding resolution. It simply reiterates something which has already acquired, and still possesses, a binding force, thanks to the operation of the law-making process through which the original rule came into being. The non-binding instrument will only add *political* force to the rule or to a given interpretation thereof.

Mention has been made of the Helsinki Final Act. As you all know, that instrument, considered by many as a non-binding, merely political document, formulates ten principles which are an integral part of the U.N. Charter. There is thus no doubt that notwithstanding the fact that the Helsinki Act was perhaps not really able to create hard law (a point I would rather leave out of the present discussion), the declaration of the ten "guiding" principles is a statement of binding principles.

Of course, there is also the hardening of non-binding rules originally set forth in a non-binding instrument. This can well happen if the necessary law-making processes are set into motion: treaty or unwritten law-making processes, the latter including mainly what is sometimes labelled actual practice. I would doubt, however, that one can speak so easily (as I have perhaps wrongly understood to be the case around this table) about any sort of certainty that soft law will become hard law. This is again part of the opium, and I do not think that scholars should join governments in serving this kind of medicine to peoples or to other States. Georges Abi-Saab has spoken of "building blocks", which is a very good image for the various elements — historical, social, cultural, spiritual, religious, moral — which make up rules of customary, or unwritten, international law. But who can say, — when confronted with a recommendation by a permanent or occasional international conference, or with a non-binding piece of the Helsinki Final Act — whether or when such building blocks (less solid, in any case, than actual practice) will turn into hard law, or law *tout court*? It is quite possible that those blocks will never get to become a building. I would thus be unable to agree with the speaker according to whom soft law "is law that does not exist yet, but is about to come into being". It may well be, in my opinion, "that it does not turn into law at all", but remains soft; my experience is that there is plenty of soft law which has not become law at all. It has remained in its original state, and perhaps has even been blown to such small pieces by actual practice that there is little hope that it can ever be used as "building material".

The point is that we must not confuse *lex ferenda* and *lex in fieri*. When one speaks of soft law as something which is "about to become" (hard) law, one assumes that what has been possibly set forth by States — all, many or a number — as *lex ferenda*, is to be considered as bound to become law. *In fieri* is a child after conception, or a tree growing from the small plant one has planted. But a piece of soft law has a more problematic future. Even *lex ferenda* is perhaps not a correct description. It is quite often *lex ferenda* for some, not *ferenda* for others.

Another eminent speaker said something to the effect that if governments agree to adopt a non-binding instrument, international lawyers have no business to criticize. They ought simply to be glad that "something" has been accomplished. Of course, I have no objection to governments, unable to agree upon a *treaty* text, resorting to a non-binding conclusive statement of desirable goals, guidelines or even rules, particularly if the content of the rules is a good one. All I ask is that scholars should not be so easily content with such results when legal development or reform is necessary, and that they should not take it for granted that what is adopted as merely desirable — namely as soft law in the current sense — will become law or will be *per se* a step in legal development. In other words, scholars should be as critical and exigent as each subject may require. Above all, they should say unambiguously — should the occasion arise — how little has been accomplished by the non-binding instrument adopted. The current use — and abuse — of the concept of soft law is open to ambiguous interpretation in the "optimistic" sense I indicated at the outset.

YANKOV

I wish to make a small point relating to *lex lata* and *lex ferenda*. This distinction in municipal law or within the national jurisdiction of States is fairly easy. What is *lex lata* and what is *lex ferenda*? Within a national legal system, it is for the institutional structure of a given State, including its courts, to decide upon any points of doubt that may arise as to the existing law or rules which purport to be legal norms. By contrast one of the characteristic features of the international legal order is that the international community is not vested with generally recognized competence to determine such things *erga omnes*. As a result, it is much more important to establish all the relevant elements of the international instrument and to know what the intentions of States were when they accepted or adopted it. In my submission this is so because the coordinated wills of the States concerned constitute the foundation of the emerging rules.

SUY

May I first of all come back to what Professor Brownlie said about the reasons, as he sees them, for *the blurring of the distinction* between *lex lata* and *lex ferenda*. To these, I might perhaps add the following one: the facts of international life, as compared to 40 or 50 years ago, have changed drastically. International relations have become more and more complicated and there are an increasing number of problems which no longer belong exclusively to the arena of national sovereignty, but overstep national boundaries. We are living in an interdependent world, where all problems are linked. And this is due not only to the fact that the international community has grown from 50 to 150 or 160 member States, but also to the fact that all these new problems the international community is facing have not been dealt with by what I would call traditional international law. On issues such as the international law of the environment, outer space, human rights and the law of the sea, the international community needs to act much more promptly than, for example, the workings of the International Law Commission permit. I think it is the feeling of the international community today that leaving the elaboration of international law to respectable institutions such as the Commission is too long a business and that solutions are required much more urgently.

As a result, recourse is being had to other techniques, and traditional international lawyers have been horrified to see that the U.N. General Assembly, for example, is adopting resolutions on a variety of topics. Some of the same international lawyers, however, are very fond of some of these resolutions: Brownlie mentioned the 1962 resolution which is very often quoted because it suits some States and some lawyers, but I am also thinking of declarations on the development of *outer space*. The hard law of outer space was put together at international conventions, but before that the international community had made a declaration of principles, on the understanding that the details would be worked out later on. The same happened with human rights; the Universal Declaration of Human Rights is another example of a set of principles upon which conventions and binding international agreements were later built. This is also true for the law of the sea; between the 1958 conventions and the 1982 Law of the Sea Convention, there was again a declaration of principles.

Some international lawyers seem to be horrified by this trend and some have sounded the alarm because they think we are now gliding into abysses of darkness and insecurity. I myself am not defending soft law, or at least not the mechanism by which this law has come into being, but I am saying that there is a need to find alternative roads to law-creation. If in the General Assembly, the international community, whether by consensus or not, adopts a declaration, what is wrong with that? Is not this, in most cases, the expression, if not of an *opinio juris*, then certainly of an *opinio necessitatis*? Furthermore, we should not forget that the U.N. Charter provides that the General Assembly shall take the lead, not only in the codification, but also in the progressive development of international law.

If we come to analyze this so-called soft law, I agree with Professor Arangio-Ruiz that it does not necessarily have to become hard law. But I have the feeling that the members of the international community are less and less interested in hard law, and that they have come to grips with living with a mechanism for a softer law. Let us look at the difference, for example, between a declaration of principles on the one hand, and an international convention which has been worked out through lengthy, painful negotiations and a series of compromises, until finally the text is adopted by consensus. The politician representing his country can go to the General Assembly and say: "Now we have obtained something". It is not ideal, it is not as detailed as it could have been, it is the lowest common denominator, resulting from compromise, and therefore some people say it is soft because it lacks teeth; but anyhow, it is law coping with an urgent situation. It is not bound to become hard law, but as I say, I do not believe that member States care all that much now whether something that has been adopted as soft law ought to become hard law, as the traditional international lawyers understand this.

A last remark. Law is not made by international lawyers. It is made by politicians, by the representatives of countries; and if they have come to realize that the classical methods of elaborating international law are no longer adequate in the face of contemporary problems of international relations, then it is certainly not for the lawyer to say that the new method found is not a true law-creating method. I think if the politicians agree, then the lawyers have to follow.

When government representatives sit together, say in the General Assembly, an international conference or an international negotiation, and after ten years of negotiations come up with a code of conduct, in the view of some of the international lawyers that text is not binding, but is just a set of moral principles or a set of guidelines; it is not hard law. But if the governments have worked on it and have come up with this set of principles on the basis of unanimity, or consensus, I would suggest, that, as Georges Abi-Saab said, these are legally relevant instruments, although they may not yet be 100% hard binding law.

VIRALLY

First of all, I wish to say to my friend Gaetano Arangio-Ruiz that of course I agree with him in thinking that there is no inevitability in the formation of law. Obviously we are to understand the phrase *lex ferenda* in Latin; the gerund, not the future. It is law that ought to be made, that is regarded as desirable; it is not necessarily law that will be made. All that I wished to say was the jurist, and by that I mean the observer of the legal phenomenon, who seeks to give as objective and complete an account of it as possible, must examine all processes of formation of law, not only those which traditional jurists took into consideration, since they were interested in law only once it was finalized, accomplished.

It was emphasized just now that there are certain processes that take place right at the beginning of a successful evolution into law which have a catalytic effect, whereas others do not. There have been questions about the reasons for these differences; I would be tempted to think that they relate essentially to circumstances. Why, for instance, was the Truman Proclamation the starting point for a very rapid evolution that led to the establishment of a system for the continental shelf? Because it came at the right time: at a time when the natural resources of the continental shelf could be used. Coastal States felt that they were the ones that ought to benefit from this manna, and the Truman Proclamation was followed by a whole series of other declarations that led to the formation of the customary law subsequently incorporated in the Geneva Convention. When the General Assembly adopted a declaration on the principles of international law governing activities in space, it also came at the right time, because these activities were beginning, and it was in fact necessary to create some rules. In other cases there has been no success because the initiative taken has been premature, or did not meet a need. I do not think it is the jurist, but the sociologist, the historian or the politician, who can see if an initiative is coming at the right time, or not.

Coming back now to the question of soft law and its formation, I am afraid that, in many cases, the word law is used when there is no real question of law. I wish to recall what I said just now. In social life it is not only legal rules that are useful; there are other rules too. I have mentioned political rules and moral rules; you will forgive me, as a Frenchman, for saying that there is yet another category of rules to which not enough thought is given, despite their usefulness, namely "recipe" type rules. You know that the French attach great importance to good cooking. What is a recipe? It is a set of rules determining a series of operations that have to be carried out if a good dish is to be produced. There is no obligation; one is perfectly entitled to do otherwise; but the dish will not taste the same. What is true of cooking is true of practically all fields where a technical problem arises. At the present time, States are encountering a multitude of technical problems in their mutual relations. In particular, in many areas they feel a need to cooperate. This cooperation cannot come about by itself, simply through a few individual initiatives. Certain rules are necessary to guide States in this cooperation. It would obviously be rather denigratory to say that they are recipes, but all the same, there is a similarity. They are technical rules recommended to States in the form of General Assembly resolutions, guidelines, codes of conduct, all sorts of things that States follow more or less closely, and on which in any case they can be said to base their behaviour. As regards the enormous need for cooperation existing in international society today, diplomats are sometimes good cooks and draw up good recipes. These recipes are followed, not because there is an obligation to do so, but because there is an interest in the result, in the dish to be enjoyed. Please do not let us call that soft law. Some other term can be found that does not bring law into it. They are rules applied in social life, which are necessary, but which are not law at all. If jurists were a little less imperialistic, if they agreed to recognize that there are many rules that are not part of their empire, of their field, they would free themselves from a lot of problems. It might be an idea to say that what has been called hard law is law *tout court*.

Cassese

Since we are running out of time I shall very quickly put forward three short platitudes. First, may I take up a few comments made by Luigi Condorelli and Erik Suy about the necessity for the international community to have soft law, and the reasons behind this soft law. In my mind the gradual erosion or disruption of the dichotomy between *lex lata* and *lex ferenda* is not to be regarded as a retrograde step. And here I strongly disagree with Prosper Weil. I believe soft law holds water. Of course the phrase is misleading, but for want of a better word, I think we should stick to it. Why is soft law so badly needed? I think that it is, as Luigi Condorelli so rightly pointed out, because the current international community is pluralistic. There is no world parliament, and real power is wielded by a minority. The majority has little power, and therefore the best way of gradually changing the law is to agree upon and proclaim general guideliness, however vague they may be, with the hope that they will gradually turn into real law. I think this is the price the international community has to pay to achieve something, and that is a gradual transformation of the general standards governing the international community.

Let me quickly turn to my second general remark. I share Professor Yankov's view that we should take a pragmatic approach when trying to assess whether a particular instrument amounts to soft or hard law. We should assess each particular instrument, resolution, code of conduct an so on on its merits, to see whether it can be considered likely gradually to turn into binding law. For this purpose we have a very useful intellectual tool at our disposal and I stronly recommend all of you to read the excellent document on the new international economic order prepared by Georges Abi-Saab for the General Assembly. In this he speaks of at least three tests — or, as he calls them, "indices" — for evaluating whether a piece of "new" law is becoming law or is still soft law. The first of these tests regards the circumstances surrounding the adoption of a resolution or any other document (whether it was adopted by consensus, whether there were objections, how strong these objections were, whether any reservations were expressed, and son on). The second index is the degree of concreteness of the contents of the document (of course, if what we have is a set of very loose formulae we cannot expect that these will ever become law). The third test is the existence of a follow-up mechanism: whether there is any device for checking that this set of guidelines is complied with by States. I think we have here a very useful intellectual tool for gauging in each particular case whether an instrument is likely to turn into international law proper.

My third remark relates to the Helsinki Final Act. It has been rightly pointed out that many provisions of the Helsinki Accord, as it is called by some Americans, or Declaration, simply restate law. Other provisions elaborate slightly upon existing law, while a third set of provisions carry only political weight; these for the most part set forth political objectives, touching on topics like family reunion, for example, and include provisions on journalists, exchange of information and so on. There are, however, a few provisions which are not loosely worded, but, on the contrary, are couched in fairly precise terms and are somewhat innovative in law. Now these were accepted by consensus, and some mechanism for supervising compliance with the Helsinki Act was set up, as we know, even if the follow-up machinery does not work very well.

The crucial point, to my mind, is that a number of States have charged other States signatories to the Helsinki Act, with violating some of its provisions. Now, this is the usual practice which occurs when there is a treaty proper and a party to the treaty does not comply with its provisions; the other party of course complains, or accuses, or takes exception. In my opinion, this sort of reaction, namely that one or more signatories have taken notice of violations, and accused other countries of failing to respect the Act, gives some relevance to those provisions of it. Here we have, I think, neither treaty law, nor customary international law, but what constitutes a core of general political standards that *de facto* are treated by States as binding rules. We could perhaps describe this as a kind of twilight situation. I think we should face this new situation, and try to find a better phrase than soft law, because here we are confronted with something that is not hard law, but is regarded by States to some extent at least as binding *de facto*.

MERON

I was very interested in the comments made by Luigi Condorelli and others, regarding the relationship between soft instrument and hard content or hard instrument and soft content. The situation, I am afraid, is, however, more complicated than that. In the first place, in many situations, it is difficult to establish whether particular rules contained in an instrument are, indeed, already hard. In other situations, we may have a soft instrument, namely a declaration with, perhaps, a soft content, that does not yet reflect customary international law, but is accompanied by an exhortation on the part of the U.N. General Assembly to regard this instrument as a normative one. Every State is thus called upon to take the necessary steps in its domestic legislation to give internal effect to the provisions stated in such an instrument (e.g., the 1981 U.N. General Assembly Declaration on the Elimination of All Forms of Intolerance and Discrimination Based on Religion and Belief). Professor Arangio-Ruiz quite rightly wonders why not all instruments containing soft law, or soft norms are likely ever to become instruments reflecting hard norms. Whether a particular instrument containing soft norms has the potential of eventually being transformed into hard law depends on the quality of the norms. When we assess an instrument as regards its prospects for eventually becoming hard law, I think there are, among others, two considerations which we must bear in mind. One is to what extent the instrument, as it now stands, is close to international practice, to reflecting international customary law. Another consideration is the extent to which a certain instrument responds to a real and urgent need of the international community. If you have an instrument which does answer to at least one, preferably both of these conditions, there is a good likelihood that you will see this soft, or softish instrument eventually turning into something that will be regarded as binding by the international community as a whole.

ABI-SAAB

I have two small comments to make. The first is on the statement that soft law is not necessarily the hard law of the future, and the second is on the question of recipes. I think these points have a common element which is the role of consciousness or intention in the creation of law.

My comment on the first point is that while we all agree that an unborn child may not necessarily be born alive, the chances are that it will. I think that what makes our present soft law a little bit like a child in the womb, is exactly the point that has been made several times, namely that soft law expresses the consciousness of the international community of the need for a certain law to that effect. I agree that this consciousness or legislative intent does not take into account all the vicissitudes which may perturb or interrupt the process of law-creation. But it greatly increases the probabilities of the intended result being reached. It is not a fortuitous or haphazard process, like throwing a chip on a roulette table with one chance in 34 of achieving the result. This is a reasonable *pater familias* investment, because the international community expresses its conscious intent to reach the result; an intent which may be resisted, but which has a weight, a chance of materialization, very different from the hope of winning by playing cards or throwing dice. I agree that the transformation of soft law into hard law is not a certainty, but I think it is a very high probability, which brings it necessarily within the realm of our interests as jurists. Here again, I agree with Erik Suy. Even classical lawyers would tell you that legislation is a political activity, carried out by parliaments, by elected politicians, not by jurists. This does not mean that the jurist should not concern himself with this activity. He has to take it into consideration; and if he can influence it, so much the better.

Intent or consciousness is relevant again with respect to recipes; Michel Virally should not worry about having too French an attitude because the British too have a very nice saying which applies here: "The proof of the pudding is in the eating"; the legal recipes we prepare have to be tested by their final results.

What is the exact role of law as a recipe? In a book that I wrote about the role of law in decision-making, I distinctly said that we should not treat law only as a series of orders or prohibitions; we have to highlight the role of law as a facilitator, permitting people who act together to do what they cannot do individually; as a blueprint. The role of law as a blueprint for cooperative action is a very important one. In this respect, for once, I may not be in total agreement with Michel Virally, for unlike him I think legal recipes make hard and fast law. The legal formulae for cooperative action are not facultative; they are legal tools: if you want to produce the desired result, you have to follow them. This is very clear in municipal law also, particularly in constitutional law.

Brownlie

I shall try and summarize the sense of the meeting, though I must, of course, set aside the question of the hierarchy of norms, which we in effect reserved. Now in the first place, what is the prognosis? My feeling is that most of us are not as gloomy as Prosper Weil, although we do think there are considerations and issues which have to be reviewed. By and large I did not sense a terrible pessimism, and I think that the consensus is probably that the issues are a practical and working problem. Law-finding is important, but difficult and it will not be by fixing on a formula or a set of principles that law-finding will be made easy; just as we draft and redraft principles of treaty interpretation and the actual work of treaty interpretation remains to be done. Speaking for myself, my approach is that of an informal or flexible positivist. Positivism is sometimes characterized as reactionary, and I recently caused a considerable furore by calling myself a positivist at a conference in London. This caused enormous upset, and yet the strange thing is that my conception of positivism is precisely one which reflects what is happening. Although I agree with Professor Arangio-Ruiz that the jurist must keep his own counsel, I think the first duty of an international jurist is at least to monitor what is going on. If you do not do that, you are lost; at least you are not a jurist, you are something else. And what is going on includes soft law, and includes the possibility that the effect of a catalyst may produce hard law, and thus you may get a constructive transition. So flexible positivism is perfectly capable of taking on board General Assembly resolutions and other such material in appropriate circumstances.

The other general feature of the discussion has been the emphasis on the sheer variety of norms, the differing types of work that have to be done, and the fact that norms emerging in response to this variety of needs are themselves various. In legal theory, for example, Ronald Dworkin has emphasized what may well be familiar to international lawyers; the fact that legal rules are of many different types. And so, as has been mentioned, even within a constitution like that of Italy, or India, you may have directive principles which are not quite hard constitutional law, but nonetheless are a part of the picture. You may on the other hand have hard instruments, like GATT, containing parts which are really soft law, or something like it. Conversely, you may have soft instruments, as far as the formal category of the instrument itself is concerned, like the Helsinki Final Act which may, nonetheless include parts which are hard rules.

However, although I would favour this flexibility, this spectrum of types of law and types of — for want of a better phrase — soft law, nonetheless, I think that the threshold still matters. Consequently I was in sympathy with some of the things Georges Abi-Saab said, and I do not think the classical criteria can be cast aside. They do not work magic, but they still have a role to play. I am not completely in agreement with those who tended to emphasize the role of soft law. It seems to me that there is still a spectrum, and on occasion, States still intend to invent hard law, and that in particular contexts (especially the context of adjudication) they rely on hard law, and behave in a very old-fashioned way at least some of the time. I think that the soft law world is very important and that this is increasingly so, but nonetheless I am not sure that the old world, so to speak, the orthodox part of the spectrum, has disappeared.

I think that many examples of the catalytic effect of informal prescriptions could be given. Professor Gaja referred to the way in which an incidental passage in an I.C.J. judgment can sometimes have quite a considerable effect, when it is picked up. At the same time I think that there is the question of why some particular informal prescriptions have that power of generation, and others do not. Obviously political accidents, and the political background, play an important role; nonetheless I think there is something more to be said. If you ask why the Truman Proclamation "succeeded", no doubt it was partly because it came from the United States and thus had a lot of diplomatic clout behind it. But there is more to it than that. It was a very intelligently thought out instrument. It had to balance the maintenance of the freedom of the seas in respect of the superjacent waters, while launching a novel doctrine so far as the seabed resources were concerned. And it was rather nicely structured from that point of view; it was clever. It was also given a certain normative shape. There is the question of the quality of the drafting which preempts law, and the Truman Proclamation was obviously drafted by lawyers. It had certain indices, certain marks, which made the prognosis a favourable one.

I would like to recall, because I think it is a very important point, Professor Yankov's reminder that there are often practical reasons, not just polititcal reasons, for producing so-called soft law, model rules, which are not to be regarded as law as such. This links up with some of the things Professor Suy said, about the need for a variety of responses to the variety of problems which the international community faces. There is quite an old-fashioned, long-standing example of this kind of flexibility in the International Labour Organization methods of law-making, some of which were designed to make things easier for federal States, which is another kind of internal control.

Lastly I would like to come to Professor Arangio-Ruiz's point about the use of soft law as political cosmetics. This is quite a favourite point of mine. I am not impressed by the way in which the right to development, which I favour very much, is taken care of, not by actual policies (States know how to transfer aid, they know what can be done) but by putting phrases into international instruments. I often attack cosmetics, but at the same time, on occasion the very use of these phrases traps politicians, traps the layman, into levels of commitment which may not be as high as we would like, but are much better than nothing.

B. Is there a Hierarchy within the Body of International Rules?

MERON

I would like to focus on the question of *jus cogens* in relation to those norms — the bulk of international law — which have not yet reached that exalted status, which our friend and colleague, Prosper Weil, has called "élite norms". To start, I should like to refer to certain propositions made by Ian Brownlie. He suggested that we should not show too much enthusiasm about pushing the notion of *jus cogens*, but that, on the other hand, we should not display too much reluctance to discuss the moral content, the ethical underpinnings of the law. I believe that these two propositions are valuable in our discussions. We should on the one hand bear in mind the importance of precision in legal thought and legal expression and, on the other, we should always be aware of the ethical principles which have been instrumental in creating concepts of *jus cogens*, still developing, still fluid, yet surely so important.

I shall discuss the area of human rights. I shall introduce this by looking very briefly at the list of the customary norms on human rights which appears in the sixth draft of the Restatement of Foreign Relations Law of the United States, an important and authoritative source. These are genocide, slavery or slave trade, murder or causing the disappearance of individuals, torture or other cruel, inhuman or degrading treatment or punishment, prolonged arbitrary detention, systematic racial discrimination and, as an omnibus clause, a consistent pattern of gross violations of internationally recognized human rights. Which of these rules would we be prepared to characterize as peremptory, as reflecting norms of *jus cogens*? Invoking the authority of McDougal, Laswell and Chen (*Human Rights and World Public Order* 338—50 (1980), Comment *1* states that the rules mentioned in paragraph 702, that is all the rules mentioned in that section, are peremptory norms and an international agreement that would violate them would be void. This poses difficulties, however, because "prolonged arbitrary detention" is not mentioned among the non-derogable rights stated in Article 4 of the International Covenant on Civil and Political Rights. While rights which are non-derogable are not necessarily *jus cogens*, can derogable rights be regarded as *jus cogens*? To the Restatement's list we should perhaps add certain norms of international humanitarian law. Even so, the number of human rights norms for which we now can claim the status of peremptory norms is fairly limited.

Marjorie Whiteman published an article in the *Georgia Journal of International and Comparative Law* (1977), entitled "*Jus Cogens* in International Law, with a Projected List". She is brave because she does not only speak in generalities, but her list mentions only three or four norms pertaining to human rights: genocide, slavery or slave trade, war crimes and crimes against humanity. The Whiteman list is significantly different from that given in paragraph 702 of the Restatement. What is the importance of this list? I ask this question because no State in the world, *jus cogens* or not *jus cogens*, would claim *in abstracto* that it has the right to engage in torture or in genocide, or to engage in arbitrary deprivation of life, and no State (let us recall Article 53 and 64 of the Vienna Convention on the Law of

Treaties) would attempt to conclude international agreements with a neighboring State which would permit resort to genocide, or to torture, or to any one of those terrible practices.

On the practical level, therefore, the importance of the list is not as great as it might appear at first sight. Is there a way of classifying the various human rights norms into two categories, merely customary, on the one hand, and those that have attained the status of élite norms, of *jus cogens* norms, on the other? What are the possible approaches to trying to categorize rules this way? I would like to mention several possibilities, simply to give an idea of the difficulties involved in such an attempt.

One approach is to view those human rights norms which are non-derogable as rules of *jus cogens*. There are, however, several important arguments why this approach could not be persuasive. First, let us remember that the principal human rights instruments contain different lists of non-derogable rights. I am speaking of the International Covenant on Civil and Political Rights and of the two regional instruments – the American Convention on Human Rights and the European Convention on Human Rights and Fundamental Freedoms. Secondly, some of the non-derogable rights mentioned in these instruments have not even attained the status of customary law, let alone *jus cogens*. As an example, I would give Article 11 of the International Covenant on Civil and Political Rights, which prohibits imprisonment merely on the ground of inability to fulfill a contractual obligation. I doubt whether it could be established that Article 11 reflects a rule of customary international law.

Thirdly, it is difficult, according to their characterization in the relevant U.N. instruments, to distinguish those human rights which are fundamental from those which are not. Reading the U.N. Charter, the Universal Declaration of Human Rights, the various international conventions concluded under the auspices of the United Nations, we discover that terms such as "human rights", "freedoms", "fundamental human rights", "fundamental freedoms", "rights and freedoms" and, most commonly, "human rights and fundamental freedoms" are used interchangeably, suggesting that there is no substantive and conceptually definable legal difference between them. Fourthly, it is equally difficult to characterize human rights by the intrinsic importance of the rule. Professor Brownlie referred to the content of the rule; surely this is a relevant element. But can we reach an international consensus on those rules which appear to all of us, or almost all of us, to be the most important ones? The prospects for reaching a general agreement on the identification of rules of *jus cogens* are discouraging. Finally, I should mention the method of enumeration. We could simply try to enumerate certain rules as constituting *jus cogens*. Here again we would not obtain sufficient international consensus.

I now come to my conclusions. The first one is this. Do we already have certain human rights rules for which a claim can be made that they constitute *jus cogens*? My answer is yes. There are a number of rules, though a very limited number, for which we can claim the status of peremptory norms of international law. Secondly, is this conclusion useful? On the moral plane there is no question whatsoever that the concept is important. On the practical level, however, the usefulness of the concept is mostly potential. We have seen already that many of the questions which we are discussing in the context of *jus cogens* are really "hypothèses d'école". States do not contest the illegality of any of the prohibited acts. Violations are justified by more subtle arguments. While potentially *jus cogens* rights are important, we must be careful not to push them unduly, so as not to endanger their credibility. Rules of *jus cogens* are especially important given the present international climate of brutal violations of human rights. We should not, however, regard the concept as applicable only to treaty-making. Obviously, as Judge Mosler and Dr Suy have emphasized, the international public order prohibits States from unilaterally derogating from rules having the character of *jus cogens*. States acting severally must not be allowed to violate rights which they may not violate jointly.

YANKOV

Due to the lack of supra-State institutions endowed with compulsory adjudication *erga omnes*, it is up to States themselves to decide whether they should submit to international rules and determine the existence or non-existence of such rules, including the binding or non-binding character of an international instrument. This applies also to the distinction between *jus cogens* and other rules of international law. It is therfore not for academics or jurists to state what the elements or parameters of *jus cogens* are which distinguish it from other rules of international law. Their opinions may help, or at times may confuse the issue, but, when all is said and done, if we want to ascertain the existence of any hierarchy among international legal norms we have to look at the intentions and the expression of the will of the law-makers, and the law-making agents in international law are basically States (although in some instances international organizations could also play a role).

Consequently, when determining the difference between *jus cogens* rules and other rules of international law we have to take into consideration the peculiar features of the international system, and in particular the lack of institutional infrastructure in the international community. I may be stating the obvious, but sometimes we need to remember this and take a more realistic approach. I personally would be in favour of general acceptance of international adjudication, but this would be wishful thinking, since the international community of today is based on the sovereign equality of States and, therefore, the consent of States is the source of international law.

Abi-Saab

I have a short comment to make which relates to the question of hierarchy among norms which I consider to be essentially a cognitive question, a question of representation of international law. We all know of Tunkin's idea of a "juridical legal system". I think this is the crux of the issue. If we are speaking of a legal system, what is it like? Is it round, a pyramid, or with no shape at all? The gist of Prosper Weil's article is that international law is a bundle of special arrangements, *inter se* arrangements, more or less. There is nothing more to it than that: indeed, the same problem was referred to by Ian Brownlie when he spoke of special relations, with regard to *jus cogens* and *erga omnes* rules. If we look at international law from the outside, not as a judge, or as a practitioner, but as a system analyst, what does it amount to? Here again, after reading Prosper Weil's article, you get the impression that the only law that is true law is that which is accepted by States; in other words, voluntarism pure and simple. And if you stop and consider this amalgam of special arrangements, it is a unicellular system; a system where all the cells have exactly the same structure. It is at the lowest, amoebean, stage of evolution.

Can such a legal system govern the international life we are living now, with all its complexities, with its incredible pace of change, with its great and increasing degree of interdependence in the material relations of production and exchange of goods and services? I am not speaking of feelings of interdependence but of material interdependence, which is with us and is rapidly increasing, whether we like it or not. Can a legal system composed of identical cells which are there with no structural relation to each other govern such an international society? I think this is an impossibility. It is no longer a matter of choice between on the one hand an existing system — however rudimentary, primitive and gap-filled, but which has proved its usefulness and which constitutes an "acquis" — and on the other a yet untried and unrealistic blueprint for the international community. The system is simply unworkable in today's world. In any case, it no longer reflects or faithfully describes the actual system of international law. Once again, I repeat, views such as Prosper Weil's are a yearning for a lost paradise, a vanished or receding *status quo*.

One last word about *jus cogens*. It has been criticized as an empty box, because once you try to decide what rules go into it, there is no agreement. This criticism is simply wrong. Ted Meron has identified a few rules about which we can say we are all in agreement, that they are *jus cogens* rules. But I think that even as an empty box *jus cogens* is necessary, because if you do not have the box, you cannot put anything in it. Without having the category we cannot have consensus on *which* rules do or can belong to this category. Anyway, there is one rule which I think we all have to agree is *jus cogens*: that is the prohibition of the use of force. Some people say that this rule has been honoured more by breach than respect, but nobody has ever said that it does not exist or that it is not binding on him. Violations of it, to adapt Rochefoucauld's famous saying, pay homage to it, while resorting to special pleading to try to explain their deviation from it.

To conclude, I think the international legal system must have a structure, and cannot avoid establishing a certain hierarchy among its norms. The hierarchy does not have to be very accentuated, but in the world we are living in we cannot avoid having a system with some specialization of functions between its rules and some structural relations between them. Otherwise, it cannot be a workable legal system.

Suy

My first point would be to underline what Georges Abi-Saab said. There is no society, international or otherwise, which can live without at least a minimum of fundamental principles that have a higher value in the legal system. Now *jus cogens* has been mentioned here. Professor Meron has given us a very interesting *exposé* about which norms could be said to belong to *jus cogens*, and he mentioned some of the most fundamental human rights. I am afraid that the notion of *jus cogens* is becoming a kind of opium of the people. Professor Virally will recall that we discussed *jus cogens* nearly 20 years ago and I should perhaps confess that my thinking on this particular topic has changed slightly, in the following way. I have come to the conclusion that *jus cogens* is a notion which has a place only in the law of treaties, in the sense that a treaty which is contrary to *jus cogens* is null and void. Now can one imagine two States making an agreement by which they will practice genocide or *apartheid*, or systematic torture, etc.? This is unrealistic.

I do not deny, however, that a specific higher value has to be given to all these rules. Now if one accepts the view that *jus cogens* is purely a treaty law institution, then the other norms of higher value could be described, in Mosler's words, as "l'ordre public de la communauté internationale". Mosler has said that this vaster idea of public international order "... consists of principles and rules, the enforcement of which is of such vital importance to the international community as a whole that any unilateral action, or any agreement which contravenes this principle can have no legal force". I would go a step further and say that if one accepts this larger notion of "ordre public de la communauté internationale", then any breach of it in the form of violations of human rights, *apartheid*, genocide, etc., takes us outside the field of the law of treaties and into that of State responsibility, and specifically of Article 19 of the Ago Draft on State responsibility. Consequently violations of the higher norms have as their consequence a higher degree of responsibility on the part of the violator than is the case with violations of normal international law.

Cassese

May I just add two small points to what has just been said about *jus cogens*. First of all Jimenez de Arechaga quite rightly pointed out in the Vienna

Conference on the Law of Treaties that *jus cogens* was not going to be a mystique that would breathe fresh life into international life nor anything very revolutionary; in his view it would be very rare for the international community to be confronted with treaties conflicting with *jus cogens*. This, I feel is a very realistic assessment. *Jus cogens* is nothing particularly dangerous nor particularly revolutionary.

My second point is to the effect that one should not however discount the possibility of treaties being in conflict with *jus cogens*. May I draw your attention to a document drafted by the legal adviser of the State Department in 1979 on the Afghanistan problem, in which the view is expressed (whether we agree with it or not) that the treaty between the U.S.S.R. and Afghanistan of 1978 was in conflict with that peremptory rule of international law which is Article 2(4) of the U.N. Charter. We do therefore have cases where peremptory rules of international law have been relied upon by States.

MENDELSON

On the points raised by Nino Cassese and Dr Suy, I am a bit uncomfortable. If you take the point Nino Cassese made, the function of *jus cogens* in practical terms would be mainly in the context of a third-party decision-maker who says that a party cannot rely on a treaty because it conflicts with the rule of *jus cogens*. But the third-party decision-maker is the *exception* in the international community not the rule: most international claims are dealt with in a bilateral context through diplomatic negotiations, and so on. If, in the context of a treaty between, say, the Soviet Union and Afghanistan, either of *those two States* were to claim that the treaty was a nullity because it conflicted with *jus cogens*, I could see some practical application of the notion. But for some other State to say that a treaty between two different States is a nullity because it is contrary to *jus cogens* seems to me to be an assertion which in normal circumstances would have no practical consequences.

That is my first point. The second point is this: for the rules relating to *jus cogens* to be triggered, quite a large burden of proof has to be discharged by somebody, as Ian Brownlie pointed out yesterday. If we follow Erik Suy's suggestion and talk about the "ordre public de la communauté internationale" as being something which is not confined to, or which is perhaps outside the context of, the law of treaties, then surely the burden of proof we are going to demand will be at least as high as that which we demand for *jus cogens*. That is to say, it has to be accepted by the international community as a whole as a norm, and as a norm of this special and superpotent type. I am very doubtful that the international community as a whole is going to be prepared to identify many norms as belonging to this category, if the result is to allow these norms to go charging around, as it were, in the world of customary international law and treaties, overriding ordinary norms. Although I think that there is nothing wrong with the principle, if I may say so with respect, I think that the practical application is likely to prove difficult.

And that brings me to a connected point. In our discussion, the great, the striking degree of apparent consensus between the various participants was partly due to the fact that people were using the phrase "international community" in different contexts. Professor Yankow takes a somewhat voluntarist view of the sources of international law, and many of us do so to a greater or lesser extent. But I think that in fact States do not simply perform acts of will; States actually act in a rather more complex way. Sometimes they do perform voluntaristic acts of will, as it were: they decide they are going to do something, and they do it. But sometimes they actually respond to what, for want of a better expression (and it is not a very good expression), I would call the legitimate expectations of the international community. I realize that these are terms which are somewhat question-begging – as to what is legitimate, and what is an expectation – but I think that sometimes States feel a compulsion to act in a way in which the international community as a whole expects them to act. However, the key here is that expression: "the international community as a whole". Georges Abi-Saab talked about the needs of the international community, the demands of the international community and so forth. I think it has to be the international community as a whole, and the danger is that we equate majorities in international organizations, for example, or, majorities of writers on international law, with the international community. They are not the same; that is the problem.

Cassese

I should like to say a few words in reply to Maurice Mendelson, who has just made some critical comments about my example concerning *jus cogens* and Afghanistan. Let us take a treaty between two countries; we can keep to the example of Afghanistan and the U.S.S.R. though I have no intention of entering into details or pronouncing on the merits of the question. If I understood correctly, what Maurice Mendelson said was this: if there is a bilateral treaty which is allegedly at odds with a rule of *jus cogens* but the two contracting parties are quite satisfied with it, and have no intention of declaring it null, what is the point of saying that the treaty is contrary to *jus cogens*, since anyway nobody else is going to challenge it on these grounds?

I do not think I can agree with this, because, at least in this particular case, we are talking about a bilateral treaty authorizing the use of force by one State on the territory of another country. This of course touches upon the crucial question of the role of consent as a factor legitimizing the use of force – consent, which is a kind of ghostly presence, never spelt out in the U.N. Charter, except in Article 51, in one particular situation. Ian

Brownlie, in his excellent book on the use of force, pointed out that consent, subject to some qualification, can legitimize the use of force by a foreign country on the territory of the authorizing country. But if this bilateral treaty authorizing the use of force is contrary to a peremptory norm of international law, as was stated by the Legal Adviser to the State Department, it follows that the use of force authorized by that treaty is unlawful, hence contrary to the U.N. Charter. So you see that the proposition whereby that treaty is contrary to a peremptory rule of international law is legally and politically relevant because, being contrary to the U.N. Charter, it can be challenged by third States in the Security Council or in the General Assembly as an illegal use of force. There are therefore instances where the doctrine of *jus cogens* has a lot of relevance for third States, not only in political but also in legal terms.

VIRALLY

To bring the debate which has just taken place to a conclusion, I should like to say that I am very pleased with what has been said this morning. There has been too much theological debate about the notion of *jus cogens*, which in the eyes of some appeared to be a miracle remedy for many evils of international society, while to others it was an abomination. *Jus cogens* is neither the one thing nor the other. The real problem, which doctrine has not yet solved or even embarked on, and which practice has in any case hitherto left on one side, is what the real use of *jus cogens* is. What is its practical function in international society? We can very well see what the intention of those who put the idea forward at the Vienna conference was, but as for the practical applications, we are still waiting for them, aren't we? My friend Cassese just mentioned the declaration by the Legal Adviser of the State Department, but his argument was at least as much political as legal, and as Maurice Mendelson has just said, the consequences are extremely slight as far as law goes. Are there consequences as regards responsibility? I would be tempted to think, along with Dr Suy, that it is one of the fields that have to be considered, perhaps in a more practical way than treaty law. We have the International Law Commission's draft codification, but we are still rather empty-handed as regards the practical consequences of the distinction between international crime and international delict, and I have the impression that the Commission has some anxieties in this connection. I very much hope that these will be put to rest; perhaps they will, but today they are still there.

I feel that jurists today ought to wonder more about the concrete problems, the practical problems, raised by the notion of *jus cogens*, rather than dispute about the concept itself, about its meaning, about the possibility of accepting it, or else the desire to reject it. The problem has been posed. It is impossible for a legal order, whatever it be, to do without any hierarchy in its norms. That is quite clear. But what are the legal consequences that should be drawn from this fact? That is not at all clear. And it may be extremely different depending on the legal order. I am thinking in particular of what Ambassador Yankov pointed out, namely that the existence of authorities capable of solving these problems is quite different in the domestic order from in the international order. This is certainly not something that one should or can forget.

Chapter II

Voluntarism *versus* Majority Rule

I. Presentation

ARANGIO-RUIZ

I shall try to be as brief as possible. I trust that the participants will understand that if anything I say sounds too drastic or unilateral, this will only be due to my wish to be at the same time brief and provocative.

I shall start by addressing myself directly to the main issue, namely "voluntarism v. majoritarianism". I shall deal with the four subtitle issues afterwards. What I have to say on the general question will help me, I think, to give clearer, albeit tentative, answers to the four specific questions.

To put it shortly, I would be inclined to reject the notion (put forward, *inter alios*, by Prosper Weil in his remarkable article of 1985) that our time is marked not just by a mere acceleration of the custom-making-process – a point on which many amongst us might agree – but by a veritable revolution in custom-making and in the theory thereof. I do not see sufficient signs that voluntarism is being superseded in any significant measure by majority rule in international law-making: not, at least – if one understands law-making in a precise legal sense. I believe, on the contrary, that contemporary States are, if possible, more attached to voluntarism than they have ever been in the past. This applies in the area of so-called customary law (which I prefer to indicate, incidentally, as unwritten or general law because I find these terms less problematic than custom in a technical sense) as well as in the area of treaty law. My inclination to believe that voluntarism is still the rule finds support in a remark made by Professor Yankov.

This applies both to general law and treaty law, although there are clearly differences (substantive and "procedural") – as well, of course, as interaction – between these two forms of law-making. To the differences and the interaction I shall return, if we have time, at a later stage.

As regards voluntarism v. majoritarianism we are nowadays in a position not all that different from the position described by the Permanent Court of International Justice, in the *Lotus* case. Insofar as some kind of consent, assent, acceptance, recognition, of rules by States is requested, the situation has not altered significantly. This statement, however, must be accompanied by two qualifications, failing which it might be badly misunderstood. One qualification relates to the distinction between sources in a *material* sense and sources in a proper legal (and not necessarily formal) sense. The second qualification is the distinction between the voting procedures through which rules are formulated within permanent or non-permanent international bodies, on one side, and the consent to, or acceptance of such rules by States, on the other. These two distinctions, the first of which is based on those very essential general concepts to which I referred yesterday as essential law-school notions, are closely interrelated and both indispensable for the understanding of any thought or discourse on this subject.

To get to the essential, when I say that some form of consent is still required for any rule to be binding upon States, I do so on the basis of the well-known distincton between the material sources of law and sources of law in a narrow sense. This distinction is often expressed in the misleading terms of material as opposed to formal sources, the category of sources in a narrow sense being thus presented (inaccurately in my view) as a category to be identified by the merely formal criterion represented, for example, by a pre-existing, constitutional or legislative rule formally qualifying the source. In my opinion, law sources in a narrow sense – or, better, in a legal sense – are not such necessarily, or merely, as a consequence of their regulation by a superior (constitutional or legislative) rule. They are such also and mainly because of the fact that they are found by States' lawyers, by judges, by scholars, to be the real, decisive, law-making procedures or factors within the international system, regardless of any specific formal rule defining them. Any factors or elements indirectly contributing to the coming into being of law rules other than the procedures or factors so identified or identifiable by the jurist remain within the class of material on merely material sources.

Of course, the distinction is not always an easy one. Easy when one speaks of municipal law statutes or contracts, or of international treaties, the distinction becomes more difficult when one moves into the realm of unwritten law, such as customary law within national societies or those unwritten, general rules of international law commonly labelled as customary international law. A treaty is far more clearly definable in its essential or decisive elements than the factors determining the existence of an unwritten, customary rule of international law. In the case of the treaty – as well as in the case of national legislation – it is quite easy to distinguish the decisive elements of the law-making procedure, on the one hand, and the merely factual and indirect factors which led to the treaty's conclusion – or to the passing of the national statute – on the other. In the case of general or unwritten international law the distinction is a difficult one because of the informal and at times not clearly discernible process characterizing the making of unwritten law. Nevertheless, and whatever the difficulties, there is also here a distinction between indirect and direct factors. A distinction does exist between the indirect factors determining the behaviours and attitudes of States in a given sphere of relations, on one side, and the behaviours and attitudes (of the same States) which directly concur to the coming into being of a rule in that sphere, on the other.

Going back to our problem, a number of new developments undoubtedly exert a considerable influence on the making of both treaty rules and unwritten rules of international law. It would be an error, however, to consider such new developments as significant alternations of the centuries-old pattern of States' consent, assent, acceptance *et similia.* And here I must explain — to the extent that it may be feasible in an introductory statement such as this — my position concerning that major contemporary development which is represented by the presence of international organizations and by the role they play with regard to international law-making.

We are all familiar with Wilfred Jenks' article on "Unanimity, the Veto, Weighted Voting, Special or Simple Majorities and Consensus as Modes of Decision in International Organizations" (in *Cambridge Essays on International Law in honour of Lord McNair*, 1965, pages 48—63). That article as well as many contributions to the subject coming from other scholars, makes abundantly clear that, unlike the League of Nations era, generally characterized by the permanence of the unanimity rule, the age of the United Nations is felicitously characterized by considerable progress in the voting procedures of international bodies. In a variety of ways and degrees, unanimity is being replaced not only by majority rule but even, in a few cases, by weighted voting. Nevertheless, in spite of the innumerable instances on which — within the United Nations, the Specialized Agencies and Regional Organizations — unanimity has been superseded by some form of majoritarianism, it is a fact that with a few exceptions, the deliberations of international bodies do not attain the threshold of inter-State law-making in a proper sense.

Of course, there are majority decisions on matters of procedure and some instances of directly binding substantive decisions of international bodies. The first belong essentially to *interna corporis* of the international body. The second are addressed directly to States and are perhaps rightly qualified, for example by Morelli, as "tertiary" law-making processes, the main example of the latter being U.N. General Assembly deliberations under Article 17(2) of the Charter. One can doubt, however, that in these cases the competent body does more than "specify", so to speak, obligations which States have already assumed directly (and voluntarily) under the relevant constituent instrument.

Apart from these two sets of normative phenomena (of relatively limited impact), the "normative" function of international organizations is confined to the adoption of mere recommendations constitutionally deprived as such (even when they are labelled "declarations") of legally binding force. Of course, the rules contained in such instruments may not only be complied with more or less spontaneously by the States to which they are addressed, but also be embodied either in treaty rules or in unwritten, customary (general or regional) international law. This will occur, however, through the normal *jeu* of such law-making procedures (sources in a proper sense) as the treaty, and that less formal process which, for lack of a more precise term, is called international custom. In either case the original recommendation will not be transformed from a set of non-binding rules into treaty rules or general, customary rules. It will remain what it was originally, namely a non-binding instrument, and as such an integral part of the "bricks" or "building material" we have been taught at school – and rightly so – to classify as material sources of law.

It follows, that the majoritarian or otherwise not strictly consensual process through which the non-binding instrument was adopted does not represent any substantial innovation in international law-making. Majority plays a role during a phase or stage which precedes law-making and may actually not even be followed by real law-making (if the contents of the non-binding instrument does not become a part of a treaty or of unwritten law).

The making of treaty rules or customary rules of international law remains thus within the realm of voluntary or consensual law-making, and I am inclined to maintain that in spite of appearances, international law-making in 1985 remains essentially what it was at the time when the Permanent Court decided the *Lotus* case. The exceptions are, in my view, either very marginal, as in the relatively infrequent cases of binding decisions of international bodies, or illusory, as in the far more numerous cases of majority deliberations which only affect inter-State law-making in a material rather than a legal sense. I could perhaps add, in order to make myself clearer, that the phase consisting in the adoption of non-binding enactments by international bodies precedes law-making properly understood even more distinctly than the elaboration of the text of a treaty – from the first proposal that a treaty be concluded up to the finalization of the text – precedes ratification or any equivalent expression of the consent of the participating States.

Georges Abi-Saab spoke yesterday of "building blocks", from the assembling of which a rule (especially an unwritten, customary rule) may come into being. Within the framework of that analogy, I would say that the activities of international organizations are part of the building material. But for unwritten law as well as treaty-law, there must always be some decisive, more or less easily identifiable phase or moment in which States create, accept, give their assent to the rule or acquiesce thereto. May I incidentally add that to my regret, I am unable entirely to ascribe to the view of international custom (or, preferably, unwritten law) as a "spontaneous law" which would, I admit, add such weight to the idea of an objective value and *quasi* "heteronomous" origin of general international law. Applicable perhaps to a few fundamental rules of unwritten law, the concept of spontaneous law, quite appropriate to the customary law of national, interindividual societies, sounds improbable, except in some instances, as the main source of law in the "society" of sovereign, collective, organized entities. Only a minority of these may, in particular circumstances, be less than fully conscious, in adopting any positive or negative line of conduct (action or omission) vis-à-vis any one of its equals, of the significance, the influence, the impact that its behaviour or attitudes may have upon the formation of the unwritten, general or regional, law of nations. Lack of time prevents me from going any further into a voluntaristic concept of unwritten international law which I consider to be not only more realistic *per se* but also more in conformity with the general theory of international law as a system of essentially inter-power rules.

In conclusion, international law-making has evolved considerably since the end of the second World War, most particularly as a consequence of the development of "international organization" and, even more, following the triplication of the membership of the "global society" of sovereign entities. But this evolution has touched neither upon the nature of the units of international relations, nor on the structure of such relations — and their law — nor essentially upon the quality of the relevant law-making processes. There has been evolution of course of a major kind, but it concerns the exigencies, the vital necessities, which urge the creation of new, written or unwritten, rules of such a kind as to meet less inadequately the needs of mankind for security, welfare, freedom and equality which much too often are unjustly postponed (if not totally sacrificed) to the interests of the sovereign entities *per se*: I mean to the *raisons d'état* of the coexisting Powers. This, for example, is the main obstacle to the development of a more acceptable international economic order. Upon the unfortunately prevailing tendency of international law and relations to sacrifice human values and needs — social, political, cultural and economic — to the hard necessities of inter-power coexistence or *Staatraison* I have dwelt more fully in my 1972 Hague Course and in its reprint of 1979. I need not retain you any longer here.

I will now get on to the more specific questions appearing in the subtitles of the item I was asked to introduce. The first question is whether "there are any circumstances in international life whereby a State may be held to be bound by a norm to the creation of which it has objected." Well, perhaps the word objected is not quite the exact word and even the word creation is inappropriate. In my view, the dissenting State cannot succeed, by its attitude, in preventing the formation of an unwritten rule, but it can succeed in escaping subjection to that rule. On this, I have picked out something from Waldock's Hague General Course. Waldock in his turn quotes Tunkin for a more conservative view, but while disagreeing with the latter, I am able to accept Sir Humphrey's opinion that in international law there is no majority rule, even with respect to the formation of customary law. I think that this is still a correct statement. Of course, even the doctrine subscribed to by Waldock is subject to qualification: in the sense that the objecting State's dissent must meet requirements of consistency and persistence, failing which the dissenting State will not be exempt from subjection to the rule.

I do believe, however – although this may be judged positively or negatively depending on the content of the rule and on the wishes of other States or of the commentator – that the "doctrine of the persistent objecter" remains an undeniable reality. In this belief I differ from our excellent colleague and friend Prosper Weil. Of course, those very factors which I indicated earlier as material sources make the position of the dissenting State more difficult today than it was in the past. In the contemporary, much more interdependent, international society, the dissenting position of a State (or group of States) may in the long run become untenable with regard to certain matters: for example, in the area of so-called North-South relations. It is absurd that we should go on living in an international society in which such blatant inequalities are maintained. This and other considerations may well contribute to inducing the dissenting States to give up resistance and (I am just indicating one example at random), take steps to establish, at least in the most vital areas, a more equitable economic order.

Getting now to the subject of silence, I would take too much of your time if I undertook a lengthy discussion of its importance. That silence plays a considerable role in international unwritten (customary) law-making is quite obvious. As McGibbon has shown very well, acquiescence is, it seems, a major element in this area. But I would find it difficult to present you now with any further generalities on a matter which surely calls for a lengthier, case by case consideration.

To conclude on customary law, a term I use with reservations within the framework of international law, I am not ready to share our colleague Prosper Weil's views concerning the "novelty" of what he seems to consider to be undue or superfluous references (by the Hague Court) to customary or general rules. Weil recalls the *Tehran Hostages* case. He seems to find it objectionable that the Court referred, in addition to the Vienna Convention on Diplomatic Relations, to a general rule of international law. I do not see anything objectionable in that. If there is a rule which was a matter of general law prior to the Vienna Convention, it is the rule invoked by the Court in that case. He also mentions, if I remember correctly, the Nuclear Test Ban Treaty and the opinion that that treaty created "instant custom". Of course no custom, whether instant or not, is created by any treaty. For an instant general rule corresponding to a treaty rule to come into being much more is needed than just the treaty itself.

A further question concerns the effects that can be attributed to world-wide Diplomatic Conferences or Conventions which claim to state or "crystallize" customary law and thus extend their binding effect to non-participants and non-signatories as well. Weil cites about six cases: the *Namibia* opinion of 1971, the *Fisheries Jurisdiction* case of 1973, the *Aegean Sea* case of 1978, the opinion on the *W.H.O. Office in Egypt,* etc. In these cases, he contends, there is on the part of the Court a reference to the 1969 Vienna Convention on the Law of Treaties, which is improper, in that it would imply the attribution on the part of the Court of a more than strictly conventional value to that Convention. This is at least what I understood from my reading. My impression is that the line followed by the Court in the cases in question does not imply any prejudice to the principle that international conventions only bind the contracting parties. The International Court, it seems to me, referred to rules of the Vienna Convention expressing in treaty form rules of general international law which pre-existed the Convention.

Another sub-issue is that of statements versus actual practice. On this also there is a lot to be said. My impression is that when one tries to weigh the "building blocks" of international custom, one should carefully distinguish between statements, especially general statements, of rules – for example in "de-fused" or more or less "de-fused" resolutions of the General Assembly (you all know what a "de-fused" resolution is in U.N. jargon) – on the one hand, and the actual practice of States, within or outside the United Nations, in given areas of their relations, on the other. Surely, and obviously, statements and actual practice are two different things. In comparing the effects of these two elements, there is little doubt that what really matters is actual practice in concrete cases. The positive or negative behaviour of States in any matter is far more important, as a factor or as a piece of evidence of an unwritten rule, than any statement or proclamation of the rule by which that conduct would be binding.

II. Discussion

BROWNLIE

The first point I wanted to make does not really arise out of Professor Arangio-Ruiz's statement directly, but I think it is a point that should be borne in mind. It involves a political statement, a factual observation which others may disagree with. I have the feeling that in this kind of debate in 1985, whether we are talking about Prosper Weil's article or the kind of atmosphere which surrounds numerous other writings and statements, there is an identification of what is called majoritarianism with the Third World, with the current majority in the General Assembly, with what is seen to be a sort of sinister combination of Third World States and Communist States, operating through international organizations.

Now my observation is that majoritarianism has always been with us, and in the politics of the United Nations in the early years, it was very strong indeed. The NATO States plus the 20 Latin American votes had absolute control in the General Assembly. When I was in Law School, I remember listening to Waldock lecture in 1952 and 1953. Waldock was a great majoritarian, and we were given to understand that international law was tremendous stuff, that decisions of the International Court were the highest possible statements, and that the doings of majorities in the General Assembly, such as the Uniting for Peace resolution, were of the highest legal significance. I remember the atmosphere; it was the height of the cold war. It was a different majority of course, but nothing turns on that. I think that we have to accept that we are talking about institutions, devices, structures, which are vehicles, and can be used by any particular majority at any particular time. It will not do to talk about majoritarianism as though it were a recently acquired virus, since it is a familiar political style. And the way in which the majority reacts to the minority or the way in which the powerful minority reacts to the majority, are long-standing questions. Lawyers, I think, should have the ability to analyze these problems as on-going problems and not some kind of temporary disease.

That was my first, rather bilious point. The second one is not so much a point, as a question, and I would like to hear what my colleagues have to say about it. I do not see an opposition really between voluntarism and majoritarianism. It is just a fact that at any point in history, some particular majority, or combination of States, at least on certain fronts, tries to get its way, because it is the majority. Although I have to point out that on the law of the sea and on various other fronts, you may have a different constellation. Geographically disadvantaged States may emerge with special interests which in the law of the sea may have a different geography of majorities, if I can put it that way, or groups. But, it seems to me that majoritarianism is simply voluntarism ... multiplied by such and such a number. That is all. Sometimes you have, as it were, multiple individualism, in the form of regionalism. So I do not quite see the opposition between voluntarism and majoritarianism, but I am willing to be enlightened.

Thirdly, I think that some of this discussion is too abstract. For example, when two States seriously get down to the business of settling a particular dispute (as the United States and Canada did in the *Gulf of Maine* case, or Malta and Libya did in the *Continental Shelf* case), whether you talk about voluntarism or majoritarianism, the fact is that in order to give operational efficacy to the effort to settle that dispute, the States have to make arrangements for themselves. The U.S. and Canada were justified in negotiating a special agreement, which had to have special features in order to give the Court a good start in settling the dispute in the most effective way. And that may involve, as it did in the *Minquiers* case, instructing the Court – in the sense that there are certain limitations on what it can decide. In the *Minquiers* case the Court in theory could have decided that the Minquiers were a *terra nullius*, or that they were a condominium by conduct, but that really would not have produced a very useful result. So instead of using the optional clause for jurisdiction, the U.K. and France made a special agreement in which the Court was told virtually not to hold that there were either *terra nullius* or a condominium. The parties wanted a useful result, and the question of operational efficacy can only be dealt with on the basis of special relations.

On the general issue, I think I am with Professor Arangio-Ruiz. The fact that the system has not changed is evidenced by what we have been saying about *jus cogens*. I think *jus cogens* has become part of *lex lata*. At the same time, as has been pointed out, the vehicle does not often leave the garage. In other words the concept does not have a lot of obvious relevance, and that seems to me to reflect the paradox that you can invent things, you cannot be prevented from inventing things by a recalcitrant minority, but nonetheless the invention may have limited relevance or efficacy.

VIRALLY

Perhaps I might add a very small point to the second question that has just been brought up. Is there an opposition between voluntarism and majority rule? I would be tempted to think that the contrary is the case. I do not wish to enter into the debate between Professor Arangio-Ruiz and Professor Ago on the spontaneous or otherwise nature of custom, but it seems to me that the formation of a custom is a very complex process. It is not controlled by States individually; it is the result of a whole set of comportments by States, not necessarily planned and pursued. Custom has an aspect that I shall not term "involuntary" (the term would be quite inexact), but nevertheless constitutes a process that largely escapes voluntary manipulation by States. To the extent that international organizations or international conferences bring together a great number of States and allow them to make majority pronouncements on legal problems, on the existence of rules or on the desirability of certain rules (and here we come back to *lex ferenda*), international law is nevertheless more marked by voluntarism. But perhaps, though, more in the political sense than in the traditional sense given to that term. The majority is the expression of a will, which does have a weight in the development of law. I therefore do not think that there is an opposition between voluntarism and majority rule. On the contrary, a step towards voluntarism is taken in the formation of law through the development of majority rule.

MENDELSON

I think that this debate depends, as do many discussions on the formation of international law, on the observational standpoint. If you take the standpoint of a detached observer, a sort of sociological standpoint, then all kinds of sources and majorities become relevant. If you look at it from the point of the third party decision-maker, then you narrow your scope, and voluntarism, for example, becomes more important. But having said that, it does seem to me that even if one tries to take a hard-nosed and positivistic attitude to this question, one ought to beware of falling into the kind of trap which our training as municipal lawyers may lead us into. I refer to the fact that most of us have been trained in municipal law to think in terms of what courts do or are going to do. But that is not the nature, as I understand it, of most of the international legal process, which is a process where the role of the Court, of any court, is sporadic and peripheral.

It seems to me that a positivistic international legal examination ought also to entail an examination of what legal advisers of governments, and governments generally in their relations with each other, are doing. In that context, with respect, I have some reservations about what Professor Arangio-Ruiz was saying. He spoke about the process leading up to the conclusion of a treaty, prior to ratification, as not being law as such, because they do not satisfy the formal requirements. Well of course, that is true. But he then went on to say that we must apply this *mutatis mutandis* to custom, and suggested that when a State acts in what we might term the customary arena, it makes a very clearly thought-out decision on political grounds on how it is going to behave, and it then performs an act of will. Of course there are cases where that is so. It is particularly so if you are the first one in the field: for example, President Truman in 1945. But it is not always like that, it seems to me. For instance, if a State is to decide how to respond to other people's exclusive economic zone claims, or whether to make one itself, then obviously it takes into account its political, economic, and similar interests, but it also has to take into account the expectations of the community as a whole. As Professor Virally said, it is a rather complex process which involves responding in all sorts of contexts to the "temperature of the water" and to the atmosphere all around; it is not simply an act of will. What the community as a whole (not necessarily a simple majority) feels is acceptable or unacceptable is an important part of the process.

Now if I can briefly return to courts. In one sense of course we can say — at least a judge ought to be able to say — that, in a given case, this particular rule binds this or that State. It is often relatively easy to find out whether it does or not; has the State ratified a treaty, or has it in some way consented to a rule of customary law? But what we actually find is that the International Court of Justice frequently talks in fairly general terms about "generally accepted principles of international law", or "a custom generally accepted" and so on. In such cases it does not (at least overtly) say "here is the evidence that this particular State has consented to this rule", although this may have been going on behind the scenes, in the pleadings or elsewhere. Now, you can of course say that silence amounts to tacit consent; but I think the reality is that the Court looks at general expectations within the community. Of course, if it finds a positive act of will — consent or dissent — on the part of a particular State in a context where that will count, that may change the picture. But otherwise, even the Court is not quite as voluntaristic as perhaps a positivist who thinks in terms of what courts do, might *a priori* expect. I think these are perhaps only nuances in relation to what Professor Arangio-Ruiz says: I do not think I have any fundamental disagreement with him.

CASSESE

I second the criticisms put forward by Professor Arangio-Ruiz against Prosper Weil's main thesis. Actually it is apparent from a careful reading of Prosper Weil's paper that its underlying theme is the fear that one or two countries should become bound by new rules in international law in spite of their opposing the formation of those rules. This fear of majority rule, and Weil's conviction that voluntarism is dying or on the wane, is not warranted, because actually dissent still plays a role in the international community, as Arangio-Ruiz rightly pointed out.

First of all, it goes without saying that this applies to treaty law; of course treaties do not bind countries which are not parties to them. But as regards customary international law, too, we have the theory of the "persistent objector". No country which persistently, consistently, objects to a rule of customary international law from its conception, can be regarded as bound by that rule. I would like to add that even *jus cogens* cannot bind a "persistent objector"; in other words, voluntarism applies even to *jus cogens*. It is my belief that peremptory norms are subject to the limitations inherent in the sources to which they owe their birth: namely custom and treaties. I think that like rules generated by these two sources of international law, *jus cogens* binds States only if the latter have not staunchly and explicitly opposed them from the start. If this is correct, it follows that a State that has clearly and consistently expressed its dissent at the stage when a peremptory norm was taking shape and has not changed its attitude subsequently, is not bound by the norm even if this comes to possess the overriding status of *jus cogens*. The obvious consequence is that the objecting State can make an agreement contrary to the peremptory norm with another State which has also consistently objected to the norm of *jus cogens*, without the agreement becoming void.

To my mind, the ultimately consensual foundations of *jus cogens* clearly indicate the limitations of this class of norm, as well, of course, as all international law-making. There is no doubt that much headway has been made with regard to this body of supreme or "constitutional" tenets: States have created an "ordre publique international". However these principles or basic guidelines of the international community are not necessarily endowed with universal force, nor are they heteronomous, for, as I have just pointed out, they ultimately rest on the will of all the members of the international community. I think this is an inherent contradiction in the concept of *jus cogens*. *Jus cogens* consists of a group of rules or principles which are more important and have greater legal force than other rules of international law, but like all other rules of international law they suffer from the limitation inherent in voluntarism.

Let me now just say a few words about the different problem of statements versus actual practice. How does one determine the position of a State with regard to acceptance of an international norm: through statements in international fora, or through its actual conduct? I do not have any general answer to this difficult question, and I do not think we can engage upon any abstract discussion. But just let me give you an illustration, taken from the recently developed humanitarian law of armed conflict. I am of course referring to what happened in the Diplomatic Conference of 1974–77 on the updating of the four Geneva Conventions of 1949. On the occasion of the adoption of the two Protocols, all the countries participating in the conference made statements concerning the new rules, either supporting or opposing them or suggesting particular interpretations they were keen to place on them. The situation, therefore, is this: we have statements made by countries on some very tricky and important subjects such as the use of weapons and the protection of civilians, but we do not have any corresponding State practice. The question is, can the statements made by States in that international forum in Geneva be taken as sufficient grounds for believing that the States concerned expressed their legal conviction, their *opinio juris*, that new rules of international law had evolved, which transcended their conventional status, that is to say, bound all States participating in the Conference, regardless of whether or not they subsequently ratified the Protocols adopted by the Conference? Or should we instead wait to see the actual conduct of belligerents on the battlefield?

I was taught when I was at Law School that there is a presumption that States are serious entities. When they make statements, they do not speak just for the sake of speaking; they should be taken seriously. Even if they do not formally state that they commit themselves to a particular line of conduct, if they put forward a legal view concerning a certain type of conduct, this view should be taken seriously as expressing their legal opinion. That is why I think that at least as far as this area of international law is concerned – and it is a crucial area – one might tentatively conclude that – as a rule – statements by countries or by governments are enough, and if there is no practice, or no conflicting State practice, these statements reflect the legal view of the countries concerned.

VIRALLY

In connection with one of Professor Cassese's assertions, I wish simply to throw in a little idea that might perhaps be taken up in the debate. This question of declarations made by States seems to be one of those that no general answer can be given to. Everything depends on the declaration and on the circumstances in which it has been made. In the case of a declaration made during a debate in the General Assembly, for instance, or in connection with the adoption of a resolution, in very general terms, and in a field where there is as yet no practice, I can quite accept that a State may be said to be seriously expressing a legal opinion. Of course, the question is what this legal opinion means, what effect it will have on law.

When the two elements of custom are analyzed, namely practice and *opinio juris*, I at any rate think that *opinio juris* always comes second. It is a reaction by States to a practice that is in the course of emerging. Consequently, if there are opinions expressed at legal level before any practice, I would say that these are opinions *de lege ferenda*, which relate to what the law ought to be. Consequently, they do not constitute an element in the formation of a custom. Even if, of course — and here we come back to the question of voluntarism — legal opinions expressed by a majority or by a great number of States, or by important States, may have consequences for subsequent practice, by bringing about this practice, and preventing its generalization from causing protest. There will then be a positive effect on the customary process, but at the point when the declaration is made, it is still not an element of custom, but simply an element *de lege ferenda*.

Yankov

First of all I would like to emphasize the significance of what Ian Brownlie said about the juxtaposition of voluntarism and majoritarianism. In my submission, unless there is some misunderstanding, we are talking about matters more relating to quantity than substance, affecting the very nature of legal rules and the process of law-making. Indeed, as he said, and I completely agree with him and with what Professor Arangio-Ruiz said in his introduction, the international system has not changed and remains a system based on sovereign States. Thus States are the main agents of the law-making process where the *Grundnorm*, the basic rule, is consent, agreement between the States parties. Whether this process takes place in conference or through the more traditional law-making technique of negotiation, the end result is the elaboration of legal rules based on mutual consent. Hence if there is no consent, there is no law. This is perhaps a simplistic way of expressing a general truth about the foundation of international law, which is a consequence of the international system being based on collaboration between sovereign States. Of course, we should not lose sight of the impact that a rule established by a majority of States, or by an important international codification conference, may have. There are other factors which may exercize an indirect impact on law-making, such as opinion.

When we speak of law-making in the international community, we have to take into consideration first of all the existing international system. With the exception of supranational institutions, as Arangio-Ruiz said, and the rules for law-making adopted by these institutions, the general pattern is the adoption of legal norms on the basis of mutual consent. Otherwise we have regional law or internal rules within international institutions. Supranational law-making has peculiar features which are closer to the municipal law-making process.

If we bear in mind the existing system of international relations and the typical pattern of international treaty-making, I do not see any kind of contradiction between so-called majority rule and voluntarism, because, in both cases, if there is no coordination of will, there is no law. From this point of view, I do not think it would be correct to hold that there is an emerging trend towards replacing law-making based on the consent of the parties concerned by some other mechanism based on majority rule. This other mechanism does not exist, because even at a codification conference when the text of a draft convention is adopted by majority, the convention becomes legally binding only upon signature, ratification or accession of the State concerned. If we take U.N. resolutions, including those adopted by consensus, undoubtedly they have a very important, sometimes stimulating role, and yet they are not law; they cannot even be called soft law, because they are just recommendations which may become legally binding rules if they go through the proper process of law-making, based on the consent of States to abide by them. I agree with Professor Arangio-Ruiz that there are not sufficient indications to admit that voluntarism as the underpinning of international obligations is being replaced by the emergence of majoritarian norm-setting.

Of course there might be instances when the international community or the majority of States took the stand that certain rules which enjoy wide acceptance were applicable in respect to all States. But this has not been the case even with Article 2(6) of the U.N. Charter, which provides that the Organization shall ensure that States which are not members of the United Nations act in accordance with the principles of the Charter. This provision has a field of application which is limited to what may be necessary for the maintenance of international peace and security. Secondly, it is not automatically applicable. I do not therefore think that it could be taken as evidence of the emergence of a new way of international law-making by majority rule.

Another argument in favour of the majoritarian concept could be Article 103 of the Charter. It provides that in the event of a conflict between the obligations of U.N. Members under the Charter and their treaty obligations under bilateral or multilateral treaties, their obligations under the Charter shall prevail. This is a good principle and a good rule, binding only on the Members of the United Nations, which establishes the hierarchical relationship in the treaty obligations of Member States. I do not know, however, whether this provision could be taken as an argument for the theory of the replacement of one treaty-making process by another.

We are all aware of the doctrine of objective legal régimes, such as, for instance the régime of navigation in international rivers. According to that doctrine rights and obligations deriving from a treaty or convention establishing an objective legal régime, could be invoked in respect of non-parties, and even of those States which are otherwise opposed to this treaty. This would be the case when they make use of the régime and therefore implicitly agree with the rules and principles constituting the legal framework of the régime. In the field of customary law the problem is much more complex. Let us take the case of the recognition of the exclusive economic zone (EEZ). This recognition took place more through unilateral actions taken by States than through the normal, routine process of codification, for what is now embodied in the U.N. Convention on the Law of the Sea is still *de lege ferenda*. The Convention, although signed by 156 or 160 States, has been ratified only by 14 or 16 parties, while 60 ratifications are required for its entry into force. Therefore, if we talk today about the exclusive economic zone as a "legal reality", it is not because a majority has introduced an international rule, but because through another procedure, namely through State practice, it has been recognized. I could also mention the draft articles constituting the legal régime for the protection and preservation of the marine environment. Even at the very preliminary stage, before the single negotiating text was called "draft convention", reference was made to these provisions in some national legislations and parliaments as though they were already in force; in fact the Convention was at an early stage of *lex ferenda*.

My last point is about the impact of world-wide diplomatic conferences and conventions which claim to state or crystallize customary law and thus bind non-participants and non-signatories as well. Here again I would come back to the fundamental concept of consent as the source of international obligation, unless we adhere to the doctrine of "objective legal régime", which I assume would not be the case. When a multilateral convention with large participation is at stake, the only reaction of the international community or the majority of States would be to try and defend their positions by all means at their disposal. But nobody could claim that non-signatory States or States which did not ratify the convention were bound by its provisions, though the convention may enjoy a very broad range of acceptance. Such a convention cannot be invoked against, or imposed on, States which are still objecting.

These considerations lead me to the basic rule of agreement, or consent, as the source of international obligation, whatever the form or the mechanism for the expression of consent: through agreements, through recognition of customary rules or through legislative actions or unilateral declarations of the States concerned.

CONDORELLI

I too should like to put myself among those who are dubious about the terminology employed in our discussion. Let us say that the question to be dealt with is whether it is conceivable for international norms to be imposed in one way or another on States that do not want them. In other words, can one maintain that a rule of general international law can be arrived at by a majority process, against the express contrary wish of a State, and end up binding it?

This issue is a burning one if ever there was one, and has been widely discussed, especially since there has been a numerical preponderancy of the Third World in the General Assembly of the United Nations. Ought we not perhaps to say, much overdiscussed? In fact, the debate, at least to the extent that it has centred around the normative scope of General Assembly resolutions (and of declarations of principle in particular) may probably be regarded as exhausted. Not only has "everything" been said on both sides, resulting in the repetitive character of discussion on it. The point is that the problem has – it seems to me – been largely overtaken by reality: that was the feeling I had when, with a view to attending this meeting, I reread Prosper Weil's article, and went back over the list of objections that he brings against "Third Worldist" theses. More exactly, my impression was of attending a boxing match during which one of the two contenders has already collapsed from fatigue, while the other – equally tired – has not noticed, but continues to fight the air.

I think in fact that the time has passed when the aggressive ideology according to which general international law might be constructed by majority action was in fashion. A lot of water has passed under the bridge since then. Today we are living at a time of strenuous search for consensus. In all international venues, whether regional or world, there is this kind of bastard unanimity called consensus which is sought after at all costs. Even – as I had occasion to say in my previous intervention – at the cost of having to be content with soft law, that is, law which for one or more reasons (to do with the content of the rules or the instrument through which they are promulgated) will not be binding, or only weakly so. In fact the lack of homogeneity of the social basis inevitably leads to soft law if major compromises covering all the groups of States are to be achieved. It is evident that there is great attachment to this idea: the proof is that the system of consensus is everywhere followed, and that in an increasing number of international venues consensus is no longer only a practice but rather the formally consecrated rule for adopting important resolutions and decisions, at least those that are hoped to have wide-reaching normative effects.

Why has consensus become so generalized? I think the reason is precisely this: there is full awareness that decisions adopted by majority in the face of vigorously hostile opposition have very little chance of producing rules of law that bind everybody. Concerning declarations of principle by the U.N. General Assembly in particular, experience shows that, leaving aside their political significance (which may be great), the legal and practical usefulness of those which have been adopted by majority is, when all is said and done, slight, at least when it appears clear that the recalcitrant minority will subsequently refuse to bow before them. In short, the fact that the group which today is very much in the majority seems fully convinced of the appropriateness, not to say necessity, of reaching consensus must in my view be regarded as nothing less than a demonstration of the failure of the majority method for arriving at rules of international law.

I would point out that I have not been speaking only of the formation of general international law. The attitude to which I have just alluded has just as deep an influence on the procedures of formation of conventional law, where similar phenomena are met with. In fact, the very largely predominant tendency in this sector too is, as far as at all possible, to avoid in international conferences the majority method indicated by Article 9(2) of the Vienna Convention on treaty law, in adopting the texts of major international treaties. Here, too, what is aimed at at all costs, whatever the conference's rules of procedure may say, is to arrive at a "consensus text", that is, a compromise on a global scale which can be acceptable to all, so that it may thereby become operational and also, possibly, capable of then "passing" into general international law. Moreover, important cases are known where the search for consensus has been rendered obligatory by the rules of procedure of the conference or the negotiating body.

In his introduction, Professor Arangio-Ruiz started by excluding from the area of our interest, and rightly so, certain phenomena of production of law that take place in a few international organizations: those equipped with bodies which, pursuant to the treaties setting them up, may by majority adopt rules of "derived law", law which binds the minority. One remark should nevertheless be made in this connection: it is that consensual methods tend to prevail even in these rare cases. Often consensuality is restored thanks to arrangements which are designated by the term "contracting out". In other cases (I am thinking here of the European Communities) what we see is simply the agreed non-application of those provisions of the founding treaty that provided for the adoption of various normative acts by majority. In the European Communities, the return to the principle of unanimity has been consecrated by the sort of gentlemen's agreement, the "Luxembourg compromise", which is the real fundamental rule of the organization, a rule which has not been gone beyond despite innumerable declarations of intent. It seems to me, in short, that majoritarianism is everywhere losing ground; perhaps one could even say it is a dead duck!

But let us return to general international law. I think that in our times there are not many authors genuinely convinced that it is possible to develop this law by majority, even in the ranks of Third World lawyers. Must one then, in view of the foregoing considerations, accept the voluntarist conception for which a number of speakers (beginning with Professor Arangio-Ruiz and Ambassador Yankov) have declared their support? I do not think so; in other words, I think that the majoritarianist opposition to voluntarism is false, because one can quite well reject the first without necessarily accepting the second. I am in fact among those who believe that the formation of rules of general international law is not based exclusively on consent, acceptance, or agreement on the part of all the addressees.

During the discussion, many people have stated their approval of a view that seems to me very close (if not identical) to classical voluntarist theory: that of Triepel, of Anzilotti, of the *Lotus* case, of Tunkin, etc. There is of course no question of my denying that the will of States, and hence their more or less explicit consent, plays a fundamental part in this connection. Nevertheless, once this has been admitted, the question remains whether only will has a role to play in this, or whether perhaps other types of social conduct may not also enter into it, as rightly suggested by Professor Virally. I am thinking in particular of a whole range of possible attitudes going from simple silence to occasional, unrepeated protest against a particular situation or claim. I feel it would be exaggerated or even unreal (and I am thinking here in particular of the "presumption of acceptance" mentioned by Tunkin) to treat this kind of attitude as being the same as consent. But at the present day, the non-voluntarist conception of general international law means just this: one must be aware of the fact that a rule of this law may very well bind a State which has never – either explicitly or implicitly – expressed its wish to accept the rule in question. In other words, the formation of the general customary rule can be established through a flexible, global evaluation, aimed at assessing in synthetic fashion the whole set of behaviours, actions and reactions of the social actors, and not at counting their acts of consent analytically and adding them up. Moreover, isolated non-acceptance by this or that State would not be enough to prevent the formation of a customary law, in the face of what the International Court of Justice calls "general recognition" of such a rule.

The point I have just touched on seems to me an important one: the legal scope of "permanent objection". In fact, classical voluntarist views are accompanied today by more flexible theories which, while still accepting voluntarism, assign to permanent objection by a State, not the ability to block the process of formation of the general rule, but the effect of withdrawing the State in question from the compass of that rule. These conceptions, which are founded on rare precedents in case law (which are, moreover, very disputable) seem to me hard to accept, not to say morally intolerable. Must it, for instance, be asserted that South Africa is not bound by the rule banning *apartheid* (and that it is therefore wrong to condemn it on that account) because it has always, consistently and continuously, disputed that rule? Is one really to believe that a State may exempt itself from a principle of international law by its attitude as a "permanent objector", when all other States regard this principle as perfectly in existence? I refuse to believe any such thing, and I shall explain myself by giving a further example: is one to believe that one State has the right to exploit the resources of the continental shelf of another State because it has permanently objected to the rule pertaining thereto?

In my opinion, permanent objection to a customary practice by an interested State is quite certainly an element to be taken into account and carefully weighed when verifying whether a general custom has in fact been able to emerge in these circumstances, or whether this emergence has been hindered. In the latter case, when the norm is not yet in force as a general norm, it will certainly not bind the "permanent objector", but might well bind *inter se* other States who have expressly or tacitly accepted it. But if, despite isolated objection, the norm in question actually corresponds to truly general practice and *opinio juris*, it is then binding on all, including, in my view, the "permanent objector". Nevertheless, it cannot be ruled out that the consistent, continued attitude of rejection adopted by the latter might have set going a process leading to the formation of a special system, derogating from the general rule; a procedure which may take place, for instance, through a combination of the attitude of objection in question and the acquiescence of other States particularly concerned.

Of course, in order for an agreement derogating from a customary norm to be validly arrived at, the latter must be capable of being derogated from. This is not the case for rules of *jus cogens*, among which must indubitably be included the one I have just mentioned in connection with South Africa, the rule against *apartheid*. The case of the Republic of South Africa, is, moreover, for me, the stumbling block that the voluntarist conception inevitably comes up against, both in its traditional version and in its revised and moderate version of the "permanent objector". South Africa is universally condemned by all international circles as guilty of conduct that has been erected into an international crime by a rule of law against which that State has always fought. This fact makes it quite plain that international practice cannot be forced into the Procrustean bed of the voluntarist thesis.

I want to end by saying a word or two on a separate point which is also on the agenda, and has been mentioned in this connection both by Professor Arangio-Ruiz in his introduction and by Professors Cassese and Virally: that of the respective weight in the process of formation of general international law of declarations by representatives of States and of the actual practice of the latter.

I wish to state my support for the following idea: without a doubt, the declarations in question are an integral part of the practice of a State in the broadest sense of the word, but one must be extremely cautious in evaluating their weight in comparison with that of other elements which normally, in my view, appear to be more significant. I refer to the actual conduct of the State in international relations, to its legislative and judicial practice, and so on.

To be sure, one cannot doubt the importance of certain declarations made by the supreme bodies of a State, which, moreover, have on occasion even been found by international judges to be able, in particular circumstances, to bind the State directly in its relations with one or more other States. There is no doubt either that solemn declarations (for instance in the form of a diplomatic note) by State representatives other than the supreme organs (for example, heads of diplomatic missions) deserve special attention when particular circumstances authorize their being regarded as actually and officially expressing the State's point of view. But can the same thing be maintained about everything said by the innumerable people who speak in the State's name in various international venues, especially since the number of these is increasing all the time? I do not think so.

Indeed I believe, more generally, that internationalists ought not only to ask themselves, in connection with State agencies, the classical question regarding treaty-making power; they ought also in my view to ask about what might be called the "custom-making power" of these agencies. The constitutions of our countries, often so careful in regulating the procedure for arriving at the will of the State with regard to international treaties, normally entrust the Executive with the handling of international relations, subject to more or less penetrating parliamentary control; but this cannot mean that the emissaries of the Executive that attend the thousands of international meetings are all empowered to express the *opinio juris* of their country with equal authority! In conclusion, these declarations seem to me normally to be of marginal importance: it is impossible to reconstruct the international attitude of a State on the basis of them alone.

WEILER

I can be brief on one aspect at least because Luigi Condorelli covered an essential point I had been meaning to make. Can one really say that if there is no consent, there is no law? South Africa never consented to the illegality of *apartheid*. Does this exempt South Africa from that prohibition? Surely not.

For the rest I have a few footnotes to some of the points that were raised. I agree entirely with Professor Brownlie. Let us leave for a minute the realm of empiricism, of what States do, and go instead to what scholars say about the international legal process. We see that the revolt against so-called majoritarianism today is due to the fact that people are unhappy with what the majority are doing, not with the fact that it is a majority. They were quite happy 20 years ago when the majority was constituted differently. Nonetheless, I think one has to qualify that in the following way. International society today is different from that of the nineteen fifties. In that period, for good or for ill, there was Western domination: international society was much smaller; there was less interdependence, and more dependence. Effectively, the majority could more or less impose its will and the minority could use devices such as that of the "persistent objector". Now – and one has to generalize and simplify because there is a much larger international society – there are three big blocks.

Here we see how our three issues merge. I think that at least to an extent the very existence of these three blocks and the fact that we do not have one dominant majority and smaller minorities is in part at least instrumental in the tendency towards so-called soft law, the tendency towards consensualism. It has been said that international society needs these devices, because otherwise, at least in certain cases, there would be stagnation of the international process.

Another little point I would like to make on consent is that it is fundamental even in supranational organizations. Supranational organizations differ from the world order in a lot of ways, but not so much by virtue of the way law is formed. What we have there is also a rule of consent, even in the E.E.C. which is the *locus classicus* of a supranational organization.

And here I should like to take up a running feud between Nino Cassese and myself. Let us take the example he used: "The international society" decides that the protection afforded by the Geneva Conventions is not sufficient, or in fact that if there is State practice, it is unsatisfactory. There is therefore pressure to revise the Geneva Conventions of 1949 and one has an international conference, with statements of consent, or agreement. Nino Cassese then makes a bold step and says that in the absence of a "persistent objector", in the absence of opposing State practice, this kind of expression of consent can create a rule. I find that troubling, because in the international legal system, if you want to create binding norms in the absence of State practice, the normal process of creation is treaty-making. But Cassese takes the expression of consent before the treaty is formulated, and transforms that into a binding rule. He forgets that often the statement of consent in this type of forum is made because it is not a binding rule: if it were a binding rule, you would not have anything like the same level of consent.

On the question of practice and statements I do not think we have had a satisfactory answer. Professor Arangio-Ruiz was too abstract and Nino Cassese did not mention hard cases, for example that of torture. The prohibition of torture has been stated here (and everyone would support this) to be a peremptory rule of international law: torture is not only prohibited by international law, but this prohibition is part of *jus cogens*. There are millions of statements in all kinds of international fora, all States agreeing that torture is prohibited. And yet torture is widespread in a large number of States, as one knows from an equally impressive number of reports. I have not actually gone and tested the truth of this in person, but there are probably more States practising torture than States not practising it. How does one deal with that in terms of the relationship between practice and statement, when you have a uniform statement prohibiting a certain practice, yet, flying in the face of it, a very widespread practice by many of the States which proclaim it to be illegal?

FALK

I am not sure whether I am suffering from intellectual jet lag, but let me try to make a couple of comments that may explain my lack of participation in the entire discussion up to now. I am troubled a bit by what I think is an excessive purity of legal reasoning in addressing these kinds of issues at this stage in the world's history. My concern can be illustrated, I think, by reference to Professor Weiler's comments on the issue of torture. It seems to me that part of the answer to the question of the status of torture under international law has to do with what will contribute most to the minimization of torture as a characteristic of State practice. In other words, I think we need to take a morally consequentialist view of these kinds of issues, rather than view them in a kind of abstract setting where tools of logical analysis and the authority of competing legal doctrines are brought to bear.

As I see it, the world as we confront it is a very dangerous place, and not to address the problems facing international society as a way of trying to interpret the role of international law seems to me to be a fundamental political error. I think we have to face the political question of how we choose to relate legal discourse to the problems confronting international society and the challenges of international life. Otherwise we international lawyers are in effect fiddling while Rome is burning (I realize that we are in Florence, but it is close enough).

For instance, if one raises the question of the legal status of nuclear weapons at the present time, I would maintain that there is no juridically convincing answer, that one can argue either way. There is, in other words, a condition of fundamental uncertainty that attaches to this issue and if one emphasizes the indispensable character of consent one arrives at a particular conclusion that seems to me politically and morally undesirable. Given the fact that one is dealing in a domain of jurisprudential uncertainty, my view is that one of the functions of law is to build a normative consensus in international society. It would be an extraordinary renunciation of responsibility to civilization to act as if this question were purely a question of jurisprudential affinity, and the right jurisprudence could give you the right answer.

The same kind of reasoning applies to the perhaps less controversial issue of the status of the exclusive economic zone. Whether one validates this extension of the control by the coastal State over the offshore waters seems to me not so much to be a question of legal analysis, as of political analysis: how one chooses to evaluate the trends that have evolved in recent years.

My final comment is on the distinction between voluntarism and majoritarianism. I agree with Professor Brownlie that these are complementary instruments that States use to advance different positions in world society. And I would maintain, following the lines of his observations about the popularity of majoritarianism when it reflected U.S. and NATO preconceptions, that we would not be formulating this issue in this way at this time if it was not for the fact that the United States is alienated from the organized international community. In other words, the very agenda we have at this meeting is a socio-political reflection of the fact that a very important State that used to be very closely involved in the construction of an organized international community is now deeply alienated from it. The fact that the Soviet Union was alienated at an earlier stage made very little difference to the pattern of juridical discourse. People would not be having this kind of discussion if the United States was still involved and certainly did not have this kind of discussion when it was. Obviously the Soviet Union was seriously threatened by majoritarian tendencies in the past, especially prior to the entry of the Third World upon the international scene.

In my opinion, then, what one is confronted with is a choice between unilateral and collective modes of realizing national interests in the world. Those who see more collective procedures as serving their national interests, necessarily tend toward majoritarian forms of legal reasoning, and those that see themselves as on the losing side of majoritarian political processes naturally incline toward unilateral and highly positivistic forms of legal reasoning. As has been suggested, all this changes with the changing complexion not only of international society, but also with changes of leadership in critical States. For instance, the existence of the Reagan administration, with its particularly strong ideology of State sovereignty, again alters the pattern of juridical discussion because it has sufficient weight to reshape the way we think about international legal issues. In conclusion, then, I would say that the way one comes down on these issues does not have a great deal to do with jurisprudential rigour. These questions cannot be resolved on a jurisprudential level and therefore I think we should be more willing to connect jurisprudential discourse with the political context of choice. The actual choices exist.

Another related point is that there is some temptation to confuse the issue of law-formation with the problems of making certain laws effective in international society. In other words, the ineffectiveness of the prohibition on torture does not seem to me to alter the basic analysis of whether or not the prohibition is valid. As I see it at least, its validity arises partly and significantly from the willingness of States to take a formal position to the effect that torture is illegal, and therefore to use that willingness as a political instrument to minimize the practice. This is the decisive issue of choice that arises in this kind of context.

VIRALLY

This brings us back to some extent to our discussion of yesterday, but poses the problem of the role and the function of the jurist in somewhat wider terms; and ultimately, the question here is whether the jurist really can establish what *lex lata* is or whether he is always bound, one way or another, to confuse it with *lex ferenda*. I think all the same that it is possible, despite changes in position made by States (even important ones) to try to establish the state of the law at a given moment as it is objectively valid, irrespective of the preferences of this or that party. But the problem is a hard one, I recognize that.

MERON

In the area of human rights, including of course the prohibition of torture, which I described yesterday as constituting not just a customary but a peremptory rule of international law, statements as opposed to actual practice of States may be of particular importance. This is not only true in the moral sense of which Dick Falk spoke a moment ago, but even in the purely legal sense, as discussed by Professor Virally. Empirical evidence may show that probably as much as half of the international community, if not more, practises torture in one form or another. Nevertheless, this empirical evidence should not lead us to the conclusion that the prohibition of torture is not customary international law, or that it is not a peremptory norm of international law. Statements can be decisive in the formation of custom when they clearly reflect *opinio juris* and the States making such statements recognize (I am merely rephrasing what was said by Professor Virally) that inconsistent or contrary practice is a violation of that law.

SUR

To the extent that questions such as that of custom, or of *jus cogens*, have been covered, I feel that it is not essential to take any special stance with regard to Professor Weil's article. These questions should be dealt with by themselves. I wish to say first of all that there are points on which I have no objection or special opinion to put forward. I think, for example that the suggestion that we should speak of individual consent and of the collective elaboration of norms rather than voluntarism or majority, is quite right. The term voluntarism is in itself somewhat ambiguous. It may give the idea that there is an expression of a precise, almost psychological, will of the legal subject, which is obviously something rather imaginary. It is therefore perhaps more logical, more appropriate, to mention the dialectic that is going on, and has been considerably enriched over the last few years, between individual consent and the collective elaboration of law. I think we can speak about a dialectic of the unilateral and the collective.

This remark leads to a second observation: one must, as has been said, distinguish between the existence of a rule and its opposability. In other words, a majority of states may perfectly well set up a rule which it may claim is a general rule. And the rule will be general, to the extent that it is not aimed at a particular situation, geographically or politically, but is called upon to govern the whole of international society. It is nevertheless the case that certain States may individually exclude themselves from application of the rule by indicating that they are opposed to it, and that in any case they do not wish to be bound by it. I therefore believe that this distinction between the existence and the opposability of the rule to some extent reconciles the apparent contradiction between majority formation of general rules and the possibility that one State should not be bound by them.

Now I wish to make a few observations regarding the two essential points which have been discussed this morning: custom and *jus cogens*. Custom and *jus cogens* may to some extent perhaps be taken together, but in another sense should be kept separate.

As regards custom, I was extremely pleased to hear Professor Arangio-Ruiz welcoming the *Lotus* case and saying that *Lotus* was in some sense still in the air, that there had been no fundamental change in international law since this decision of principle. In fact it seems to me that voluntarism, or let us say, the principle of consent to customary rules, has always been sacred to international jurisprudence. To be sure, one may then say that this principle is no barrier to asserting the existence of custom, and of a remarkable complexity in the formation of customary rules. But I would say that in a certain sense this does not interest the lawyer, or interests him only indirectly. The way in which custom is formed is clear for the lawyer, and unequivocal: the customary rule is formed and becomes opposable in virtue of the consent of States. This consent may take extremely diverse forms. One might even speak of juggling with consent; but there is always a "mask" that allows the customary rule to show, and that "mask" is consent.

One might then say that it is only a mask, a fiction. In reality we see behind the action of social forces, we see pressures, tensions, technological or political needs, whatever you want. But this does not interest the lawyer, strictly speaking. It might interest the politician or the moralist, but as a lawyer, I look at the way the system functions and not at what is outside the system. Accordingly voluntarism, or more exactly consensualism, very clearly appears as the rule which operates the system. Of course, this consensualism is adapted to the particular form or the particular constraints of custom. But I would perhaps not be in complete agreement with Professor Virally when he makes an opposition between treaty and custom, saying that a treaty may be controlled by States while custom is much less so. It seems to me that this statement must at least be qualified.

A treaty can in fact be controlled by States but a State acting individually is subject to the consent of other States. In cases of multilateral treaties, it may happen that their entry into force is dependent on the consent of a certain number of States — for instance 35 States for the Vienna Convention. It is quite clear that one State does not individually control or manipulate the 34 other States that have to consent. There is, then, a sort of independence, a sort of exteriority of the treaty vis-à-vis the States acting individually. And analogously, in a certain way, the State may act upon custom, either by rejecting it or by taking the initiative of suggesting its creation. I therefore feel that the situation of custom and treaty, from the viewpoint of the action of States on these two ways of arriving at rules, is much closer than one might think.

I was likewise struck by Professor Mendelson's remark regarding the role of the International Court of Justice in connection with the assessment of customary law. It is true that the Court shows great freedom in the treatment of custom; it is thereby participating in this manipulation of the customary rule. But it seems to me that several different hypotheses may be distinguished. There are cases where a custom is itself the object of dispute, where its applicability is directly at issue, where the parties to the dispute do not agree as to the opposability of the rule. When the Court is faced with such a hypothesis, it indisputably gives the palm — with the sole exception of the *Nottebohm* case — to the consensualist solution. But when it has to do with customs which are not in dispute, customs which are simply an element in its reasoning, it utilizes them in a much more flexible manner. One might give several examples of this, but I do not wish to extend my presentation unduly. Briefly, these customary rules are not disputed, and it is indeed very probable that they will not be a factor in the decision. They will simply play a part in the legal reasoning and will have no definitive legal authority. This formulation of custom will not be vested with the authority of *res judicata*. What one can say is that, when the Court formulates such customary rules, in some sense it is proposing its participation in the customary process. It puts forward a proposition, and States react to this formulation. They accept, or do not accept, the formulation of the customary rule put forward by the Court. In so doing, they perhaps give it the status of obligatory rule. One might take the famous instance of the *Fisheries* case of 1951, in which the Court formulated rules relating to the territorial sea, giving indications which were subsequently accepted and taken up by States.

Voluntarism or consensualism, then; but some flexibility has to be introduced. I am struck by the fact that in treaty law, flaws in consent are accepted, if aimed at protecting the authenticity of the State's consent, and hence at protecting its will, by giving this term quite a special meaning, specific to the international legal system. As far as I know there is no theory of flaws in consent to custom, which shows that there is less protection of consent to customary law.

I should like to make a few more very brief observations. It might also be said that this consent is limited by the fact that it is tacit: I shall not go back over what has been said, but will perhaps make one brief point regarding practice and *opinio juris*. I think that the distinction between these two factors is an entirely academic distinction, which in international legal life is completely relative. Practice always contains an *opinio juris*. As for the *opinio juris*, how could it be known independently of practice, since the *opinio juris* is itself practice? If we take a General Assembly resolution presented in the form of a declaration, in a certain way it is also practice. It cannot simply be considered as *opinio juris*. It is at the very least practice in the context of the United Nations, laying down, for instance, the competence of the General Assembly to intervene in the area it is concerned with. Accordingly, the notion of practice and the notion of *opinio juris* are very relative notions, generally jumbled up together in international legal life.

Since I am speaking of practice, I shall make one last observation in connection with *jus cogens*. For a very long time I believed that *jus cogens* was a stronger variety of custom. In other words, that there had to exist a general customary rule to which was subsequently attributed the higher status of a rule of *jus cogens*. In this case, the process of formation of *jus cogens* would have been a tougher version of the formation of custom. But today I am not entirely certain that that was the intention of the authors of the Vienna Convention. I wonder whether *jus cogens* presupposes, in order for it to exist, a practice. This is not, it would seem, required by the terms of the Vienna Convention, specifically articles 53 and 64. A rule of *jus cogens* is a peremptory norm of general international law, recognized and accepted by the international community of States as a whole. There is no reference to any element of practice. It may be that the recognition, the acceptance, takes place in solemn, declaratory, fashion, but it is in no way required that there be a corresponding practice. Should one then consider that the formation of the rule of *jus cogens* is identical to that of a customary rule and that *jus cogens* is a strengthened form of custom, a higher derivation of custom, or is there an autonomous, original mode of formation, which perhaps does not form part of practice?

Brownlie

I wanted to say a few words about the problems of statements in relation to actual practice which I did not deal with before. It seems to me that the proposition that practice is the determinant of the formation of custom is simply unattractive on the grounds of common sense. In the first place, many States which try to conform with international law for all sorts of practical reasons, may wait 10 or 15 years before a particular episode arises in which they can display practice on the basis of a certain rule. It simply is not common sense to say that their commitment to various rules cannot arise until they have actually been involved in some pertinent incident. In the same context it seems to me to be contrary to common sense and supremely unattractive to suggest that because large numbers of States do not conform with the norm prohibiting torture, torture may have become lawful.

Secondly, as a matter of fact, it is generally held that the properly articulated statements of States on matters of law form practice. Most experts think that. I know there is an attractive counterthesis, expressed by Anthony D'Amato in a very well-written book, but the general view is quite otherwise. When States have responded after careful consideration to questionnaires from the International Law Commission or other bodies, to say that these are mere pieces of paper seems to me again contrary to common sense. On the other hand, I do think that actual practice may in certain circumstances have relevance. Let us revert to the Truman Proclamation. As some of you may recall, in fact there were two Truman proclamations, one was the famous one, and the other (on fishery conservation zones) was immediately put into the cupboard. It was not followed by a single executive order, as far as I know, and the United States seems to have regretted it, as it had repercussions in Latin America. There is no doubt that the complete inaction on the basis of that proclamation must have had some weakening effect on the significance of the proclamation.

Lastly, Professor Weiler's torture example seems to me to create confusion because the problem he was posing was the problem of efficacy, not the problem of formation of custom.

CASSESE

I apologize for speaking yet again, but I would like to take up a few points made by Luigi Condorelli about South Africa, on which Joseph Weiler and Giorgio Gaja also commented. This is a very important example, but it does not, in my opinion, upset the theory of consent. Not at all. What Condorelli said is correct: that is, that consent is not the only indication of a State's acceptance of new rules. There are other pointers, but in my view the key to understanding the international situation as it really is, is the concept of tacit, or implicit consent.

This may seem trite, but the concept of implicit consent covers situations such as South Africa, as I think I can show you by a brief look at the question. We all know the U.N. documents on South Africa and also the *South African Yearbook of International Law*, which contains South African practice connected with international law. Well, to the best of my knowledge, South Africa has never denied in the United Nations that the principle of racial equality exists or that it constitutes one of the fundamental principles of contemporary international law. I remember that the time when the *Namibia* case was before the International Court of Justice, one of the Counsel for South Africa said before the Court: "We do not violate the principle of racial equality. In actual fact, what we do is simply promote and effect separate development for different communities". He then pointed to the example of Switzerland and said: "In Switzerland women do not have the right to vote, and this is not regarded as discrimination. Similarly, in South Africa, blacks do not have the right to vote, and this does not amount to discrimination". That is, he very cleverly evaded the issue, without denying the existence of the principle of racial equality. In other words, the South Africans uphold the principle but maintain that in point of fact the (abominable) system of racial segregation is not contrary to it. Of course we cannot agree. The fact remains, however, that from a legal point of view they have never explicitly opposed the existence of the principle. In my opinion, then, South Africa implicitly consents to the fundamental principle of the international community forbidding racial discrimination.

On the other hand, what South Africa does make plain is that it objects to the U.N. Convention on *apartheid*. Like a majority of Western States it does not accept this Convention, but for very obvious reasons. As we all know, the Convention makes *apartheid* an international crime in the strict sense of the word and consequently carries the implication that the perpetrators of the crime of *apartheid* bear personal responsibility. But this is not the same as a violation of the general rule of racial equality. I would conclude that the example of South Africa does not demonstrate that consent plays no role, so long as consent is understood in the broad sense to cover implicit consent too. This is Tunkin's theory, and I would tend to agree with him.

VIRALLY

I am not sure that the last remark on *apartheid* closes the debate, because the problem, ultimately, is not whether South Africa does or does not accept the principle of equality and non-discrimination. It says it does. The question is what interpretation it gives this principle, and whether this interpretation is accepted by other States, and I think that we have a problem here. But I find it very remarkable that, in this quite fundamental debate on what international law is, how it enters into force, the practical problems facing us are those of torture and *apartheid*. Perhaps that ought to make us do some thinking on the true nature of international law.

ARANGIO-RUIZ

I hope nobody expects that during the midday recess I have been able to put sufficient order in my thoughts as to be able to reply to all the remarks which have been made following this morning's statements on voluntarism v. majoritarianism. I shall do my best not to leave any remarks unanswered.

Starting in a way from the last question, let me make clear that nothing I said this morning about the distinction between sources in a *legal* sense, on one side, and material *sources* on the other, implies a formalistic or conservative approach to law. On the contrary, I belong to the not very numerous class of international lawyers who do not even accept, as an accomplished legal development, the existence of an international legal community in a proper sense. In order to try to look at the matter more optimistically I re-read Hermann Mosler's "International Society as a Legal Community" on my way to Florence. But this effort was not, alas, successful. I still believe that there is no such thing as a real international legal community, either as the community of mankind, or as a community of States. Far less do I believe that there is, even in our time, an organized international community. One or two of those present may have taken a look, with respect to this, at the Appendix to my Hague Course of 1972 on "Friendly Relations" (or its 1979 reprint). On the question of the organized community, particularly on the United Nations, especially in paragraphs 132–147, I went (and still do) decidedly beyond the relatively realistic approach of Sir Gerald Fitzmaurice (paragraph 139). My views thus differ quite substantially from those of our friend Prosper Weil, who while criticizing a few current overstatements about international law, seems really to share the current (and in my view misleading) belief in the actual existence of an international legal community, which is in a way the very foundation of some of the theories which give him cause for concern.

A second point is the attitude of the lawyer to law, and in particular, of course, to international law, written or unwritten. While believing that there must in principle be a sharp distinction in the mind of the lawyer both between what the law is (*lex lata*) and what the law ought to be (*lex ferenda*) and between sources in a narrow or legal sense and sources in a material sense, I certainly do not deny that the lawyer should be concerned as much with *lex ferenda* as with *lex lata*. In addition, I do not believe that the lawyer should confine his task to a more or less strict interpretation of existing law. On the contrary, he must look far beyond. He must consider — I agree with Professor Falk — the political environment from which the law stems, and in which the law operates. Nor should he hesitate to pass judgment on the conduct of governments. I have no doubt, for instance, about the necessity of condemning such episodes as the American decision to stay away from the *Nicaraguan* case before the International Court of Justice. I felt equally critical, during the *Nuclear Tests* case, of the attitude of the French Government in that respect. I actually believe that the more a country is a free one and claims to be attached to the rule of law, the more its government should avoid having recourse to legally poor excuses to stay away from the International Court of Justice. I join the criticism which has been widely voiced in the American press about the United States decision. I also blame the Government of Italy for not having managed yet to submit a declaration of acceptance of the Hague Court's compulsory jurisdiction under Article 36(2) of the Statute.

I am equally concerned with the necessity that when one tries to see whether a legal rule exists or not, or when one interprets a treaty rule, one should also consider that for any legal rule to be such — namely a binding rule — it must be applied with a minimum of *consistency* by the States which invoke it. If, on the contrary States pay only lip-service to the rule and apply it unilaterally against, one, two, or a few given States, forgetting about the many other States which do the same or even worse, they weaken the rule. To use a rule of conduct with bias or partiality — especially within an organic system which has neither a regular judge nor a real policeman — undermines respect for and jeopardizes the very existence of the rule. Unfortunately, this is a very frequent practice of States.

This leads me to the further theme: the relationship between statement of rules and actual practice. Assuming that by statement one means the formulation or declaration of a rule or principle (for example, by a resolution of the U.N. General Assembly), while actual practice would mean that States (or a given State or group or States) concretely conform their conduct to the rule or principle, I believe — as I stated this morning — that actual practice is by far more relevant. Insofar as general, unwritten or customary rules are concerned (namely, rules or principles other than contractual rules), the essential evidence is what States actually do (or do not do) in their concrete relations, rather than what they say that they (or others) shall or should do. The statement of course, will have its bearing. However, while the mere statement would not be adequate evidence of the existence of the rule, actual practice can well be, as I understand it. I must add immediately, however, that by actual practice I mean more than the mere "externally visible" conduct of States. Actual practice can be, as I understand the expression, not only the best evidence of the so-called material element of general law, but, unless it appeared that the conduct in question was held as a matter of courtesy, also the best evidence of *opinio juris*. It can certainly be more valid evidence of such *opinio* than a mere statement or proclamation of the corresponding principle or rule.

This applies, in my opinion, whatever the form or channel through which the statement of the rule took place. The simplest possibility is that the statement of the rule should take place orally or in writing, unilaterally or bilaterally. A frequent occurrence it that the rule be stated — evoked, declared, proclaimed or invoked — at an international conference. An even more frequent case, in our time, is the statement of the rule through a permanent, multilateral body. The most important instance are the declarations adopted by the General Assembly of the United Nations: and I have attempted to make some distinctions with regard to this aspect of international practice in a wide sense. In the 1972 Hague course – I apologize for mentioning it again – I attempted, in particular, not only to discuss the relationship between statement (or declaration) of the rule on the one hand and actual conduct on the other, but also the relationship between "United Nations practice" (as a particular aspect of the practice of States in general) on one side, and what I call "State practice at large", namely the practice of States outside the United Nations (I refer to paragraphs 22–30 of that 1972 work). It is certain, in my view, that if the statement so understood is not accompanied or followed by actual practice (in the comprehensive sense I have indicated), there will not be a rule by the mere strength of the non-binding statement. If the stated rule was already a binding rule it would naturally be another matter.

One last point is to mark some perplexity with regard to the opinion expressed by Professor Virally that practice comes first and *opinio juris* later. As I understand actual practice, this may or may not be so. There may well be cases where an *opinio* is so strongly entertained as genuinely to manifest itself in a statement prior to any material conduct as a factor and evidence of the rule. The idea that material conduct comes first in time is connected to the rather "scholastic" distinction between those two elements of custom (especially of that national or interindividual custom in which I am inclined to see a much more genuine species of custom than in most international unwritten rules), which are currently known as *diuturnitas*, on the one hand, and *opinio juris* on the other. It is on the basis of the consequent artificial separation between an external material element and an internal psychological element that one is led to see the unwritten rule created, so to speak, through two distinct phases, the first phase being one of mere conduct, the second the elevation of that conduct to the higher status of legally due behaviour. Even assuming that this picture corresponded to the real phenomenon in municipal law, I doubt that it would be a good description of the far from identical creation of international unwritten rules. The latter, in my view, is a much more, if not fully, conscious process than the interindividual one. And within this more conscious law-making process the States' *opinio* can well precede – provided it is a genuine *opinio juris* and not just a platonic statement – the corresponding behaviour.

Another necessity is to clarify the relationship between statement on the one hand and *opinio juris* on the other. I would strongly reject any identification between the two. A government may well make or vote the most emphatic statement on a rule, in the legal force of which it does not really believe.

Turning to other points, Condorelli referred to attitudes towards such crimes as torture and *apartheid.* He seemed to make too much of the attitude of the "culprit" State, whose negative position is not necessarily based on a rejection of the rule or principle it is violating. South Africa, for example, contends (in my view quite wrongly) that its conduct is a matter of domestic jurisdiction or that the rule is inapplicable. It does not claim that the rule does not exist. Leaving on one side the obviously negative position of the condemned State — the State resorting to torture or *apartheid* — one should be concerned with what other States do vis-à-vis the torturing State, or the State practising *apartheid*. The most important thing, within an inorganic fabric like the international system, is — I insist — that delicts or crimes meet an adequate, *impartial* reaction from other States. That the violation be acknowledged by the culprit is naturally desirable. But it is not, relatively speaking, the main problem.

On the question whether majority rule (with the limits and with the understanding I indicated this morning) is a relatively new invention in the General Assembly, I am inclined to agree with Professor Brownlie. Within the limits set forth by the Charter, that rule has been there since the very beginning of the United Nations. It operated then to the advantage of a certain group of States just as well — and just as legally — as it operates at present to the advantage of the so-called Third World.

Another question raised concerned the relationship between a bilateral treaty and *jus cogens*. On the subject of *jus cogens* I wish I could find the answers to doubts that will stay with me for the rest of my life. My mind is clear neither with regard to the general definition and place of *jus cogens*, nor with regard to the identification of the single rules qualifying as such. As to the question raised, I would say that if two States conclude an agreement in a sense condemned by a rule of *jus cogens*, there are two possibilities. One is that the parties comply with the agreement (for instance an agreement envisaging aggression against a third State): in which case obviously the fact that they comply with the agreement does not exclude that they violate a rule of *jus cogens*, or, more simply, a rule of general international law binding them towards other States, whether as a matter of *jus cogens* or not. The second possibility is that one of the two parties refuses to comply. It seems obvious that the other State cannot reasonably claim compliance before an international body, if such a body is bound to apply the rule in violation of which the treaty was concluded. This possibility, however, is not restricted to the case of *jus cogens*. A similar impediment would presumably arise within the framework of any multilateral system (for example before a U.N. body) whether or not the violated rule qualified as *jus cogens*.

With regard to so-called supranational organizations, I have for some time held a position similar to Professor Yankov's. In my opinion, the European Communities are not supranational. They do not constitute superior legal systems encompassing the legal systems of the Member States in any sense comparable to that in which federal law embraces the legal systems of member States as its subdivisions. European institutions are just common institutions of the various member States, operating as such —

by virtue of the several legal systems as adapted to the constitutive European treaties – within each one of those systems. I would classify the acts of European institutions (insofar as they operate directly within the legal systems of the member States) as vicarious State activity of international bodies (as distinguished from the international activities in a narrow sense normally carried out, for example, by the U.N. General Assembly or the Security Council, by the International Court of Justice, or by an arbitral tribunal). It follows, in my opinion, that European Community Law is more a matter of common or uniform municipal law (constitutional, administrative, procedural) than a matter of international law. The function of international law is essentially to bind the member States to set up the institutions and to confer upon them the given functions within their respective national systems. There is no direct reaching of the *subditi* of the Member States on the part of international law; or, for that matter, on the part of a European federal, as such supranational, law.

Another question raised was the relationship between custom and will (or consent). No doubt, the kind of consent embodied in general (or unwritten) international law is not quite the same kind of consent which characterizes treaty-making. For unwritten, customary international law, silence or acquiescence are more probable ingredients. As I stated earlier, however, I am not inclined to accept the current identification of all international unwritten (or general) law with a customary law of the same kind as municipal law custom. I am inclined to believe, in particular, that general (or unwritten) international law is not such a spontaneous growth as the custom of municipal law. The international custom-making process is a far more conscious and, in a sense, wilful rule-making process. Basically, some form of acceptance – and in that sense of consent and will – is involved in the attitudes of the States participating in a law-making process. The difference from contractual law is far less pronounced than in the case of interindividual customary law.

The next point made by one or more speakers, was that the existence of blocks in contemporary international society favours recourse to soft law devices. I believe this to be quite correct; and it may also be a positive factor for the survival of cooperation amongst States, of international organizations, ultimately of international law itself. However, I repeat the warning I gave yesterday: one should not rely unduly on soft law devices, as if they could really solve problems.

Someone mentioned the possibility of a piece of soft law possessing binding force. I think this is what you would call begging the question. Obviously, if a rule is treated *in concreto* as a binding rule by the relevant number of States, whatever its source, it is a binding rule. I would not say that it is a *de facto* binding rule. It is simply a rule of law, either by virtue of a treaty or by virtue of tacit agreement or custom.

Of course I am troubled, and I should like to hear more from Professor Falk, about the question of lawyers fiddling while Rome is burning. I do not see myself doing this, nor would I encourage any other lawyer, or any student, to fiddle while Rome is burning. On the contrary, I criticize the international system and its contents as much as I can: up to the point of wishing it to be substituted by something entirely different.

With regard to nuclear weapons, I will simply reply to Professor Falk by referring to what he wrote about the *Shimoda* case, with which I am sure you are all familiar, in the *American Journal of International Law*. My opinion is that there is probably enough in the *Shimoda* case, and in the comments of Professor Falk, to conclude that nuclear weapons shall not be used because they are condemned by international law. Of course, there is no rule of international law which states in express terms that nuclear weapons are outlawed. But nuclear weapons are implicitly outlawed by the outlawing of weapons of mass destruction, or which cause wanton destruction. It is quite possible to argue that in the case of Hiroshima or Nagasaki — with all respect for the lives of the Japanese, Americans and other nationalities saved as a consequence of recourse to those devices — the horror of the consequences was such that it could well be maintained that military necessity did not really justify that choice. This was, if I remember correctly, the gist of the *Shimoda* decision: for which, I must say, the Japanese Court — and I join Professor Falk again here — should be complimented.

Chapter III

To what Extent are International Law and International Lawyers Ideologically Neutral?

I. Presentation

FALK

To orient the comments I shall make on this specific topic, I should start by saying that I am not so impressed by Prosper Weil's article. In fact I would welcome it if someone could enlighten me as to why it is considered such an important formulation. It strikes me as being, to put it rather strongly, a slightly hysterical effort to stop the world from changing. I see it as the work of a highly intelligent person who dislikes what is happening in the world and is translating into jurisprudence a kind of ideological nostalgia for an earlier period of certainty and consensus; he dislikes the problems of tension and diversity that exist in the world. I would stress that I am putting this so impolitely because I would really like to understand why others find the article so important and useful. In my opinion it is a gross overstatement of what is happening and makes use of extremely emotionally loaded language in order to express a highly nostalgic view of international political life. The final point I would make is that it is more about politics than law, despite appearances to the contrary, and I am opposed to political elements being introduced.

I should now like to start by taking up a topic Professor Arangio-Ruiz touched upon when he expressed the view that nuclear weapons are illegal as a consequence *inter alia* of the *Shimoda* case. Although I welcome this as a conclusion, I do not feel that it follows from the jurisprudential perspective that emphasizes the voluntaristic character of international law formation. The U.S. Government, at least, definitely does not think it has consented to the formation of any such rule prohibiting even the first use of nuclear weapons, and it takes the position in its Field Manuals, and elsewhere, that so long as there is not a specific rule of prohibition, these weapons can be legally used.

Now the existence of this kind of position is precisely why I feel that a strictly voluntaristic or positivist view of law-formation is unacceptable at this stage of international society. I think the issue of nuclear weapons is probably more important to the future of the world than the question of *apartheid*, and I think the power of a single country to dissent from the general consensus cannot be reconciled with an acceptable jurisprudence, or with an acceptable juristic stand.

The question of how one deals with ideology seems to me to be closely connected with the professional identity of the jurist — a point that Professor Virally made, I think in response to my comment this morning. In approaching the question of ideology and ideological neutrality, it is therefore important to clarify one's idea of the relationship of juridical science to values. I would begin by saying that a doctor is not supposed to be neutral towards disease, and drawing the analogy, which I think is close, with the jurist, who should not be neutral about violence, torture, genocide, ecological decay, and a further list of important menaces that confront international society. If one decides that *jus cogens* provides a neutral, or more professional, way of handling this type of responsiveness to these challenges, this is fine, but one should recognize that this is itself a kind of ideological rationalization.

I think it is very important to be clear about this connection between legal analysis and an ideological perspective. I am not, in any sense, saying that one should become an ideological mercenary and represent partisan positions under the guise of scholarly autonomy or objectivity. I think there has been a lot of legal analysis of this sort, on such issues as the Arab—Israeli conflict, where competing interpretations of international law are invoked to serve a set of unacknowledged political interests. I am trying to oppose this kind of suppression of perspective in the name of legal analysis. It seems to me that we confront the issue of ideology only when there are important conflicts among leading political actors in the world, and particularly when the *status quo* is being challenged by emerging social, political and economic forces. These challenges are then characterized as ideological to denigrate them, and weaken their claim to a par in the law-creation process. One of my objections to Professor Weil's article is that I think he is fundamentally doing this.

In our historical period, there seem to me to be three kinds of ideological struggle that are of importance. The first and most obvious is the struggle between socialism and capitalism as an informing perspective on the substance of international law, particularly in the area where property rights are at stake. The second is an ideologically phrased struggle, principally between the Third World and the developed countries, on whether some kind of structural revisions to the content of international law should be made at this time, as a matter of distributive justice and of rectifying certain distortions from the past. Finally, and most important in terms of ideological perspective in my view, is the contrast between those that accord to the sovereign State almost exclusive control over the law-forming process and those who challenge this exclusiveness from a number of points of view. Now this is probably treated on the whole as the least important of the three levels of ideological struggle, but I regard the conflict between State power and civil society as the fundamental political conflict of our time, east or west, north or south.

To the extent that international law is interpreted to reinforce exclusive control over the law-forming process by the State, it is serving an ideological role of a negative sort. Maybe I can make this clearer by reference to efforts to invoke the Nuremberg principles, that were enunciated and accepted at the end of Word War II and can, I think, legitimately be said to form a valid element in modern international law by almost any criteria. Now these principles have been systematically repudiated, not in the legal discourse of States, but in their practice. The question therefore arises of the degree to which non-State actors in the world can try to implement the Nuremberg principles or the fundamental standards of human rights. This will often take the form of domestic struggles between society and the State and one of the most important roles of international law in these very non-technical areas must be to legitimate domestic claims upon government. For instance one finds the Solidarity movement in Poland invoking the standards of the International Labour Organizations (I.L.O.) to provide legitimacy for its claims. One finds dissenters in the Soviet Union calling on the U.N. Covenants on human rights accepted by the Soviet Union to back up their claims against the Soviet State. One finds opponents of the nuclear arms race in the United States referring very widely to the Nuremberg principles when objecting in domestic courts to various aspects of reliance on first-strike weapons.

What I am trying to say is that one of the least appreciated ideological battles concerns the degree to which a traditional view of the law-making process continues to be attributed validity by international jurists. My argument is that this is inevitably a political choice. There is no technical solution to this choice, and we must have the integrity not to hide behind professional arguments, but to confront its implications directly and honestly.

Let me just say two more things. The first is that in this period of complex ideological tension — and there is no way of ridding present day world conflicts of ideological elements — there is what I might call a meta-ideological quest, an attempt, that is, to agree on a common framework that transcends these ideological issues. The U.N. Declaration on Friendly Relations could be taken as a summary of what I would call the meta-ideological framework; relatively meaningless in behavioural terms, but establishing a common legal discourse that can be used by all sectors of the international community. And this is very important to the extent that one of the things that international law facilitates is communication across these ideological barriers. Indeed, in my view, a large part of the functional agenda of international life is also meta-ideological in this sense, and serves as the practical foundation for the international order.

Let me end by saying that I think the insistence on the distinction between *lex lata* and *de lege ferenda* is again a way of falsely and misleadingly restricting the identity and proper role of the jurist. The real issue facing jurists is how to behave in a set of circumstances beset by legal uncertainty. The boundaries are so blurred between what the law is and what the law ought to be in all of these areas of active controversy, that to rely on this distinction is in effect to take sides in the legal argument, and the distinction itself does not seem to me to rest on any objective legal ground. In fact, what I see happening is the emergence of a kind of neo-naturalist perspective to describe the content of what the law is; and a neo-naturalist perspective that objectifies certain values by its very character blurs the distinction between what the law is and what the law ought to be.

Again this is a matter of political choice; there is no jurisprudence that can give an authoritative answer to the question of what the place of natural law-thinking and legal positivism is in an appropriate science of law. Positivism served the 19th century very well, because States were in agreement and in control, but it serves the second half of the 20th century very poorly, because States can no longer be in control, either in normative or in practical terms. It therefore seems to me that the most appropriate jurisprudence is the one that serves the needs of a particular historical period. We should not be prisoners of the past; we should try to invoke the past in order to solve the problems of the present, and move towards a preferable future. International legal activity cannot avoid this normative or ideological dimension, that is crucial to its identity. I think we can either equate ideology with the normative dimension, and therefore find no fault with it, or we can use the word in a pejorative sense to signify types of politics and morality we do not like. There is nothing wrong with doing this, but if we do we should be clear that we are making this kind of statement. The important thing is to face up clearly to this relationship between values and law in this period of tremendous international ferment and of great danger to the stability of international life.

II. Discussion

WEILER

It is not an easy task to speak after Dick Falk, but for the sake of argument I shall at least try to deal with some of the issues he raised.

As I stated in my intervention, it is my belief, a belief which in my view is a commonplace, that no law can be neutral. International law in this case is no exception. It was the emergence of competing ideologies which highlighted the ideological changes in the current situation of international law. In his critique of Weil, much of which I agree with, Falk seems to fall into the same trap, or, rather, Prosper Weil seems to be following Falk's own prescriptions. Weil takes an ideological stance (although one with which Falk and I disagree) and he tries to be very effective, by presenting it in a scientific attire and with the same kind of jurist's commitment. Falk is right in claiming that we cannot be ideologically neutral; that being a jurist is to be involved in the world and concerned with what is happening; and that we should try and use our profession in a skillful way to advance our aims. But in this committed way, although from the other side of the ideological barrier, it could be said that Weil is doing just that. There is a certain measure of intellectual dishonesty in criticizing him for his method. At the end of the day the Falk critique of Prosper Weil really says "I do not agree with your ideology"! Basically Falk and Weil are the same type of lawyers, with a certain disagreement about the means which a committed lawyer, an ideological lawyer, should or should not use.

My second point goes a bit more *au fond.* Can one not draw the opposite conclusion, that precisely because we are in a world scenario with competing ideologies, one has to be even more sociological and detached, and that the only relevant question that one can ask is really "Are there norms which States and others in the world order accept as law?" I agree that "positivism" is a word that evokes a different era. But we could be empiricists, and ask: "What are the laws that are really operating?" Implicit in the Falk critique of scientific jurisprudence – in fact a negation of scientific jurisprudence – is the proposition that in all the critical issues, the boundaries are so blurred that it is a fiction to maintain a position on the basis of scientific analysis. If this is so, either you openly say: since everything is blurred one should be motivated by a moral commitment or by neo-naturalism, or one should at least be aware that scientific jurisprudence is a pretence, maybe even a deception. But here I think the Falk agenda, which is powerful and persuasive, can only exist in a society of lawyers where the majority are doing scientific jurisprudence, or pretending to do scientific jurisprudence, and there are only one or two mavericks who call their bluff. In other words Falk's agenda depends, even relies, on others accepting cynically, or otherwise, the premise of scientific jurisprudence. Why am I saying this? Because by using the word law to advance an agenda Falk relies on a certain fiction which that word and discipline carry with them. If we explode it completely, and destroy the fiction of scientific jurisprudence, we might be doing a good thing in terms of improving the world, or destroying the world, according to our set of values, but we will not be able to enlist, in our aid, the whole set of normative associations that the word law carries with it. So in a way, Falk's challenge depends on the fact that there is a society of lawyers, for good or for bad, who are keeping up the fiction that law is real, that there is some way of discovering principles, and so forth. He can then challenge this, shoot it down and explode it and evoke a more overtly ideologically moral commitment as a strategy of what lawyers as responsible citizens of countries of the world should be doing.

Arangio-Ruiz

First of all, I would like to take the question of nuclear weapons. When I stated that the use of the A Bomb could be looked at, in my view, as a violation of a rule of international law, I referred to rules of international law existing at that time. And I do not see how such a tentative view (obviously a matter of interpretation of the rule on weapons of mass or wanton destruction) could not be compatible with a voluntarist or a positivist concept of law or law-making. The voluntarist or positivist concept of law-making does not mean that, once a rule has come into existence, a State can dismiss it at will. Such a possibility would of course be open within the framework of the theory of self-limitation, namely the theory according to which international rules are created by States merely as a matter of self-restraint, so that each State could withdraw from subjection to the rule *ad nutum*, as soon as it did not feel like living under it any longer.

Going back to the question of resort to the A Bomb, notwithstanding the fact that certain considerations might have led me to decide as President Truman decided on that terrible occasion, I believe as a lawyer (and a human being) that the decision might well be found to be condemnable under the rules of warfare at that time in existence.

On the wider issue raised by Professor Falk, I find his approach far too political when he contends that at some point the lawyer must not shun, or hesitate before, political choices, if those political choices can have good results from the political or moral point of view. Although I believe that the lawyer must be critical and look at the law not only as it is but also as it ought to be (from a moral or jusnaturalistic point of view), I do believe that there is a vital distinction between those two aspects of his task. Whenever the lawyer is asked to give an opinion or to decide a case, he is bound to place himself on the basis of *lex lata*. It is only at a different stage — this is elementary — that the lawyer may feel called to argue about what the law ought to be, and indicate a political choice.

Strangely enough, although Professor Falk is extremely concrete in his approach to law, he seems to come near to Hans Kelsen in certain respects. I refer to Kelsen's tendency, particularly clear in his "The Law of the United Nations", to offer at times more than a single interpretation of a Charter rule (which is, of course, perfectly justified in certain instances) and to add that the choice is a political one, as such beyond the task of the lawyer (a point I would not find equally justified).

My humble view is that the lawyer finds himself quite often before alternative solutions, whether as a judge or as a scholar. I also believe that in any such case he will tend in practice to be conditioned, in some measure, by feelings, opinions, outlooks which can generally be indicated as political factors. It will thus not always be easy for him to be as neutral as he should be in deciding the case or expressing an opinion. I also believe, on the other hand, that the scholar's duty is to resist any political conditioning and to seek the objective legal solution. Much as this solution may be difficult to grasp, it does exist, and it is the lawyer's task to look for it as a legal, not as a political solution. Nor should he give up his task and leave the matter too easily in the hands of the politician.

YANKOV

Dick Falk insisted primarily on the dichotomy aspects, on the ideological division and their impact on today's international society. I think, however, that we should also try to search for the modalities (legal, sociological, or others) that will prevent this world from falling apart, and enable it to survive and overcome the divisions. I am not asking for panaceas or practical solutions, but I think this intellectual exercise would be more productive if, without neglecting the negative elements, we see what could be the modalities of convergence from the lawyer's point of view.

VIRALLY

I do not intend to speak about Professor Weil's article. A great deal has been said about it, much in the way that cinema critics speak about a film; that is, by seeing in the director's intentions a lot of extraordinary things that the director perhaps did not have in mind when he was making his film. Prosper Weil is not here to tell us what he was thinking; I think it is perhaps better not to make him say too much.

Perhaps I might try to bring what we are discussing down to simple terms. It seems to me that our problem, the one we are studying this afternoon, has three aspects. I would define them in the following way: there is the problem of the relationship between politicians and ideologies, that of the relationship between jurists and ideologies, and that of the relationship between law and ideology.

Politicians and ideology is a subject that a lot has been said about, and Professor Falk made some very interesting points about it. Clearly, our world is at present ideologically divided, and it is undeniable that the various governments often defend their interests under the mask — a word we have heard already this morning — of ideology. There is a real struggle here which is continuing, the effects of which we see every day. And it will of course have consequences for law.

Jurists and ideology is the subject which interests us most, I think. Here the problem I mentioned this morning arises: that of the jurist's function. More exactly, I think the plural should be used, the functions of the jurist. For the jurist does not always do the same thing. He may be an observer of the legal phenomenon, of the system of law, as it is presented to him, and may endeavour to describe it in the most exact way possible. In other words, he seeks, with greater or lesser success, to do a scientific job of describing reality. I recognize that we are weak, and that we have our prejudices, often ideological ones, that we are not neutral; but I nevertheless think it is our duty to try when we do that job, to do it I shall not say objectively, but in the most intellectually honest way possible.

For my part I am not ready to give up that role. But we may also think that in today's world, especially in international society, there are a number of problems that have been raised, and that have not to date found a suitable legal solution. Here the jurist will take a *de lege ferenda* approach and formulate solutions that seem to him to have to be applied to these problems. Here he will of course very often be inspired by a particular ideology. I think that none of us would agree to be hived off into that role of somewhat disembodied observer that I mentioned just now, and to be only a kind of cartographer of existing law. All of us, I think, also try to make proposals to advance the law. In this respect our position regarding our ideologies is quite different. We are committed. But I think — perhaps it may be rather idealistic or naïve on my part — that we must strive to keep these two jobs quite distinct. And to distinguish them still more from the job we sometimes have to do, a rather different one from those I have just described. It is no longer that of solving a legal problem, for the good of international society, but that of working for a government that has asked us to defend its interests and maintain a thesis. Then the jurist becomes an advocate; and here I think it is not so much the ideology that concerns him as the interests that he has to represent and defend. It is a jurist's job and an important one, but it must be very clearly differentiated from the foregoing ones.

For my part, then, I would be a supporter of a particular deontology of the "legal trade" based precisely on a clear distinction between functions that ought in my view not to be confused.

There remains the question of law and ideology. On this point, I think that there has been a very marked evolution over the last few decades in international law which has brought ideology increasingly into international law. This is an observation that we can make as academic jurists and therefore in the first of the roles I have just mentioned. Classical international law was doubtless inspired by an ideology, but an ideology that was nevertheless a fairly legal one, with the idea of legal security playing a very big part. The idea of legal security obviously benefited some more than others, but this was not very apparent in the context of a vision of the ideal society, which seems to me inseparable from the notion of ideology. Today, by contrast, with the development of human rights, the rights of peoples and the struggle against war, international law has a much more considerable ideological content. Despite the confrontations existing today between north and south, east and west, between those in favour of the State's monopoly in international life and – here I take up what Professor Falk said just now – those who on the contrary think that private individuals and the groups they make up also have a part to play; all the same, it seems to me that a certain number of convergencies have finally emerged. They are no doubt fragile and limited. Hence the difficulties we have encountered here in describing the state of international law; and it must be recognized that there still exists a wide margin of uncertainty. It is a fact that must be recognized; there may be convergence on a number of principles, but there is divergence on the scope and meaning of these principles. Here we find the problem of *apartheid* again, from another angle.

Perhaps the jurist's role is to recognize this reality and – here I am very pleased to come together with Professor Yankov – to seek to broaden by his proposals the areas of agreement, of convergence, that may exist and if developed may promote the development of law. But the jurist has to know what he is doing in this case: he is not simply confining himself to describing realities; he is trying to contribute to changing the law, which is also the role of doctrine.

SUR

I should like first to say a few words about the relationship between ideology and lawyers, and to indicate immediately that I find myself in rather complete disagreement with Professor Falk. I can perfectly well understand the anxiety he shows in connection with the maintenance of peace, in connection with this or that scandalous, inexcusable violation of humanitarian law. But I wish to argue here purely as a lawyer, and still more a man of doctrine, sticking closely to the distinction between the different functions of the lawyer just presented by Professor Virally. As a man of doctrine, I in no way feel, to refer to the analogy he made in his presentation, like a doctor. Professor Falk said that a doctor is not neutral with respect to an illness. I do not feel in any way a doctor, I feel more like a biologist, and it seems to me that the biologist does not choose between the microbes and the patient. The doctor's mission is to cure; he is concerned with eliminating the microbes. But the biologist studies the microbes' conditions of existence, and properly speaking, there is no professional ethic that brings him to a choice between microbe and patient. Accordingly, personally, I endeavour to make no confusion of genres. This does not mean that I do not in other respects feel myself a citizen or that I have no reactions. But they are part of my general political competence and not of the technical capacity I hope to have as a lawyer. This then is the first accusation I am putting forward, that of confusion of types.

There is a second one, which, it seems to me, is located on Professor Falk's own ground. It is that of the ineffectiveness or limited effectiveness of the approach he advocates. I have the feeling that we, as lawyers, and as men of doctrine, tend to be divided as to the analysis of positive law *tel quel*. The arguments we have show that there are a certain number of points of disagreement, though we argue on the basis of the same normative material. What will happen if we argue on the basis of different material, namely, the ideal organization of international society? We are likely to end up with a downright war of religion. There will be those who will plead for supranational organization, for the wearing-away of the sovereignty of the State, for the universal community of individuals; then others will plead for quite different forms, but equally ideological ones. I therefore believe that, far from reaching a normative consensus among the internationalists, we will be doing nothing but pursue a war of religion among ourselves. From the viewpoint of the efficiency sought for, this is perhaps not the best result that might be hoped for.

Still arguing along these lines, I add that I wonder if Falk's attitude is not founded on an overestimation of the role of law. Can we think that changes in legal rules will all of a sudden deeply transform international society? I take one example, that of the banning of nuclear weapons. It is clear today that there is a threat of use of nuclear weapons, and that this threat seems if anything to have increased over the last dozen years. Would proclaiming that nuclear weapons are contrary to international law, supposing that this is the positive law – which I for my part do not at all believe – deeply change behaviour, would it by enchantment, by a stroke of a magic wand cause the disappearance of existing stocks of nuclear weapons? I think that is rather doubtful. To the extent that this attitude carries with it the illusion of the independent effectiveness of a change in rules it departs from its object.

There is a second aspect of the matter, perhaps the most important one for this afternoon's discussion. That is the way in which ideology plays a part in the formation, the existence, the application of rules of law. In other words, what is the place of ideology in the legal system? This is an entirely independent question on which I should also like to make some observations.

It seems to me that in any organized legal system, there is an ideological element, hidden or apparent. But if there is an ideological aspect in every legal system, there is also another, which is the organizational aspect; and a third, which I propose to call the notarial aspect, namely the dimension of recording a given situation of fact.

Let us, for instance, take a constitution. An internal constitution certainly contains an ideological aspect; when it refers to such and such a model of political system, or proclaims given individual rights as human right. It also contains an organizational aspect, when it lays down public powers and organs. One might also say that it records a given factual situation, since this constitution is located at a certain stage in the historical development of the country, and therefore cannot be understood outside the situation which it transcribes.

The same thing might be said of the U.N. Charter. There exists an ideological part, found in the preamble, and also, to some extent, in Article 2. There is an organizational part which deals with the creation of the institutional machinery. And then there is also a part that records an existing situation, which one finds, for instance, in the composition of the Security Council, or in the voting rules. There are thus, in a sense, three levels in the legal system, but they are not located at different places in the system, and it is not even necessary to consider it as a whole in order to see them. They can be found within each rule taken individually, in varying amounts, and more or less obviously. They are the three dimensions of the system or of the rule.

Coming back to international society, it seems to me that one of the consequences of its ideological dislocation, or disruption, is a dissociation among these three levels. This means that relationships which in an optimally functioning system would take on ordered shape in an articulated fashion, in contemporary international society are disrupted. In other words, the international legal system can be read from an ideological point of view, and a certain number of rules will be found in it. It can be read from the viewpoint of organization, and other rules will be found, perhaps partially the same, but from a different viewpoint, differently interpreted. And it can also be read from the viewpoint of the situation of fact which it results from and which it transcribes.

One might take two examples to illustrate and conclude this idea. A first example from a rather special area, but one that has frequently been dealt with, is that of peace and security. We might say that there is an ideological vision of both peace and security in the United Nations, that there is an organizational vision, and that there is a purely notarial vision, that is, one that restricts itself to recording a given situation, a situation that exists independently of the rules.

The ideology of the maintenance of peace is disarmament. In the United Nations Charter and also in the resolutions adopted later, notably the 1978 resolution of the General Assembly, we have references, which are manifestly ideological, to universal, total disarmament. It appears here that the objective is to realize peace through disarmament. That is one level of the system; but not the whole system. For, partly in contradiction with it, we have the organizational level, which is that of collective security. This is represented by an endeavour to set up collective security mechanisms, organized round the Security Council. We therefore have a sort of dissociation or contradiction between the level of ideology and the level of organization. But there is still a third level, namely that which records the actual situation. In this case, it is the policy of arms control, which is in effect a mere recognition of the reality of the power relationships between the principal nuclear States, especially the United States and the U.S.S.R.

This is an example from a rather special area, but it seems to me that it can be taken to illustrate the disruption between these three levels in international law in general; it being understood that what takes place in the United Nations is a reflection of the situation of international law as a whole.

It might be said that there is an ideology of the United Nations. I am of course, oversimplifying, but it might be said that the principles of Third Worldism today constitute the basis or essentials of the ideology of the United Nations. This ideology makes international law into a law of the weak, whether these be individuals, peoples or minorities. Side by side with this, we have an organizational vision of international society, which makes it a law of equals, since it is States, and the principle of sovereign equality among States that dominate here. This is what conditions the formation of the rules that have binding value and are considered as binding by the States themselves. Then we also have the reality, the third level of the system where the law merely records a situation that it cannot control. It might be said that in this context international law is the law of the strong, the law of the powerful. It seems to me that a number of difficulties we are familiar with come from this dissociation between the ideology of the system on the one hand, and the regulation that it seeks to bring to intergovernmental relationships on the other; and finally, the purely material rules that record the real facts of international life.

Mendelson

I think a great deal of what I was proposing to say has already been said by Professor Sur more eloquently than I could say it myself, so I hope to be able to confine myself to a few quite brief remarks. In the first place, I would like to take objection to the statement in the position paper, that it is a commonplace that no law can be neutral, and the corollary from this dubious proposition which has been drawn by some today, including I think Professor Falk – that no lawyers can be neutral.

To take the easier part of the proposition, that no lawyers can be neutral, it is just not true. Professor Sur preferred the metaphor of biology to that of medicine; I think that metaphor in legal discourse is perhaps something suspect in itself. But if I can pursue Professor Falk's metaphor, if I were the doctor, and if I thought that cancer were a bad thing, I would not be doing my duty to the patient by misdiagnosing the illness as cancer when he had influenza! Secondly, I would not be doing him any service by operating on him for cancer if he had influenza. And thirdly, I would be acting quite wrongly if I let him die because I thought he was a bad man. In other words, we must try to see things objectively, and keep values in their proper place. Lawyers as citizens can express their own views; but if

I expound to my students what the law is on a particular aspect of, shall we say, the law of the sea, then I think I can do it in a neutral way. I may want to go on and express a view as to what I think the law ought to be, or what its deficiencies are; in the first place I am a citizen, and a citizen of the world, and secondly, I may have spent more time studying the problem than somebody who has spent his time doing something else. And therefore I do not think we should be too modest about this. But still, as Michel Virally said, we ought to strive to identify when we are speaking personally, and when we are trying to be scientific.

The more difficult part of the proposition is that law cannot be neutral. Now, I think that is only partly true. Obviously, for example, the Soviet or the Italian law of property is not ideologically neutral, in that it is based on a certain ideology about how property should be distributed in the community. But once you get to a certain point the rules become technical-legal and do not have any additional ideological charge. What is more, I think that even though ultimately a rule may have an ideological basis, it is quite possible for the law to be applied neutrally. And anybody who takes the oath to be a judge (not just an academic like us, but one whose job it is to apply the law), has a duty to apply that law in a neutral way. If he does not like the law, he should not be a judge. He must endeavour at least in clear cases – and I shall come back to the unclarity in cases in a moment – to apply the law neutrally.

So I think this is an incorrect proposition, and just to show that those who belong to the school of critical legal studies do not have a monopoly of self-righteousness, I should perhaps say that I think it is profoundly important that the law be applied in a neutral way, because without neutrality the law is nothing, the law is the embodiment of naked force. Its virtue is that it is neutral and that it can be applied in a neutral fashion. I do not think we need to be apologetic about this, or to feel that we are hiding behind any sort of professional cloak in order to avoid confronting the issues. There is an important contribution that lawyers can make to society by pointing out, as citizens and students of international relations, the defects in the way the international system works. But at the same time, we must retain our intellectual honesty. And I think it is quite unfair to accuse those who attempt to do this of academic dishonesty or lack of intellectual honesty, or anything of the sort.

Now, there are certain intellectual and philosophical underpinnings of Professor Falk's position which one cannot go into in great detail here, but I think there are two further things that I would just like to mention. One is that, if I understood him rightly, he said there is no mechanism whereby we can establish the correctness or falsity of positivism or natural law. Now, a great deal of what Professor Falk has told us today and on other occasions has been ultimately premised on the belief that there are some right answers somewhere, and even he purports to be giving us some. So there seems to be a contradiction in his position. By the same token, of course, it is true that some of the law is blurred; it is true that the law is fuzzy round the edges. But is is not fuzzy everywhere, and it does seem to me with the greatest respect (and I have great respect both for Professor Falk's intellectual powers, and also for the integrity with which he puts forward his views) that the kind of enterprise that he is encouraging us to engage in is a kind of self-fulfilling prophecy, because it is that kind of thing which helps to blur the law even further. But surely, to adapt what Wittgenstein said, at least part of the task of legal study ought to be to try and show the fly the way out of the fly bottle, not to introduce yet more flies and mosquitoes. It may be — I am sure it is the case — that, as Professor Falk has repeatedly told us, the world is on fire, and it is quite right that we ought not to be fiddling while the world (not just Rome) is burning. But equally I do not think that spitting in the wind is a way of putting out the fire. I think it is important that we keep our techniques as effective as possible in the hope, however vain it may be, of being able to contribute to the fighting of the fire.

BROWNLIE

I think I agree to a considerable extent with what Dr Mendelson has just said, but I would express it in a very different way. The matter can be approached by way of a performance evaluation of lawyers like Dick Falk, on a sort of curve. I think that for a very large part of the curve the performance is positive; we need people like Dick Falk; they keep public issues in focus, they expose hypocrisy, they challenge governments, they promote high-quality public debates (like the debate Falk promoted in the course of the Vietnam war), and they generally play an important public role. Now the point on the curve where the quality of the performance changes is when the question arises: where does this lead? Lawyers are like other professionals, like government officials, like people in the private sector. They have interests, they have religious views and views of other kinds and we are all, so to speak, framed by background. And of course it is necessary to point out the interests which lie behind ideas, so that even the concept of human rights is often used as a weapon, as a front for particular interests. The real question is, though, where does this lead? I would say that it does not lead to anything very positive; true, it avoids pointless idealism, it generates a certain level of constructive scepticism, and it gives us intruments for analysis. But only up to a point, beyond which in some ways it is destructive; because, although I would not go as far as Maurice Mendelson in taking the view that law is pure, nonetheless, the rules and institutions are the poor things we have available. They are an attempt, they are moving towards something new.

Dick's approach tends to lead us to the point where either law does have some imperfect but nonetheless objective role (it is a sort of new social reality, a form of dialectical change that does actually produce something valuable in itself), or we are, so to speak, only playing a part. We are like failed monks, who only live on in the monastery because the standard of living is good, and we keep the garden in some sort of order. Perhaps we are better gardeners than we are monks, and really we should be gardeners; we should give up the pretence. We should stop pretending we are lawyers and take up morality instead. And if in fact it is the case that law does have an objective role, that there is dialectical change, that the difference between morality and law is real, and law does provide imperfect but nonetheless valuable instruments, then Dick's approach beyond a certain point on the curve is negative. It causes demoralization. It criticizes the imperfect vehicle, almost to the point of saying the vehicle should not be used simply because it is imperfect. And there is even sometimes a certain tendency to say, because things are impure, because they are imperfect, they really should not be tolerated.

In real life, is it the case, for example, that the Law of the Sea Treaty (which is an attempt to mediate between all sorts of interests and which was worked out over a period of 8 or 9 years) is so tainted with ideology that it is of no use at all? It was a deliberate attempt to mediate between interests, and it is the expression of differing, but nonetheless to some extent convergent, ideologies – which is what a multilateral treaty is all about. And in the same way if you look at the institutions for the peaceful settlement of disputes which are not often used, you will see that there is quite a queue of material not just before the International Court, but before *ad hoc* tribunals, some of which are not even known about; but they are there, they are used, and quite important disputes are disposed of. For example, if two States of quite different backgrounds like Malta and Lybia take a case to court on the basis of a special agreement, it is interesting to analyze the different backgrounds of those two States. But the whole point of the adjudication is to try and cut through the differences of approach, the differences of culture, and to produce something new. There is a social value in adjudication. There will be compromises, but that is what the law is about: mediation between differing interests.

Lastly, I think that Dick takes a two-dimensional view of governments. It is very fashionable, especially for liberals, to attack governments almost as if they were obscenities in themselves. Some governments are. But some political organizations and some private organizations are obscenities in themselves too, and governments are often the vehicles of reform, and often prevent groups within the State from genocidal attacks on one another. In international law, whether we like it or not, the government of a State has a certain legitimacy. And a major power at the moment is intent on subverting the government of at least one small State precisely by challenging its legitimacy, and using externally supported groups to subvert it. I think, therefore, that we have to take a rather more discriminating view of the role of governments.

Abi-Saab

So many of the points raised deserve comment that it is impossible to do them all justice or to do it in a coherent way. I would like to tackle a few.

First, on the question of objectivity, I would like to recall Gunnar Myrdal's famous dictum that the only way of approaching objectivity in social science, within which I include law, is to reveal one's own subjectivities. There can be no absolute objectivity. Otherwise, we would not be needed, there would be computers which could process all legal propositions and come up with neat mathematical legal conclusions. Fortunately, judgment cannot be totally disposed of, and whenever there is judgment, there is an element of subjectivity, whether we like it or not.

Dick Falk was taken to task because he said that Prosper Weil's article was a piece of special pleading, prompted by nostalgia for a quickly receding world. I would like to come to his assistance on that point. If I may, with your permission, refer to a personal episode, Professor Weil presented the main lines of his ideas in a remarkable series of lectures at our Institute in Geneva before the article was published. In the seminar that followed the lectures, Professor Weil took the very strong position that resolutions have no effect at all. I threw at him the very famous paragraph of Lauterpracht's separate opinion in the *Voting Procedures on South-West Africa* case (1955), where he says that States have an obligation to consider in good faith the resolutions addressed to them, and that if they do not abide by them, they are under an obligation to explain why. His answer was: "If Lauterpracht was in the Court now, he would have said something different, because the majority of the General Assembly has changed". So much for objectivity.

Turning to Michel Virally's comment, I would say that there is always an advocate in the jurist, even when he tries to act as a dispassionate scientist. In this discussion we have called on biology, on linguistic philosophy, and even on the church; I would like in my turn to call on physics. We have been told that the jurist is not a doctor, he is a scientist like the biologist. But why does the biologist study microbes? Isn't it because, in the final analysis, he wants to find an antidote to them? Someone once asked Einstein – and this is where physics comes in –: "What is the difference between fundamental (i.e. theoretical) and applied science?" His answer was very simply "Twenty years". Why is it that fundamental research addresses certain problems? It is not "de l'art pour l'art", it is always because of the awareness that through it there is a social function that can be fulfilled later on.

This is why I think we should not really make too much of this so-called scientific attitude. We all strive to be objective, but within parameters which themselves are not completely objective. These parameters are values, and we cannot abstract ourselves from them. Now the positivists say "We act exclusively as scientists, making abstraction of values, and we only take reality as it is". But the way we see reality is affected by our values. Michel Virally says that classical international law was less ideological. Well, yes and no; because what was highly ideological (hence controversial) was kept out of the system. Most of the world was under colonial domination, and the Latin Americans, whenever they objected to any part of the system, were kept in their place by so-called "peaceful blockades" and other such "peaceful" means. If you remove the controversial issues from the system, by saying that they are not subject to the law, you reduce law to a relatively simple and seemingly objective set of rules of the game. But even these apparently innocuous rules were used or abused by those who subscribed to them against those who were excluded from their ambit. In other words, they served as a means of legitimizing and consolidating the interests and ideology of one group and its domination over the rest. Taken in this wider context, can they really be considered as less "ideological" or more "objective" than our present day international law?

On another level, I think that while the jurist has to be aware of the subjective elements, he has to strive to identify what is commonly perceived as objective, otherwise we cannot have an international law system accepted by everybody. But law does not have an embodiment except in words, and if we speak of custom it is not even embodied in words. So here we run again into a cognitive problem: how do we take cognizance of law? We perceive it through our eyes, which are subjective, whether we like it or not. There is always an element of interpretation in any rule, however clear we think it is, and most rules of international law are not that clear, whether they are written or customary.

It is here that the question of the role of the jurist comes in. How does he interpret a rule? Isn't he supposed to interpret it in the light of the general context within which it evolves? This is the famous intertemporal principle of interpretation that was formulated by the International Court of Justice in the advisory opinion on *Namibia*. Doesn't he have to take into consideration also the purpose and object of the rule? We speak of teleological interpretation of a rule; how about teleological interpretation of the system as a whole? It is not enough to posit your ideological wishes for them to become law; we all have certain constraining parameters within which we have to work. But these parameters leave us some margin, and within this margin, I do not think we can abstract values. If we do, we are in fact just sweeping them under the carpet. The so-called positivists, who say that they do not take anything into consideration but existing reality, really mean that we should uphold the *status quo*. But which *status quo*? In fact, their argument is much more ideological than it first seems. It reflects a basic contradiction with their premise. It is not consistently for the maintenance of the *status quo* whatever it may be; only the *status quo* which is compatible with their ideology and interests. In the library of the nostalgic, apart from Weil's article, you will find the famous piece that Sir Gerald Fitzmaurice did for the centenary of the Institute of International Law, as well as an article by Krystina Marek (in the *Annuaire Suisse de droit international* of 1982) entitled "Sur la notion du progrès en droit international". And what is progress for her? A return to the Congress of Vienna system. The Nirvana of such international lawyers is from Vienna to Versailles, the apogee of European colonial domination. This is a very political choice; and I do not think it is objective in any way.

To conclude, I would take an intermediate position between Dick Falk and the others. I would say we have to accept that rules are constraining, that we cannot really do violence to certain elements; but there is always a large margin for interpretation, and here we all interpret according to our own values. We cannot abstract values from interpretation. Nor can we avoid influencing the system through such interpretation, for there is no standing still in the dynamics of social systems. Isn't it better, in these conditions, rather than holding desperately to the mirage of objectivity (which is unattainable anyway), to recognize that all interpretation is more or less teleological, but to consider that it should be guided, not by the individual values of the interpreter, but by the values of (or emerging from) the international community itself at the moment of interpretation?

HAZARD

I have enjoyed hearing what everybody has said today, and I particularly liked Dick Falk's expression of "meta-ideology" about the struggles of East and West and North and South. I suspect that the third example that he chose (that is the struggle of mankind to protect itself against its States) is really the primary battle of the moment; and it is really what Ted Meron has been talking about all the time we have been here: that is, the human rights struggle. It is an effort to utilize international law, and hence international pressure, against one's own government, because internal forces have failed. This applies all the way across the board, East or West, South or North: everywhere there is the problem of protecting citizens against their own governments, and this effort is now spreading into the international world. I am reminded of the International Law Association struggles of years ago. Henry Cocheau created a committee to try and resolve some of the debates which were appearing within the Association between the East and the West; through his efforts that committee finally prepared a sort of code of peaceful coexistence, which finally took form in the U.N. Declaration on Friendly Relations, which Dick has held up as one of the examples of the right way to do things.

I quite agree with Professor Brownlie that international law does provide a medium for handling some of the concrete problems. He gave the Law of the Sea Convention as an example. Certainly there are many other concrete cases of this kind and the whole purpose of the Declaration on Friendly Relations, and the result of the discussion in the International Law Association, was to lead us to what Ted McWhinney of Canada always argues is the only thing that international law can do when there are struggles of this kind, that is take a step-by-step approach to concrete problems. That certainly appeals to me, but I find that we are not helped in our efforts by what the statesmen keep saying.

The Soviet jurist Professor I. Tenkov wrote that "Among the major aspects of this problem are methods of using the principles and norms of democratic international law in the interests of a revolutionary transformation of the world". Well, that frightens the West to death. If Igor Tenkov would withhold his rhetoric, from my point of view, it would be better, and of course the same thing may be said of a great many of the scholars in the West. My feeling is that we should all appreciate that the other side uses rhetoric to satisfy its own people: rhetoric is designed for the people at home. Unfortunately when it gets into the international arena, it only exacerbates conflict.

Of course we all do have an ideology, if ideology is defined in terms of a goal towards which we are moving, but to my mind we should not allow that ideology to blind us. I think Dr Mendelson is probably right when he says we can find areas of international law which are relatively neutral in which we can work, and I would leave to the politicians and the Foreign Offices the ideological struggles which they feel they have to conduct in order to satisfy their people.

VIRALLY

I am impelled to take the floor again by what Georges Abi-Saab said a moment ago. I am very largely in agreement with him, he will be surprised to hear, but with some qualifications that I should like to bring out. First, I am in complete agreement with him on the subjectiveness of the jurist. He mentioned physics; physicists themselves are at present wondering about the consequences of the scientist's subjectiveness on his science, however remote from the taint of subjectivity physics may seem. The important thing is to be aware, not only of our subjectiveness, but of our prejudices, which largely guide our thinking. This being said, I do not feel that one should give up the fight for greater objectivity.

Abi-Saab mentioned Einstein's saying that what separates fundamental research from applied research is 20 years. But 20 years is a long time, especially in science. It may mean that the person doing the applied research will be quite a different person from the one that did the fundamental research; there will have been a change of generations. In any case it indicates that there are two stages, and I think these two stages ought not to be confused. Before trying to be a doctor, before trying to apply remedies or make a diagnosis, one has to know the disease well. The biologist comes before the practioner. This is really what I meant just now when I spoke of the different functions of the jurist. If the jurist wants to participate effectively as such in the progress of international law, he must first of all understand what is not working well in international law, the real problems that it is facing, and therefore must look at reality in the most thorough, the most complete way possible. If he does not do this preliminary work, which is a thankless and difficult task, his proposals will probably remain mere wishful thinking, without much effect.

I have one other little point, in connection with the share of ideology in classical or modern, or recent, or contemporary, international law. There always is ideology, to be sure, but have we really asked ourselves today – perhaps this gives our debate a certain imprecision – what there is behind this word ideology? The word can be seen to have different meanings. We have taken it mainly – and I think this is the line that Professor Falk set us going along at the outset – as a synonym for values or system of values. This is one possible definition of ideology, but there are many others. When we speak of the ideologies confronting each other in international society today, we are using the word in another sense. Ideology here is a certain representation of the way society ought to be, or else, to take up the term used already, a mask placed over reality to cover up what it is. We have to agree, then, on what we mean by ideology.

It is clear that in a relatively unified world, as was the case in international society in the 19th century, ideology was not spoken about. There was no reason to speak of ideology when one more or less agreed on the dominant values of the legal system. Ideology begins to be spoken about when there is disagreement, as in the present situation. If values have to be spoken of, I think that, after having tried to get to know the law as it is, the jurist must seek to make proposals to improve it, and he must of course refer at that point to a number of values, which, I hope, he will formulate in precise fashion. But if the jurist is to enter the ideological fight, then that is quite a different thing. What I meant just now is that the jurist ought to avoid launching himself into the ideological fight. He ought rather to try to broaden the convergences that may exist between the various tendencies that are today fighting with each other in the world, rather than put himself in the pay of one of the fighting camps. These are the reasons for my reticence with regard to the adoption of an ideological position for the jurist. Once again, that does not mean that as soon as he ceases to be an observer and wishes to play an active role, he is not to stand up for his values.

I wish to finish with an appeal to modesty. Because we are jurists, because we have the feeling that we have a certain body of knowledge, that we represent a certain set of values, we hope to influence the development of international society through the changes that we propose to international law. Very well and good. But please don't let us entertain too many illusions; we must see that we probably have a more useful role to play trying to make others understand the state of law as it is today, with all its imperfections, rather than putting forward marvellous ideas that may be dear to us, but perhaps have no chance of ever penetrating into reality.

ARANGIO-RUIZ

First of all I want to join Michel Virally in what he just said on the distinction between the various tasks of lawyers. As I stated earlier, I believe in the triple distinction. There is just one point I should like to add, about values, also with reference to what was stated by Georges Abi-Saab. There is one particular value of which the jurist is a depository: stressing something which is probably in the minds of many, I would say that it is the value of existing law itself, and the necessity of respecting law as it is. That is an important, essential value. Certainty about existing law and the exact determination of the content of law at a given time in order to evaluate the conduct of States, is an essential function of the jurist. But that function would be lost if the jurist mixed up three different standpoints from which he should view things.

Professor Hazard made a reference to something said by Professor Falk about the Declaration on Friendly Relations being an example of the right way to do things. Now, I do not know exactly on what grounds Professor Falk believes the Declaration on Friendly Relations to be an illustration of the right way to do things. All I know is that on the prohibition of force, the only novelty in the Declaration is an express (interpretative) statement condemning armed reprisals; one and a half lines. The rest is merely repetition of what the U.N. Charter states: and there is not one word of precision on the permitted uses of force, simply because there was no possibility of reaching an agreement.

On self-determination, there is just a little bit of progress towards the express assertion of that universality of self-determination which is also surely embodied in the Charter. Anyway, even the explicit emphasis on universality was not made in such clear terms as those which were later to be used in the much shorter formulation of the principle in the Helsinki Final Act and in the Algiers Declaration on the Rights of Peoples, where you clearly have the universal conception of self-determination for every people, North, South, East or West.

There is a rather imperfect text on non-intervention, with regard to which the Special Committee was unable to proceed to a serious drafting effort as a consequence of a not unavoidable misunderstanding between the States rightly most concerned with that prohibition, on one side, and the United States and other Western delegations, on the other.

A serious step backwards was taken on the principle of peaceful settlement of disputes. Although the diffidence of a number of delegations towards the Hague Court was at that time justified by the Court's inadequately representative composition, it was absurd that no mention should be made of judicial settlement at all. In addition, while no step forward was accomplished in other "third party" settlement areas (such as compulsory arbitration and conciliation), the formulation of the principle unduly emphasizes the voluntary character of the procedures listed in Article 33 of the U.N. Charter. Finally, very little was accomplished — as a matter of progress — on the principle of cooperation; and nothing at all on the primacy of international law over municipal law.

How a "critical" progressive-minded international lawyer could be satisfied with such a meagre achievement I am frankly unable to tell. Of course, it was a diplomatic success, in the sense that a Declaration was "consented" to. But where does Professor Falk find the substance so satisfactory as to point at this as an example to be followed? I would be much more exigent in the search for a substantial enrichment of the Charter formulations.

Abi-Saab

There is a point I wanted to raise but forgot in my previous intervention; a point Professor Hazard has touched upon as well. It is the third ideological controversy or conflict: the "statist" versus the "grass-root" approach to international law. I am in great sympathy with the latter, but in this respect there is perhaps a difference in degree between Dick Falk and myself. My problem is that I have not found the way of squaring the following circle. International law is international, that is, between nations; it has been structured, tailored, constructed basically in this way. Of course it would be fantastic to find a way of having more individual initiative in putting into motion the mechanisms of international law. But how can it be done within the present system? This is a technical problem and I do not like paper victories, or people who say that because the individual can seize the European Commission on Human Rights, he has become a subject of international law. No. The individual will become a subject of international law only when it is a normal and usual thing for him to have direct access to the international level, which is not the case now. Is there a strategy of transition in that direction?

Yankov

I wish to refer again to the modalities and means that international law and international lawyers may offer to provide a better *modus vivendi* in this pluralistic and divided world. I myself have no prepared answers; perhaps Professor Falk could come to the rescue. The political and ideological dichotomy has occured in the last 5 or 6 decades since the emergence of the Socialist State and subsequently the international system of Socialist

States. The East-West relationship has indeed been a relationship between two social and political systems with their respective ideological implications and with the impact that this division has had on the international community. Nevertheless the world has survived and even during World War II, this ideological division did not prevent States from the different social and political systems from coming together and meeting the common danger to their own existence and the preservation of our civilization.

Are we not facing a world in such a critical situation that the very survival of mankind is at stake? What are the positive factors, or the constructive driving forces, which can challenge the imminent dangers? What should be the role of international law? A nuclear conflict of global dimensions would not result in winners and losers under the traditional concept of warfare. Everything would be at risk, including the very existence of mankind and its civilization. The contemporary world is facing a new challenge. Not to speak of other global problems which cannot be solved alone by any group of States, no matter how powerful it may be: global problems such as the protection of the environment, the rational use of energy resources, or raw materials, and the supply of food to the population of our planet, should be solved by common efforts of the international community as a whole.

FALK

What Professor Yankov has just said in fact about the degree to which our present situation is defined by a challenge that goes to the whole foundation of human survival, really underlies my whole perspective on the issues that we are discussing today. And it is precisely because Prosper Weil seems either indifferent or insensitive to that conditioning circumstance that I felt it was important to challenge that way of thinking about the role of law and lawyers; that it is not just a matter of one polemic versus another polemic. There is a historical situation that needs to be interpreted, and responded to, and some responses are constructive, others are evasive, and still others are actually regressive in their overall social impact.

I feel very challenged by many of the remarks and comments that have been made. I cannot possibly respond to them in any systematic way, but let me try to divide my response in this way: I shall first address myself briefly to what I feel are misunderstandings, then to disagreements, and finally to this challenge of Professor Yankov's to say something about the positive potential within the present setting.

As far as misunderstandings are concerned, my whole emphasis on what I called the meta-ideology domain, was intended (though perhaps I did not elaborate enough) in fact to affirm the importance of allowing international law to play a problem-solving role, and not in any way to denigrate that function. In fact the purpose is to try and expand it. But it was a misunderstanding to suggest that I thought the Declaration on Friendly

Relations was a great thing. All I meant was that I thought it was an expression of the maximum statement of East—West consensus on a framework for international law at this stage, and therefore illustrated this attempt to get even questions as seemingly political as are contained in that Declaration on to a meta-ideological level. I think the law of the sea and the kind of achievements that Ian Brownlie spoke of are extremely important, and nothing I have said was intended to denigrate in any way the importance of those achievements.

Furthermore, I completely agree with the view that there are different roles for the jurist to take and that the context shapes the form of legal discourse that is appropriate. If one is trying to convince the U.S. Government not to intervene in Nicaragua, one talks about the role of law in a different way than if one is talking about the legal issue to a group of Americans who are being asked to fight in that war. And it seems to me important to realize that we are often addressing different audiences. Putting it very bluntly again, there is a leaders' bias within the international law fraternity, particularly at its highest levels, that the only important audience are governments. That I reject on political and ethical grounds. Because if you accept that notion, then there is only one form of legal discourse, which of course emphasizes voluntarism and consent, and basically does not threaten a statist's view of the world in any fundamental way. But I think that is a profound disservice at a time of this overall international crisis. It is perfectly appropriate when addressing the International Court of Justice, to adopt a discourse that will be effective within that setting, but what I am really trying to say is that often international lawyers are reductive in their view that only one discourse is appropriate, and that is the discourse that is used in the highest levels of communication directed at governments.

Now, as far as disagreements are concerned, I think the biggest disagreement that I have been able to identify here is whether one should play the game of pretending objectivity and neutrality. I think that is a real disagreement. Again I am not suggesting the unimportance of trying to establish stable bodies of law in as many areas of international life as possible. But what I am suggesting is (and I think Georges Abi-Saab expressed it very succinctly by referring to Gunnar Myrdall's observation about suppressed and revealed preferences) that as jurists at this stage, confronted with a world that has much torment and many dangers, we cannot afford to reduce our perspective to one that purports to be only objective, and not to have important preferences built into the perspective that is adopted. It seems to me that the way one addresses these issues, for instance in an academic setting, is of course to indicate the various perspectives that can be taken, with regard to the controversial issues, but also to indicate those courses of legal development that seem to have the best prospect of fulfilling the positive or constructive role of international law in human affairs.

Again this brings me back to Ambassador Yankov's quite correct appeal to us to think positively and constructively and responsively on this survival agenda that exists at the present time. If I had to indict the legal profession at this point, it would be for its failure to devote sufficient attention to that survival agenda. This seems to me partly a choice that is dictated by an unwillingness to appear to take sides, to take on controversial questions, and by the greater vocational safety in appearing to be technical, to deal with a subject matter that is not threatening to governments or to other centres of power.

I suppose what I am appealing for in one sense is a recognition that a different set of priorities should determine the agenda of enquiry for the international legal profession, whether or not they agree with the particular preferences that I have associated with myself. Part of my criticism, and part of the reason why I expressed these views as strongly as I did, is that I think a lot of the international legal literature of the last 20 years is open to the criticism of tremendous trivialization of concern, given the problems of the world. It is that turning away from the real challenges of the real world that I think is a professional, moral failing. Again, I think that that turning away is in a sense turned into an ideology in the paper by Prosper Weil. I am sorry he is not here, or I would be even more direct. I don't like to talk behind his back, but I just feel that his paper is very good for the purposes of provoking a strong response, is a sort of centre-piece for discussion of this sort.

Let me finally come to this issue of what can be done positively. I have already suggested that the objective setting within which international law is unfolding at this time is one that suggests that the survival agenda be given tremendous importance, and that international lawyers should try to bring into the meta-ideological domain some very important and concrete issues. I agree very much with John Hazard that real progress is made when highly emotive issues can be reduced to concrete issues that can be solved. And I shall just mention three. First, the one we have discussed at different points during the day: to mobilize international legal opinion upon the importance of the unconditional prohibition of the use of nuclear weapons would seem to me to be an enormously important contribution to the future of humanity at this stage in history, and something which I think international lawyers in all political systems, should focus on. I think it could make a difference to the way in which governments perceive their choices. It would not be a determinative factor, but it would be a factor in the process of arriving at or sustaining official policies. Second, I think that the defence of the environment and the protection, conservation and development of resources in the world is a subject that could easily become meta-ideological and achieve tremendous practical results, if the efforts of lawyers were focussed upon it. And finally, the area of human rights, in its various dimensions, seems to me to be an extremely important one to emphasize. We should try to build as strong a meta-ideological foundation as possible beneath the demand for the effective implementation of human rights.

The final thing I want to touch on is this third dimension of the ideological battle-field, the State-society dimension. I was encouraged in the discussion by the fact that others felt, as I do, that this is really where the future lies, in the outcome of this ideological struggle. It is a very uneven world in this regard and there is no one right way to address the problem, which is different in the Socialist world, in the Third World, and in the liberal democracies of the West. I think one could develop a legal strategy within each of these settings, designed to take account of the realistic constraints and also the opportunities of working towards a stronger capacity of civil society to control the state. I am not sure that I accept Georges Abi-Saab's view that the essential victory would be achieved by individuals being given direct access to international institutions. That would certainly be an enormous symbolic and substantive achievement, but it seems to me that at this stage, part of what is at stake is the notion that governments are representing society and are not themselves autonomous, and that law in that sense ultimately belongs to society, it is not just the property of the State.

Part of what has happened during the period of the growth of the State is that is has become progressively detached, even in democratic societies, from its roots as a delegated body of authority that derives its ultimate legitimacy from civil society itself. It seems to me that part of the problem is associated with revitalizing democratic forms themselves. The most important issue, at least in the liberal democracies of the industrial world, is in the national security area, in the degree to which society has unwittingly created in these militarized States extraordinary arbitrary power that is not accountable to anyone. It is my belief that the reclaiming of that power is absolutely essential to the future functioning of democratic society. This brings me back to what Ian Brownlie said, namely that I seemed to be indicting the State as such. What I would really say is that the State is supposed to represent society and, to the extent that it is failing to do that, then it is very important to use whatever instruments we have (and I think international law is a very important one) to try to condition the behaviour of the State.

One of the things that is important – and here I speak somewhat provincially about some developments in the United States – is the idea that citizens have a direct legal interest in a lawful foreign policy. I would regard it as more important than the access to international institutions that individuals should have the right to insist on a lawful foreign policy, and that right was respected within the constitutional order. It would address many of the most severe abuses of State power in the world today. In my opinion jurists have been very slow to identify and articulate this as an important arena of struggle. The substantive importance of giving citizens in their own territorial domain the right to insist on a lawful foreign policy, and from the point of view of the Nuremberg principles, to make governments accountable in this way, was the basic attempt of positive international law after World War II. I think jurists have been very slow, because of the political sensitivity of this issue, to try to assert those ideas in an effective political way.

Part III

General Round-Up

by *Antonio Cassese*

1. Purpose of these Conclusions

As we pointed out in the Preface, the purpose of these concluding pages is not to summarize the whole discussion, much less to draw conclusions from the various views that emerged. As the participants dealt with the major themes from different angles, appearing to do so under different headings, my principal aim has been to bring their views together so as to offer the reader a fairly organic survey of the opinions expressed on each issue. I shall also emphasize major points of agreement or disagreement, to show the direction taken by the discussion and highlight the general trends that emerged.

2. The Classical Sources of International Law

In "revisiting" the sources of international law, custom undoubtedly attracted by far the greatest attention. By contrast, "general principles of law recognized by civilized countries" were widely played down as a law-making process that has proved sterile and is on the wane. As for treaties, the reason for the scant attention devoted to them in Florence lies perhaps in the fact that nobody casts any doubt on their importance; furthermore, after the adoption of the Vienna Convention of 1969, misgivings or apprehensions about the scope and consequences of treaties are gradually disappearing. Precisely the fact that this source is now consolidated, becoming relatively less problematical, probably led us to focus on other, more questionable or challenged sources.

As far as treaties are concerned, the role of "interministerial agreements" was the principal question raised (de Fiumel, Meron); in particular, it was asked whether they are different from inter-State agreements proper, and whether they belong to municipal law or to public international law. The other issue touched upon by some participants was the question of State succession with regard to treaties (Hazard, Abi-Saab, Graefrath).

3. Custom

Four major issues relating to custom were debated.

The first was the new role played by custom, or the *new "vitality"* of custom as it is sometimes called. It was generally agreed, in the wake of

Professor Jimenez de Arechaga's introductory remarks, that, far from being totally supplanted by treaty law, custom is enjoying "a new youth" in the world community. While in the fifties it was regarded by many States and scholars as a symbol of traditionalism, of *status quo* and stagnation, "it has functioned as an efficient mechanism, not just for law-making, but for law-reforming and the adaptation of fundamental rules to the new circumstances and requirements of the international community of today" (Jimenez de Arechaga). To a great extent this vitality is due to the proliferation of international diplomatic conferences in which all or most States of the world participate. These conferences serve as an important stimulus to the generation of customary law, in addition to the treaties agreed upon in these fora: "customary international law is thus secreted by the procedure for codification and progressive development, on the basis of the equal participation of all States and not by the *fiat* of a few preponderant States".

According to Jimenez de Arechaga (but his view was supported by others) the growing importance of custom is also due to the contribution of the International Court of Justice, which has played an important part in the "contemporary resurrection" of custom. Indeed the Court has dealt more with customary rules than with treaty norms; by so doing, it has helped greatly both to enhance the role of those rules and to clarify their import, the process by which they are formed, as well as their nature and constitutive elements. In particular, the Court has pronounced on regional custom; what is even more important, it has passed upon whether a customary rule should be supported by universal consent (according to Jimenez de Arechaga, the Court has rejected the voluntarist conception of custom, by not requiring "strict proof of the specific acceptance of the defendant State" – this view, as we shall see, was not shared by all participants in the dicussion).

A sort of summing up of the present role and configuration of the custom-creating process was given by Ted Stein, who took pains to contrast, "as a set of paired opposites", the "classic" and the "contemporary" process generating customary rules. Traditionally, general international law was unwritten, and unconscious; it was "accreted" (namely "generated over time through the accumulation of discrete instances"), and in addition it was generated through bilateral interchanges. Today custom is written, conscious, "instant and captured in some legislative formulation", and – what is even more conspicuous – it is generated "in settings where formal procedural rules of the forum have a tremendous influence", namely within diplomatic conferences.

The second major point stressed by many speakers was the *interaction between custom and treaty* (an issue on which Jimenez de Arechaga, Hazard, Graefrath and Abi-Saab particularly insisted). Everybody agreed that codification treaties, while they restate, clarify and supplement existing general rules, also contribute to the formation of new ones; in turn, customary processes on new matters often make it necessary for States at a later date to agree upon treaty rules that will provide the nuts and bolts of the matter, especially the mechanisms for ensuring compliance with the substantive rules. It was also emphasized that the respective roles of treaty and custom are in a way different from what they were in the past. As Hazard put it "customary law is taking the ascendancy at the moment. Treaties are now looked upon as a first step towards the creation of customary law, instead of the reverse. It used to be customary law that was put into treaties through the codification process, and now, to many people's minds, customary law is apparently created by the negotiation of a treaty; and even if not everybody signs the treaty, they are all bound by it, because it is custom". Graefrath stressed in particular that this interaction is made possible by the "common ground" of the two sources, "this common ground being agreement between States of one form or the other" (a conception of custom as "tacit agreement", that most participants, either implicitly or explicitly, did not share).

A sub-issue on which general consent emerged was the tripartition outlined by Jimenez de Arechaga — on the basis of the famous pronouncement of the International Court of Justice on the *North Sea Continental Shelf* case — by which a treaty can have a *declaratory, crystallizing* or *generating* effect; that is it can restate a pre-existing rule, or it can have the catalytic effect of consolidating an emergent customary rule, or it can constitute "the focal point of a subsequent practice of States which, in due course, hardens into a rule of customary international law".

By contrast, a third issue proved very divisive: that of *the role of the "persistent objector"*, in other words, the question whether a State can opt out of a nascent customary rule by manifesting its consistent dissent from the outset. It is apparent that this question is yet another facet of the question *consensualism v. universalism*, that is, the question whether international custom is based on (tacit or implicit) consent, or whether it is capable of binding even those States which oppose it from the outset. (Indeed this issue, discussed in the first round-table conference from the viewpoint of the functioning of the classical sources of international law, was taken up again in the second round-table conference, when the more general theme of voluntarism was tackled: see *infra*, para. 8).

A markedly consensualist approach was taken by some (Cassese, Graefrath, T. Stein, Weiler, Meron). Cassese stressed that the International Court of Justice seems to uphold the notion that a State cannot be bound by a general rule if there is solid evidence that from the moment when this rule emerged it consistently objected to being bound by it. He also emphasized that an important segment of the international community, namely Socialist States, insist on the voluntarist nature of customary law, and are not ready to bow to general rules to which they have not explicitly or tacitly manifested their consent; this should constitute a further element corroborating the consensualist approach, in view of the importance of this group of States. That Socialist States take this view was borne out by the comments made during the discussion by Graefrath, who pointed out that one of the basic trends of the present international community is the "continuing importance of the principle that States cannot be bound against their will, that a practice which is said to have a law-creating feature must also be the practice of the State concerned".

Ted Stein propounded two other reasons in favour of the notion of "persistent objector": first, "the consent idea has, and always will have, an enormously powerful moral as well as social strength; second, we have moved into an era where the most powerful States are no longer capable of controlling the customary international law process, as they once were".

On the other hand, Weiler drew attention to an apparent paradox, which in actual reality is easily accounted for by power politics: while in the traditional legal system Western countries, which set the pace of the international community, were "universalist" (hence tended to oppose any idea of a "persistent objector"), now they insist on this idea, for they are at present in a minority. Meron added that because of the "growing interplay of emerging treaty rules, and the many doubts being thrown on the past practices of forming customary rules, the role and the function of the 'persistent objector' not only continues to exist, but will be a very vital one".

A critical view of the notion at issue was instead taken by Jimenez de Arechaga and Abi-Saab. The former pointed out that at least some qualification was necessary. He observed, in particular, that "at least with respect to certain very essential norms of international law, there is a contemporary tendency not to allow individual 'persistent objectors', but only certain groups of States, to veto the establishment of a customary rule". He referred to the rule prohibiting *apartheid*, which, in spite of the opposition of South Africa, must be regarded as binding on *all* States (a point which was taken up in the second round-table discussion by Condorelli, Arangio-Ruiz and Cassese: see *infra* para. 8). In his view opposition can only come from *groups of States*; this is indeed so because the rule on *jus cogens* laid down in the Vienna Convention on the Law of Treaties (Art. 53), as well as Art. 19 of the Draft Convention on State responsibility (concerning international crimes of States), indicate that what is required is the consensus of the three worlds, for a general rule (of *jus cogens*, or on crimes of States) to be binding on all States. The inference was that also for "ordinary" customary rules such consent is necessary and sufficient. Jimenez de Arechaga also underscored an important point: to admit the possibility of "persistent objection" by a group of States, is not equivalent to holding a voluntarist view of customary law.

The notion under consideration was also considerably qualified by Abi-Saab, who stressed that, although in the beginning, when the rule is *in statu nascendi*, a State can oppose it, one should look at the process as a whole: "consolidation through widening acceptance, through the progressive 'erosion of oppositions', may come gradually as a cumulative process. In other words, what we cannot have immediately in final shape, should not be rejected completely, i.e. dismissed for being incomplete, as it may still be perfected, given time".

A major disagreement emerged both in the first and in the second roundtable dicussion on how the *International Court of Justice* approached the role of "persistent objectors" in custom formation. While according to Cassese and Sur the court basically upheld the doctrine of "persistent objector", Jimenez de Arechaga, Mendelson and Condorelli held the contrary view; in particular the latter stressed that the Court tends to emphasize the need for "general recognition" of State practice, for it to be regarded as the subject of a customary rule; this implies that the Court does not take either a strict voluntarist or a consensualist approach but tends rather to a middle-of-the-way view between voluntarism and majoritarianism.

A fourth issue also proved divisive: the question, to which De Witte drew attention, of the *role of the actual conduct of State agencies* vis-à-vis *formal pronouncements or declarations* of States in international gatherings in determining the formation of a customary rule. Various participants (including Gaja, Cassese and Meron) pointed to the difficulty of determining the role of the volume and consistency of State practice as distinct from official pronouncements in international bodies. In particular, Meron stressed the question of constitutional restraints on the power of State delegates to participate in a customary law-making process: in many States constitutional provisions do not allow State representatives to bind the State in a manner that could have repercussions on the fabric of municipal law. This could be a further argument for reducing the value of official pronouncements in international fora as opposed to the actual practice of State agencies (courts of law, State officials, combatants on the field, etc.).

This issue was discussed again, in the course of the second round-table discussion, under the general rubric "voluntarism v. majority rule". When this general theme was tackled, and the question of the role to be assigned to the actual conduct of States (as opposed to formal pronouncements in international fora) in the assessment of State acceptance of customary rules came up again, once more there was general disagreement. Cassese stressed the relevance of statements made by States in international gatherings, maintaining that even if they are not buttressed by actual State conduct, they may often be taken to express the legal view of States (Brownlie also implicitly took the same view). By contrast, Arangio-Ruiz, Virally, Gaja, Condorelli, contended that the decisive element is State practice, or the actual conduct of State authorities. Formal statements in international organizations or similar fora should be played down, for a number of reasons. Sur, in turn, considered the distinction between *opinio juris* and practice to be entirely academic, for the two notions are always bound up together and cannot be separated. As he put it, with regard to General Assembly resolutions, "If we start from a General Assembly resolution presented in the form of a declaration, in a certain way it is also practice. It cannot be considered *opinio juris*. It is at the very least practice in the context of the United Nations, laying down, for instance, the competence of the General Assembly to intervene in the area it is concerned with".

4. "General Principles of Law"

On "general principles of law recognized by civilized nations" opinions turned out to be divided. A group of participants took a very restrictive view of this source of law (Riphagen, Abi-Saab, Cassese, de Fiumel, Gaja). According to Riphagen, these principles constitute merely a starting point; their function is twofold: they take some rules deriving from other sources to their logical consequences, and they counterbalance rules deriving from other sources. In either case they do not provide solutions to conflicts between other rules; in other words, Riphagen felt the principles under consideration do not play any autonomous role in international law. Abi-Saab, in turn, emphasized that this is a source that in the last 20 years has not proved to be very fertile, probably because of the increasing tendency to emphasize voluntarism. The tendency of the International Court of Justice not to resort to principles was also stressed by Gaja and Cassese. The latter pointed out that the source created in 1920 as a result of the adoption of the Statute of the Permanent Court was partly conceived as a sort of heteronomous source, and this ran counter to the consensualist basis of international law. This, coupled with the present tendency of Socialist States to deny any role to those principles as a distinct source of law, should induce us to recognize a decline of this source. Probably, Art. 38 of the Statute of the International Court, in the provision referring to the principles, should be taken to mean those fundamental principles of international law which govern international relations (substantially the seven principles embodied in the 1970 Declaration on Friendly Relations, plus the principle on respect for human rights). A similarly negative attitude towards general principles was taken by de Fiumel who, however, played down their role for different reasons: in his view Art. 38 of the Statute of the Court "was conceived not so much as a catalogue of sources of international law but as a catalogue of sources of decisions of the Court". E. Stein, though he expressed his argument in dubitative terms, in fact contended that what appears on the surface as a promising method for determining the law, should in actual practice be discarded because of the "vast ideological differences in the world" of today, differences that do not allow for any common ground between States as diverse as the Socialist, Western and developing countries.

A more favourable attitude towards principles was taken by Jimenez de Arechaga, who stressed that, although rarely invoked by international courts, the principles referred to in Art. 38(c) may serve the useful purpose of stop-gaps in cases where treaty law and custom contain a *lacuna*; in this connection, he mentioned the equitable principle quoted by the Court in the *North Sea Continental Shelf* case.

5. The Role of General Assembly Resolutions

In addition to traditional sources of law, participants in the round-table discussion also focussed on the possible role in international law-making of resolutions adopted by international organizations, with special emphasis on resolutions passed by the U.N. General Assembly.

It was unanimously agreed that resolutions *per se* do not make up a distinct source of international law. However, beyond this common proposition, views differed. While a rather negative stand on the "normative" role of resolutions was taken by Condorelli (particularly in his introductory remarks on the subject), Gaja and Yankov, by contrast, and Jimenez de Arechaga and Abi-Saab drew attention to the remarkable contribution that resolutions can make to other law-making processes. In particular, the former made two points: first, resolutions may constitute "an appropriate vehicle for reaching consensus and determining the agreement of States on certain rules governing their conduct"; second, they can have the same effects treaties have vis-à-vis custom: "declaratory" (they restate existing rules), "crystallizing" (they consolidate emerging rules) and "generating" effects (in that they constitute a "model of conduct" that can subsequently become an established standard of behaviour endowed with legally binding value). Abi-Saab, in turn, drew attention to two possible roles of resolutions: first, they can have a "destructive effect" on existing rules, in that they show that the majority of States no longer considers a certain customary rule to be supported by the requisite *opinio juris* of the whole world community. Second, they can constitute the "building-blocks" for the creation of a new rule, in that they register how positions of States converge and reflect the emergence of some form of consensus on a given matter.

One special issue was also the subject of some discussion: the question whether a resolution can be regarded as an *agreement* concluded, in simplified form, between the States voting for it. I have just recalled that this was indeed one of the possibilities envisaged by Jimenez de Arechaga. De Fiumel, though he agreed to some extent, felt however that this sort of agreement can only be concluded within the context of regional organizations based on economic and political integration (and he quoted Comecon as an example). By contrast, two other jurists, Gaja and Condorelli, did not agree at all. They both emphasized, among other things, that normally the State representatives who participate in the discussion and adoption of resolutions within international fora do not possess the full powers normally required by their respective constitutional systems for entering into internationally binding agreements.

6. Lex lata and lex ferenda: still a viable Distinction?

Of course, the role and significance of resolutions adopted by international organizations came up again when the discussion moved on to the crucial issue of the distinction between *lex lata* and *lex ferenda* in the international community. The debate revolved primarily around the question whether this dichotomy still plays an important role in international law, or whether it has been gradually eroded by the emergence of new forms of standard-setting which beget precepts that, though devoid of legally binding value, are nevertheless more compelling than moral or political guidelines.

Various questions were debated. First, it was pointed out by Ambassador Yankov that the aforementioned distinction is fairly easy to apply in municipal law, where the State apparatuses (and, in particular, courts of law) are called upon to decide whether certain standards of behaviour have turned into binding law; by contrast, in the international community no international agency is vested with the power to make such a determination *erga omnes* with binding effects. As a consequence, while the distinction remains crucial, it proves difficult to apply. In Yankov's opinion the ultimate test must of necessity be "the intentions of States", because "the coordinated wills of the States concerned constitute the foundation of the emerging rules".

A second point, eloquently made by Brownlie in his introductory remarks, is that the emergence of "*soft law*" (that is that corpus of standards living in a twilight area between non-law and law proper) has come about because diplomats (and politicians) decided that it was convenient to create this sort of precept. In other words, soft law was not invented by jurists, but was deliberately chosen for reasons of expediency by diplomats who thought it fit to argue upon vague and sometimes even ambiguous tenets, devoid of that special force which characterizes legal rules. Jurists only coined the phrase (which goes back to Lord McNair, as Abi-Saab recalled, adding that the great British jurist used it in a context and with a meaning that were slightly different).

A third point was made by several participants, who stressed that we are now witnessing *a blurring of the distinction between lex lata and lex ferenda* in international law (Brownlie, Arangio-Ruiz, Condorelli, Suy, Cassese). Some considered this phenomenon negative in some respects, for among other things, it helps to complicate the body of international law or to cast doubts on certain existing rules (because of the claim that new standards — termed soft law — are now replacing them). Instead, according to Abi-

Saab, one should not be afraid of soft law making its appearance on the international stage, if only because one ought to take a broad view of law. As Abi-Saab tellingly put it, law is not created as a result of a "big bang": it would be unsound to believe that "there is a legal 'vacuum', then suddenly there is a big bang bringing with it something into 'being', and that something is the law". Rather, when scrutinizing law, one should take into account the preceding steps as well, that is the whole process that leads to the solidification of normative standards of behaviour into norms endowed with binding force. If one broadens his perspective so as to include the whole norm-creating process, the appearance of soft law becomes the crucial stage if we are to understand what law is and what its contents are.

Despite slight differences about the positive or adverse effect of the emergence of soft law, it was generally agreed that its existence cannot be denied. The important issue then became, in the eyes of many, to *ask why this class of law is so conspicuous in the present international community*. Answers were principally given by Condorelli, Suy and Cassese. Although their arguments were more or less elaborate and detailed, their explanations boiled down to the following proposition: the present world community is riven by deep tensions; it is too conflict-ridden to allow for any possibility of easily hammering out rules of law acceptable to all member States, especially in such new areas as outer space, human rights, environment, economic relations. Whenever there are too many insurmountable clashes, yet the political will of States exists to endeavour to reach a modicum of unity, that is to agree upon some loose blueprint for political action, States fall back upon soft law, i. e. guidelines of a sort which might, in the long run, harden into binding rules of behaviour.

Another important issue dealt with by various participants related to *methodology*. As Brownlie pointed out, and Virally, Abi-Saab and Condorelli stressed, to grasp the purpose of soft law one ought always to distinguish between the *content* of the standards (which may or may not make up soft law) and the *instruments* by means of which those standards are enacted. If one bears in mind this distinction, the identification of soft law becomes much easier. For there may be provisions which, though contained in such legally binding instruments as treaties, are so loose in character or so woolly that they cannot be regarded as belonging to the domain of law proper. By contrast, there may be international acts such as the Helsinki Declaration, and at least some General Assembly resolutions, which include stipulations worded in precise and accurately drafted terminology. They can either restate existing law, or contribute to its formation, in particular by the "catalytic effect" to which Brownlie and Gaja drew attention (as the former rightly noted, some "informal prescriptions" of unilateral declarations such as the Truman Proclamation, may have a "catalytic effect" in that they gradually prompt authoritative decision-makers to uphold their normative elements as legal rules; Gaja underscored in particular the role of the *dicta* of the International Court of Justice). Another point made by various participants, also related to methodology, concerned the *tests for ascertaining* under what circumstances a certain standard ceases to be soft law and becomes law proper, (or hard law). Here Cassese drew attention to the importance of a three-pronged test expounded by Abi-Saab in a U.N. paper. Abi-Saab had stated there that one ought first of all to look at the circumstances surrounding the adoption of a resolution or a similar document, so as to infer the intentions of the parties concerned about the value they intended to assign to the instrument. Second, one should examine the degree of concreteness of the contents of the document. Third, one should see whether some sort of device exists for ensuring compliance with the set of guidelines laid down in the document. The basic ideas behind this tripartite distinction were upheld by Meron, among others.

In addition to these distinctions and clarifications general agreement emerged on three points. First, soft law constitutes an "intermediate stage" (as Yankov put it), between the realm of political and moral standards and the area of legally binding rules. Yankov stressed that "in some instances States themselves prefer to establish rules which may entail certain political commitments but do not provide for legal obligations"; in these cases it may prove "more fitting to work out general guidelines or recommendations which, *strictu sensu*, are not binding, but would be at the disposal of governments for use at an appropriate moment". Second, guidelines and standards belonging to soft law do not necessarily become part of the *corpus* of legally binding norms (special emphasis was put on this point by Arangio-Ruiz, Suy, Virally and Meron). Third, as Brownlie emphasized in his concluding remarks, whatever school of thought one may belong to, what matters is that jurists still think that there is a "threshold" between non-law and *lex lata*, between soft law and law proper; in other words, one of the principal postulates of legal positivism is still widely upheld, in spite of the differences in emphasis on the importance of the standards of behaviour that inhabit the twilight zone we now term soft law.

7. Is there a Hierarchy of Rules within International Law?

It is apparent that the question whether a nucleus of international rules or principles that rank higher than other rules exists at present, coincided with the question whether *jus cogens* exists in the world community.

Several points were made here. First, a few participants emphasized that no society with a minimum of structure can live without granting a higher value and rank to some fundamental principles, placing them above the main body of legal rules (Abi-Saab, Suy, Virally). In particular, Abi-Saab reminded critics of *jus cogens* (who object that no real consensus has emerged on the contents of this class of principles) that even as an "empty box" *jus cogens* is necessary, "because if you do not have the box, you cannot put anything in it. Without having the category we cannot have consensus on *which* rules do or can belong to this category". He also pointed out that if one considers international law from a purely voluntarist view-point as an amalgam of agreement, a "unicellular system", "at the lowest, amoebean, stage of evolution", one may well wonder whether "such a legal system /can/ govern the international life we are living now, with all its complexities, with its incredible pace of change, with its great and increasing degree of interdependence in the material relations of production and exchange of goods and services". That such a primitive and rudimentary legal system could govern current international realities, was, in his view, an impossibility.

A second point concerned *the way peremptory principles or rules can emerge*. In this connection, Yankov stressed that the ulitmate test is always the will of States, which are basically "the law-making agents in international law", although to his mind, international organizations as well can play a role in some instances. This view was echoed by Virally and Mendelson. The latter drew attention to the fact that the international community *as a whole* must be agreeable to a certain principle having the nature of a peremptory rule. Cassese pointed out that *jus cogens* suffers from the limitations inherent in any sort of international law-making: only those States which do not object to the emergence of a certain rule are bound by it; consequently, even peremptory rules cannot be imposed on those States which, from the outset, consistently objected to the formation of the rules.

A third issue, on which a fair amount of agreement emerged, was the *scant importance* of *jus cogens* (Arangio-Ruiz, Brownlie, Meron, Suy, Cassese, Virally). There was agreement that this class of rules constitutes neither a miraculous cure for the ills and deficiencies of the international community nor an abomination capable of disrupting the very fabric of that community. The difficulty of identifying those principles on which real consent exists to the effect that they belong to *jus cogens*, makes for the scant importance of this category. At any rate, it is beyond doubt that hitherto *jus cogens* has not played a major role. As Brownlie put it, "The vehicle does not often leave the garage", and Meron observed that "on the practical level ... the usefulness of the concept is mostly potential". However, individual participants gave illustrations of what they regarded as undisputed principles of *jus cogens*. Thus, Meron cited the rules on torture, genocide, arbitrary deprivation of life. Arangio-Ruiz, Abi-Saab and Cassese mentioned the prohibition of the use of force.

Another important point was the impact that the inconsistency of a treaty with a rule of *jus cogens* can have on *third States*; if a bilateral agreement is contrary to *jus cogens* and neither contracting party relies upon *jus cogens* for the purpose of disregarding the agreement, can a third State claim that the agreement is null and void? Cassese said it could; he mentioned the case of the 1978 treaty of alliance between the U.S.S.R. and Afghanistan, on the strength of which Soviet troops used force in Afghanistan; he recalled that in 1979 the legal advisor to the U.S. State Department stated that that treaty was contrary to a principle of *jus cogens* (the prohibition of the use of force). He added that that statement could be (and probably had been) used in the United Nations to object to the Soviet resort to force (at least to the extent that such resort had been justified by the U.S.S.R. on the strength of the aforementioned agreement). This view was attacked by Mendelson, who contended that for a State to say that a treaty between two other States was a nullity on account of its being contrary to *jus cogens* was an assertion which "in normal circumstances would have no practical effect". Virally shared this view, and pointed out that in the instance made by Cassese "the consequences are extremely slight as far as law goes".

Finally, a few participants (Suy, Virally) thought that, in view of the scant importance *jus cogens* currently has in the field of the law of treaties, one should probably raise the question of whether it can play a more useful role in *the area of State responsibility*, where the distinction between "international crimes" and "international delicts" appears to a large extent related to the concept that a *corpus* of peremptory principles enjoys a higher status than other international rules.

8. Voluntarism versus Majority Rule

In the position paper circulated to the participants by the two convenors of the meetings, the general question was raised whether the international community is still governed by a law resting on the will of all member States, or whether instead some form of law-making process has evolved that is capable of binding even those States which have either refrained from expressing their consent or have even objected to the formation of the relevant rules. In particular, the issue of the "persistent objector" was raised. Another issue discussed was how to determine the position of a State and its acceptance (or refusal) of an international norm: through its statements in international fora or through its actual conduct? On the general question of voluntarism versus majoritarianism, several trends emerged.

According to some participants (Arangio-Ruiz, Brownlie, Yankov, Sur, Cassese) there are no signs to show that *voluntarism* has, in any way, been superseded by majority rule. However, within this general approach, only a few participants (Yankov, Cassese) went so far as to assert that all international law is still based on State consent. Yankov, in particular, pointed out that the international system has not changed from its 19th century structure and remains a system based on sovereign States: they are "the main agents of the law-making process where the basic rule is the consent between them".

A moderate or revised version of voluntarism was instead advocated by others, who insisted on the concept of "persistent objector" (Arangio-Ruiz, Sur).

They felt that, although one cannot say that all rules of international law rest on the (explicit or tacit) consent of States, still a State can opt out of a customary rule by consistently expressing its dissent at the moment when the rule is being formed. Both Arangio-Ruiz and Sur took pains to emphasize, however, that the present conditions of the international community make the role of "persistent objector" more and more difficult, thus minimizing the role of dissenting States vis-à-vis emerging rules of customary law. As Arangio-Ruiz pointed out, "in the contemporary, much more interdependent, international society, the dissenting position of a State (or group of States) may in the long run become untenable with regard to certain matters: for example, in the area of so-called North-South relations. It is absurd that we should go on living in an international society in which such blatant inequalities are maintained. This and other considerations may well contribute to inducing the dissenting States to give up resistance". Sur added that some flexibility has to be introduced into consensualism. By way of illustration he recalled that while in treaty law flaws in consent are accepted if they are aimed at protecting the authenticity of the State's consent, there is no such rule concerning flaws in consent to custom, and "this shows that there is less protection of consent to customary law". In addition, he stressed a more general point; in his view, one ought to distinguish between the existence of a rule and its opposability. A majority of States may well set up a rule which it claims to be general; if, however, a State has consistently objected to such a rule from the outset, the rule cannot be opposed to it. In Sur's opinion "this distinction between the existence and the opposability of the rule to some extent reconciles the apparent contradiction between majority formation of general rules and the possibility that one State should not to be bound by them".

A different stand was taken by Condorelli. In his opinion the majoritarianist opposition to voluntarism is false, "because one can well reject the first without necessarily accepting the second". In his view, the formation of customary rules is not exclusively dependent on the consent or acceptance of all the addressees of a rule. When appraising whether a customary rule has evolved, one ought to take into account not only consent or agreement proper, but also a whole range of possible attitudes "going from simple silence to occasional, unrepeated protest against a particular situation or claim"; in his view, these various attitudes could be regarded as in some way playing the role of consent. The conclusion he drew was therefore that a rule of general international law "may very well bind a State which has never – whether explicitly or implicitly – expressed its wish to accept the rule in question. In other words, the formation of the general customary rule can be established through a flexible, global evaluation, aimed at assessing in synthetic fashion the whole set of behaviours, actions and reactions of the social actors, and not aimed at counting their consents analytically and adding them up. Moreover, isolated non-acceptance by this or that State would not be enough to prevent the formation of a customary law, in the face of what the International Court of Justice calls 'general recognition' of such a rule". Condorelli added that the doctrine of the "permanent objector" is unsound, as is proved among other things by the fact that the rule prohibiting *apartheid* binds South Africa in spite of the latter's opposition: actually, Condorelli felt the case of *apartheid* was the "stumbling block that the voluntarist conception inevitably comes up against" (this instance was however interpreted in quite a different way by Cassese and Arangio-Ruiz, who gave a "voluntarist interpretation" of the behaviour of South Africa, even though they reached the same practical conclusions as Condorelli).

Yet another view of the voluntarism-majoritarianism opposition was expounded by Falk. He considered that one is actually confronted with a "choice between *unilateral* and *collective modes of realizing national interests in the world*. Those who see more collective procedures as serving their national interests, necessarily tend toward majoritarian forms of legal reasoning; those that see themselves on the losing side of majoritarian political processes naturally incline towards unilateral and highly positivistic forms of legal reasoning".

9. Can International Law and International Lawyers be Ideologically "Neutral"?

The position paper circulated by the convenors of the round-table discussion, stated bluntly that international law, just like any other form of law, is bound to be loaded with ideological or political values. In other words it is not neutral — although in the past there was considerable harmony between the ideological underpinnings of international law and the principal actors (the European States plus their offspring, the United States). The position paper then raised the question whether international lawyers can be neutral, faced, as they are, with conflicting values and political postulates in a divided world. This approach gave rise to a sharp difference of opinion both as regards the neutrality of *law* and that of *lawyers*.

As to whether international law can be neutral, two main trends emerged. Many participants (Falk, Weiler, Virally, Sur, Abi-Saab) contended that at present international law is strongly marked by ideology, although views differed, as I shall soon show, on which values make up the ideological content of law. Before turning to this point, let me emphasize another disagreement. According to Virally, classical international law was less ideologically loaded; although it was admittedly inspired by an ideology, this was nevertheless "a fairly legal one, with the idea of *legal security* playing a big part". Instead, — still according to Virally — present international law has a greater ideological content, chiefly as a result of the doctrines of human rights and the rights of peoples and of the struggle against war. A different view was put forward by Abi-Saab. For him, classical international law appeared to be less ideological only because highly ideological (that is, controversial) issues were kept out of the system: most of the world was under colonial domination, hence it was unable to propound ideas and doctrines at odds with those upheld by the dominating European or American Powers; in addition, even the *corpus* of law created by those Powers was ideological in that it served to legitimize and consolidate their dominating position.

The content of the ideology or ideologies currently inspiring international law was also the subject of interesting differences of view. According to Falk, at present there are *three kinds of ideological struggle* of importance: the rift between socialism and capitalism, the tension between the industrialized and the developing world, and the conflict between State-power and civil society (the tendency of governments to monopolize the whole life of their societies and the conflicting struggle of individuals, private groups and the community at large to participate in some way in international action or to condition the foreign policy of their governments, in particular, by making them respect certain fundamental international standards).

A somewhat different stance was taken by Sur. In his view, any legal system is on *three levels*: ideological, organizational and "notarial" (in that it records a given situation of fact). In the international community, the present ideological disruption brought about by the existence of conflicting ideologies causes a "dissociation" among the three levels (for instance, in the field of peace the U.N. Charter is based on the ideology of disarmament, while at the organizational level it has established a system of collective security, which in turn does not correspond to what law — as the registration of reality — really provides for, namely a policy of arms control).

All the participants I have mentioned so far took the view that at least in its present form, international law is not ideologically neutral. An opposite view was advocated by Mendelson. He felt that although some segments of the *corpus* of international law can be ideologically loaded, beyond a certain point the rules become purely technical, without any additional ideological charge. Furthermore even though a rule may ultimately have an ideological basis, "it is quite possible for the law to be applied neutrally".

So much for the question whether international *law* can be neutral. However, the bulk of the discussion concentrated on the related question of whether *international lawyers* can or ought to be neutral. Here three basic positions emerged. Falk took the extreme view that the lawyer can never be neutral or objective. On the opposite side, Arangio-Ruiz, Virally, Sur and Mendelson contended that if the lawyer does not at least endeavour to be as impartial and independent as possible, by putting his ideological leanings on ice, he can help to disrupt the international community or, at any rate, does not respect the role with which he was entrusted. A third, intermediate stand, was taken by Weiler, Brownlie and Abi-Saab. Let us briefly survey these three different views.

According to Falk, the jurist is like a *doctor*, who is not expected to be neutral toward diseases: likewise, the international lawyer cannot be neutral about violence, torture, genocide, ecological decay, the nuclear threat, and so on. In particular, the nuclear threat and, more generally, the issue of nuclear weapons, makes it impossible for the jurist, at this stage in international society, to take a strictly voluntarist or positivist view of law. This however, does not mean for Falk that the jurist should become an "ideological mercenary" or "advocate partisan positions under the guise of scholarly objectivity". Rather, he maintains that the boundaries of international law are currently so blurred, the international community is beset by so much legal uncertainty, that any lègal enquiry into the major issues confronting the international lawyer today presupposes a political choice. In particular, the jurist can no longer be positivist, for positivism was well suited to 19th century society, when States were in agreement and in control; today, *non-State actors* have emerged and to stick to positivism could, among other things, lead the jurist to neglect or, even worse, to sweep under the carpet, this important novelty of the 20th century world community.

This view was criticized by Weiler, Arangio-Ruiz, Virally, Sur, and Mendelson. According to Weiler, Falk's critique of scientific jurisprudence as being a mere pretence to scientific objectivity can only be justified to the extent that it is made in a society where lawyers are at work who keep up "the fiction, for good or for bad, that law is real". Should the "society of lawyers" be destroyed along with their pretence to scientific jurisprudence, then we would no longer be able to enlist "the whole set of normative associations that the word law carries with it". More radical was the criticism levelled by other participants. Thus, according to Arangio-Ruiz, the jurist must always resist any political conditioning and seek the "objective legal solution". As a citizen, he can of course propose changes in law and even take action to achieve these changes; but in his capacity as a scholar, he must always shun political choices. This stand was taken by Virally as well, who also pointed out that the jurist should try to keep the two jobs (as interpreter of existing law, and as the proponent of legal changes) quite distinct. Although the jurist cannot of course "be hived off into the role of somewhat disembodied observer" nor into the role of "a kind of cartographer of existing law", still it is his duty, when acting as a scholar, to do his job "in the most intellectually honest way possible".

Sur took exception to Falk's definition of the lawyer as a doctor. In his view, the jurist was to be equated with the *biologist* instead, who does not choose between the microbes and the patient. The doctor's mission is to cure the patient by eliminating the microbes; the biologist studies the microbes' conditions of existence and virulence. A second criticism put forward by Sur was that the approach advocated by Falk has limited effectiveness. While at present jurists tend to argue on the basis of the same normative material, a downright "war of religion" would break out if jurists were to argue on the basis of "other material", namely the desirable or ideal organization of international society: "there will be those who will plead for supranational organization, for the wearing-away of the sovereignty of the State, for the universal community of individuals; then others will plead for quite different forms, but equally ideological ones". A third criticism was that, in actual fact, Falk's approach to law was founded on an overestimation of the role that law can play and actually plays in the world community. In Sur's view, changes in legal rules, or their possible perfecting, cannot deeply transform the international community all of a sudden. As an illustration of his view, he mentioned the case of nuclear weapons: "Would proclaiming that nuclear weapons are contrary to international law ... deeply change behaviour, would it by enchantment, by a stroke of a magic wand, cause the disappearance of existing stocks of nuclear weapons?" His reply to this query was at least doubtful.

Another critic of Falk's stand was Mendelson. In addition to taking up the arguments put forward by Arangio-Ruiz and Virally on the need to keep the different roles of the jurist distinct, he emphasized that a great many of Falk's arguments were ultimately premised on the belief that there *are* some right answers. This Mendelson considered to be a contradiction: on the one hand, Falk argued that there is no mechanism whereby we can establish the correctness or falsity of positivism as opposed to natural law or to meta-legal tenets, but, on the other hand, what he himself stated was ultimately premised on the belief that there are some right answers, and he purported in fact to give the right answers. A second criticism was that, in a way, Falk helped to make law even more blurred than it actually was.

An intermediate position between those of Falk and his critics was taken by Brownlie and Abi-Saab, although with different motivations.

Brownlie observed that Falk's arguments should not be dismissed out of hand. These challenges were very helpful in keeping public issues in focus, in exposing hypocrisy, in challenging governments and promoting high quality debates on law and legal institutions. However, for Brownlie, this sort of approach was only helpful up to a certain point; beyond that point in some ways it became destructive because, among other things, it generated demoralization. In a way, Falk's contribution could be drawn as a curve: up to a point the performance was good, but then at a given point of the curve it became negative, and this was the point where the question arose: where does this sort of approach lead? The destructiveness of Falk's approach lay in this: "It criticizes the imperfect vehicle /i.e. law/ almost to the point where the vehicle should not be used simply because it is imperfect".

The middle-of-the-road stand taken by Abi-Saab was somewhat different. To emphasize that there can be no absolute objectivity he recalled Myrdal's famous dictum that the only way to approach objectivity in social science is to reveal one's own subjectivities. However, while the jurist ought to be aware of the subjective elements underlying his views, he should strive "to identify what is commonly perceived as objective; otherwise we cannot have an international legal system accepted by everybody". In his view, there are always in the legal system "certain constraining parameters" within which the jurist can play his role as an interpreter; these "parameters" cannot be waived or ignored, if one intends to uphold intellectual honesty and impartiality; however, within the margin left by these parameters, the jurist tends to interpret rules according to his own values. "We cannot abstract values from interpretation. Nor can we avoid influencing the system through such interpretation, for there is no standing still in the dynamics of social system. Isn't it better, in these conditions, rather than holding desperately to the mirage of objectivity (which is unattainable anyway), to recognize that all interpretation is more or less teleological, but to consider that it should be guided, not by individual values of the interpreter, but by values of (or emerging from) the international community at the moment of interpretation?"

10. Final Remarks

The foregoing survey is of necessity incomplete, nor does it do justice to the flavour and richness of the lively discussion which took place in Florence, a discussion which was not at all a dialogue between the deaf, but a vivacious and animated exchange of views. This survey, therefore, cannot in any way replace a reading of that debate; it was intended merely to bring together, in a summary fashion, points dispersed throughout the discussion on the various items, and to reveal the main trends of the debate.

I believe it is apparent from my survey that on practically no major issue was there fundamental agreement between the participants: even jurists from the same political and geographical area appeared to hold differing views on many a point. This however, should not be disconcerting at all. The purpose of the round-table discussion was not to reach consensus, but simply to bring together jurists with a different cultural background and a different ideological or political approach, so as to elicit their views on some of the more fundamental features of the international legal system. The purpose of the convenors was certainly attained: to provoke a true exchange of views, so as to permit each participant both to understand the opinion of others better and to put forward his own view. In a way, the differences that came to the fore, and that no one was meant either to overcome or to iron out, reflected the political and ideological constellation of the world community, riven as it is by so many conflicts and divisions. I believe, however, that in spite of those differences, on one point at least all participants agreed unreservedly: the usefulness of getting together and having a candid discussion. In a way — in spite of the huge difference between the difficulty of settling political and military conflicts and that of coming to grips with scholarly divergences — this scholarly enterprise might be taken as a model for the settlement of international disputes. It showed that by making an effort to achieve mutual understanding, by openly pitting the various viewpoints one against another, points of friction could be gradually reduced or — should this goal be regarded as unattainable — at least "co-exist" in spite of all the cleavages. Over and above the scholarly value of our exercise, this was probably the final message of our Florence round-table discussion.

Analytical Index

Index of Statements

J. Brownlie

A. CASSESE

L. Condorelli

H. DE FIUMEL

B. DE WITTE

R. R. FALK

G. Gaja

B. Graefrath

E. Jiménez de Aréchaga

J. Hazard

M. Mendelson

T. Meron

W. Riphagen

Edward (Ted) Stein

Eric Stein

S. Sur

E. Suy

M. Virally

J. H. H. Weiler

A. Yankov

Bei Fragen zur Produktsicherheit wenden Sie sich bitte an:
If you have any questions regarding product safety,
please contact:

Walter de Gruyter GmbH
Genthiner Straße 13
10785 Berlin
productsafety@degruyterbrill.com